JAMES

CAGNEY

THE AUTHORIZED
BIOGRAPHY

DOUG WARREN WITH
JAMES CAGNEY

ST. MARTIN'S PRESS / NEW YORK

JAMES CAGNEY: THE AUTHORIZED BIOGRAPHY. Copyright © 1983 by Doug Warren and James Cagney. All rights reserved. Printed in the United States of America. No part of this book may be used or reproduced in any manner whatsoever without written permission except in the case of brief quotations embodied in critical articles or reviews. For information, address St. Martin's Press, 175 Fifth Avenue, New York, N.Y. 10010.

Design by Manuela Paul

Library of Congress Cataloging in Publication Data

Warren, Doug.
    James Cagney, the authorized biography.

    Includes index.
    1. Cagney, James, 1899–   . 2. Moving-picture
actors and actresses—United States—Biography.
I. Cagney, James, 1899–   . II. Title.
PN2287.C23W37 1983   791.43'028'0924 [B]   83-6643
ISBN 0-312-43956-3

First Edition

10 9 8 7 6 5 4 3 2 1

Thanks to Marge Zimmermann,
who opened the Cagney doors to me,
both East and West, and
to Jimmy himself, who consistently made me
feel welcome once the doors were opened.

CONTENTS

Sections of photographs follow pages 80 and 176.

PREFACE

After James Cagney's many years of retirement from movies, and with his built-in penchant for privacy, his persona was more or less relegated to the distant-memory department. There were the occasional screenings of his more classic films over the years, and, on a few rare occasions, he blinked into the limelight to accept awards. But, for the most part, the feisty little screen giant contented himself with painting pictures and working an eight-hundred-acre farm in upstate New York.

Then came a day when, much to everyone's surprise, the fabulous Cagney agreed to do what he had sworn he would never do: sign up for another film role. He agreed to portray Police Commissioner Rhinelander Waldo in Milos Forman's turn-of-the-century epic *Ragtime*. The publicity that followed his surprisingly facile performance in the film once more turned the Cagney name into something of a household word.

With this in mind, and considering the editor's own admiration for James Cagney the actor, St. Martin's Press thought it a good idea to include a Cagney biography in the following season's catalog. An author was given the assignment. The author wrote several letters to Cagney's better-known friends but received only one reply. It was courteous but succinct, making it clear that since it was common knowledge that Cagney preferred his privacy, it was unlikely that his close friends would cooperate with the author.

The letter had scarcely been digested when the author received a telephone call from upstate New York. It was from Mrs. Marge Zimmermann, who had been watching over the Cagneys for the past dozen or more years. One of the author's letters had come into Cagney's hands, and Mrs. Zimmermann was calling to let the author know that Cagney had been disturbed by past intrusions on his privacy and was not happy with the prospect of yet another biography.

The author pointed out that the book would definitely be written, because there was a signed contract, and that if Cagney placed obstacles in the way, it would simply be a dull book. Its publication could, however, give Cagney an opportunity to set the record straight, to correct errors made by previous biographers. The conversation took a positive turn, and before it ended Mrs. Zimmermann said that she would discuss the matter with Cagney and get back to the author.

Her first call was made on January 21, 1982. On January 25 she called to say that there had been a change of attitude and that she would help the author reach many of Cagney's old friends. The Cagneys and the Zimmermanns would be coming to Los Angeles within several weeks, at which time the arrangements could be made.

Mrs. Zimmermann called the author on March 19 to tell him that the Cagneys' two-car convoy had reached Los Angeles safely, but that Jimmy was in the hospital with a severe case of sciatica. On March 22 Mrs. Zimmermann and the author met for a lunch that resulted in the author's invitation to meet Cagney. During the meeting three days later, it was agreed formally that the book would be a cooperative effort.

There were several interviews at the hospital, and the visits continued at the Cagneys' home in Beverly Hills after he was discharged from the hospital on April 22. A total of fifteen hours was spent interviewing him during the Cagneys' two-month stay in southern California; that is not much time when it comes to filling the pages of a book, but the quality of the information was good, and Cagney seemed more than willing to reveal it. He is not a man who takes pleasure in talking about himself—in fact, he hates it— but he was never hostile in the slightest degree. He wanted very much to cooperate.

The author was made to feel welcome at a number of gatherings, the last of which was noteworthy. A few of Jimmy Cagney's friends joined him at his home for lunch and a couple of hours of friendly conversation. Following cocktails in the living room, the group was ushered into a sun-bright dining room, where Cagney sat at the head of a long table. To his left was a pal of sixty years' standing, Pat O'Brien. Beyond O'Brien was a friend of more than thirty years, Jack Lemmon. Next to Lemmon sat a youthful-appearing man of music, Frankie Carle. At the end of the table, opposite Cagney, was a man very tall in the saddle, Joel McCrea. The three chairs on the other side of the table were occupied by an extremely fit-looking Ralph Bellamy, Charlton Heston, and the author.

The accumulated ages of the guests came to about five and a half centuries. How many achievements does that represent; how many moments of anguish, of joy, of embarrassment; how many hours of boredom spent awaiting their turns on soundstages, on locations, or in recording studios? Consider the millions of dollars earned by the guests, the tens of millions made by their investments, and the billions generated by them for the studios for which they worked.

The only smoker in the room seemed to be Jack Lemmon, and his choice was a long cigar. Pat O'Brien drank some beer, and Heston and Lemmon had some white wine; the others abstained. Frankie Carle was wearing glasses, but some of the others took theirs out for reading.

The storytelling was led by Pat O'Brien, who was polished in his delivery. The most physically demonstrative in joke telling was Jack Lemmon. Bellamy and Heston had several amusing anecdotes to offer, with Heston intermittently introducing politics into the conversation. Frankie Carle was quietly receptive, and Joel Mc-Crea was the most soft-spoken of the group. The host laughed heartily at the funny stories and later shed a tear or two when Pat O'Brien sang a favorite Irish song. The music took place in the living room after lunch was served. Frankie Carle accompanied Pat O'Brien on the piano and then played medleys of older popular songs, including two of his own, "Sunrise Serenade" and "Oh What It Seemed to Be."

The first guest to break away was Jack Lemmon, who said that he was en route to the airport for a flight to Israel, where he was meeting Walter Matthau. He said it as casually as if he were headed for the corner drugstore to pick up a fresh packet of his skinny cigars. Heston was the next to leave, confessing that he was already late for a date with his son. Pat O'Brien soon followed, explaining that he and his wife were in the process of packing for a freeway trip to San Clemente, where they would appear for several weeks in a dinner-theater engagement of *On Golden Pond.*

Then it was Bellamy's turn to say thanks and farewell, and the get-together broke up at about three-thirty in the afternoon. It was just another lunch hosted by Cagney, of which there have probably been thousands over the years, but "Oh What It Seemed to Be."

The author referred to above is the person writing this, but it doesn't seem proper to use a first-person approach to an occasion at which I was merely an observer. The only statistic to which I could make a contribution was the total-age category; I was out of my class but was never made to feel that way.

Had the luncheon occurred fifteen years earlier, there would have been a number of people included, such as Spencer Tracy, Frank McHugh, Lynne Overman, Robert Montgomery, Victor Jory, and a few others with whom Cagney felt a close affinity over many years. But they are gone, and he must miss them. At this lunch, however, it was almost as though all of his old pals were there in spirit, that the scene was much the same but that some of the faces were different. It was easy to see, at a moment such as this, how Jimmy Cagney has attracted such firm and loyal friends over so many years. He is indeed someone special.

INTRODUCTION

He thinks of himself as a farmer, and in terms of time he has probably been farming almost as long as he was an actor. But it was his career in movies that made James Cagney one of the world's most recognized human beings, not his expertise in breeding Morgan horses and Scottish Highlander cattle, his ecological activism, or his deft touch with brush and palette.

In the eyes of the world, Jimmy Cagney is remembered as the all-American champ of the hoodlums; the personification of Depression-era gangsterhood; the unyielding man of the streets; one who was fast on his feet, swift with his fists, and deadly with a gat. No such thing as chivalry inhibited his freedom of expression with the fairer sex; if they encroached, they got cuffed. If they displeased persistently, they got fruit in the face. That was the image projected in so many of Cagney's films, and he has spent much of his long lifetime trying to balance it out. He did manage to portray other less venomous characters, and there were a few musical gems interspersed. The latter served to amaze his fans, who regarded their idol as a perfect hood who could also sing and dance.

If Cagney had a choice, he would prefer to have been recognized as a song-and-dance man, because that was what all his early training and experience consisted of. His favorite movie is *Yankee Doodle Dandy,* for which he received an Academy Award for his portrayal of George M. Cohan. He liked it because it demonstrated the results of all the early years of bone-aching rehearsal-hall drills and practice.

He has always considered it ludicrous for the public to lionize performers, and he disdains the label "superstar," especially if it is applied to him. Over the years he has insisted that he was only doing what was necessary to put meat and potatoes on the table; the fact that he was able to do it as a performer was his good luck. He would have been as happy, he has said frequently, if he had earned his living as an artist, but that would have been even harder than acting. If all else failed, he is certain that he would have found happiness by working the land. Although his origins are urban, his instincts have always been agrarian. It was as if Providence had nestled him in the mean climes of the city as a tempering process while his perfect place in the country sun was being prepared to receive him.

His early years of struggle and street survival molded his tough facade, but his inner sensitivity felt most at home in a pastoral setting. On the surface, Cagney is the rock-hard street ruffian so graphically displayed on the Warner Brothers screen, but only a thorn scratch beneath the surface dwells a gentle gent with a green thumb and an affection for animals, a sentimentalist in his relationships with family and friends.

To be admitted into the ranks of the Cagney friendship club has frequently amounted to lifetime membership, because the initiation can be stringent. His doors have always been open, and he greets everyone with cordiality, but passage beyond acquaintanceship rests on his instincts. Some pass readily; some do not. As a guard against Hollywood sycophancy, he has evolved a kind of radar device that automatically culls the chaff from the wheat. He has always dodged phonies and the places where they congregate. His close friends over the years have ranged from fellow actors to farmers and fishermen, and his friendship list includes many active members from the streets of his childhood. If their essence is right they remain friends for life, as though members of his own family.

As Cagney approached his eighties, he was slowed to a walk by a stroke, and it was during treatment for this that he learned he was diabetic. The two ailments rendered him minimally ambulatory; the old hoofer's legs would hoof no more. Those who ministered to him could see that invalidism for someone so previously active might be as lethal as the stroke could have been, perhaps even worse. It was important to make him active again, to stimulate interests that would bring him new goals.

Despite Cagney's retirement from films, and his stubborn vow to stick with it, the doctor's warning of creeping death from inactivity caused second thoughts. When neighbor Milos Forman offered him a role in *Ragtime,* he eventually said yes.

There would be no bucks-and-wings and stiff-legged clogging for Cagney; in fact, he scarcely walked. But he acted. The Cagney charisma, that magic screen energy, had not been tamed by time or illness. The white hair and handlebar mustache of Rhinelander Waldo was the character, but there was no doubt that it was Cagney under the facade.

Cagney has come out of retirement, and he promises no future retirements. He plans to bid this planet farewell in pancake makeup, with the lights full-up and cameras rolling.

The Yankee Doodle Dandy rides again!

PART ONE

The Kid from Yorkville

CHAPTER 1

arolyn Nelson, born of an Irish mother and a Norwegian father, married James Francis Cagney when she was eighteen, but she was not a child bride. Reared in the depths of poverty on New York's Lower East Side, the beautiful red-haired youngster was forced to leave school at twelve to contribute to the support of her family. She had been working for six years at the Eagle Pencil Company when she and Cagney, Sr., decided to marry.

Carolyn was innocent but not naive after the years of working among adults, yet the young man charmed her beyond logic or reason. All women seemed to be taken with the athletic handsomeness of this young second-generation Irishman with the curly black hair, ready wit, and gift of pure blarney. It was small wonder that Carolyn saw in this twenty-one-year-old man a future of all good things.

His work at the time was bookkeeping, which promised a sound and stable livelihood for a wife and mother, and if Carolyn was sure of anything at all in her accumulation of experience, it was that almost anything offered more future than a career in pencil manufacturing. All she asked was a good home with a kindly husband who would provide for her and their children, and, most of all, who would earn enough money to assure that the children had proper educations. She had been a talented and scholarly student, and her teacher had cried when it was necessary for one so promising to leave education behind.

There is no way of knowing whether the young Irishman confided his fantasies to Carrie during their courtship, but soon after they were married she learned of his discontent with the benumbing functions of office work. He had charm, intelligence, a way with people; what he aspired to was something more in keeping with these attributes, perhaps a business of his own. A logical arena for such expression, since there were limitations to his experience, might be a restaurant where the gentry could come to dine and imbibe. As a first step in that general direction, Cagney took a job as a bartender, a position that could provide training in dealing with the public. He had had considerable experience drinking in neighborhood saloons, so it was second nature for him to gravitate to that line of work.

He found a job in a saloon at Avenue D and Eighth Street, and moved Carrie into a flat nearby. Harry, with hair as dark as his father's, was born in 1898. A year later, on July 17, came James junior; he looked a great deal like his older brother, but his hair was the same flaming red color as his mother's.

Jimmy retains no memories of his first home, because his family moved uptown to East Seventy-ninth Street, near First Avenue, before he was two; but he disagrees with the frequently published notion that he was born in an apartment above his father's saloon. In the first place, his father didn't own that saloon, and he remembers his mother mentioning the flat they had occupied not far from his father's place of work.

He recalls a great deal about life on East Seventy-ninth Street because it was there, in multinational Yorkville, that his character began to take shape.

During his infancy he had been frail, almost becoming part of the high child-mortality rate of the Lower East Side. But there was nothing sickly about the cocky scrapper from Yorkville. From his earliest recollections, Jimmy took on all comers, whether the fights resulted from his own personal disagreements or from disagreements instigated by bloodthirsty cohorts.

Jimmy's older brother, Harry, held no such fistic inclinations; nor did Eddie, Jimmy's next younger brother, who was born in 1902. Bill, born in 1904, would later show a willingness for physical expression, but while he was growing up, Jimmy watched over him with both fists cocked. Both Harry and Ed were athletic, but they left most of the fighting to Jimmy.

Jimmy takes genuine pride in recounting his innumerable street skirmishes. When he was young, fighting was something he could do extremely well; there was little else to satisfy a hungry ego. He was small; he was poor. By using his fists Jimmy could cut the big kids down to size, and fists were also an equalizer when it came to social disparities.

Carolyn Cagney, having survived a childhood in the slums, encouraged her sons to stand up for themselves. It was her philosophy that to rise above substandard beginnings one had to fight and claw. Whether it was stated or implied, this basic message came through to Jimmy. His fighting continued long after he stopped using his fists.

Jimmy adored his mother, and he gives her full credit for keeping him and his brothers out of serious trouble on the streets. She was a demonstrative, loving person, with much laughter and affection available whenever the children needed it. But she was also steadfast in meting out discipline. When she established a law, the boys never questioned it. They did what they were told.

Jimmy had no less love for his father, but it was love of a different kind, almost a kind of awe for a visiting dignitary or deep admiration for a visiting relative, one whose visits were far too infrequent. James senior was consistently good-natured, warm, and loving. When he was at home he enjoyed playing roughhouse games with the boys, and he was not reluctant to hug and hold them. But his stronger interests lay beyond the home, and as time passed his homecomings became more and more sporadic. He was unredemptively self-indulgent and shamefully irresponsible, and from an early age the boys were aware of it. He was dearly loved but could not be counted on.

Jimmy was the favorite son of both parents, but the favoritism was not made manifest necessarily by reward. It was always Jimmy, for example, who would be called upon by his father to run to the corner on hangover-fuzzed mornings to get a whiskey eye-opener. "When my old man wanted to get up, I'd get the job. I'd go to the saloon and pick up a twenty-five-cent bottle of rye whiskey. He'd take a few shots and then he'd feel better." Jimmy explains that in those days whiskey came in casks, from which the bartender would draw whatever amount was ordered. "It was awful, as I think about it. Here I was, about nine years old, going into a bar and buying a bottle of whiskey."

There were other times when his father's absences would leave the family without food. When it reached the point of emergency, it would be Jimmy his mother would call upon—not Harry or Ed—to go to the saloon to try to bring his father back, or to try to extract from him enough money to overcome the crisis. "Dad was happy, happy, happy," says Jimmy. "When I'd go to get money, he would laugh and pick me up and put me on the bar. If I had learned a new song he would want me to sing it, and he would give me a glass of sarsaparilla. Eventually, out would come a big roll of bills and he would hand it over."

It wasn't always that simple. On many occasions Jimmy would be drawn along with his father on his long, circuitous route back home. It meant stopping at saloons along the way and gathering drinking cronies as he progressed. Jimmy loved his father's attention, but he hated these drunken odysseys. He had also to deal with his own sense of responsibility. His mother had charged him with the task of bringing home his father or the much-needed money. Jimmy felt that he was failing her as he was drawn along by his father and his friends. "I remember on this one night," says Jimmy, "I hung back when they went into this bar. Then I ran like hell and got on the Third Avenue El. I took the wad of bills home to my mother."

Jimmy says that he knew nothing about his father's parents, except that they had come from County Leitrim, in Ireland, and that the family name was Americanized from O'Caigne. Jimmy once met his father's sister—whom his father disliked—and there was at least one brother, of whom Jimmy can recall very little. "He was just another guy."

On his mother's side of the family there was an abundance of interesting and colorful family members. Carolyn's father had been a seaman who moved up through the ranks to the coveted position of river-barge captain. "To be a captain of a barge," Jimmy says, "you also have to have navigation, how to run a ship—all that kind of thing. Grandpa Nelson had all of this."

Jimmy recalls exciting episodes on the Nelson barge even before his earliest memories of school. The barge would traverse the Hudson, picking up and delivering coal. He would frequently travel with the Nelsons, sleeping near them in the snug, one-room cabin. He particularly recalls the tasty doughnuts his grandmother would make, and he remembers his fascination with the scoop that would dig deeply into the barge to bring out the coal. The only discipline he can recall came when he would wander too far from the cabin. "Hey, Jamesy," the Captain would call. "Go back where you belong." The command was always obeyed.

Captain Nelson had lost an eye on one of the occasions when he was forced to work ashore. He had a factory job that involved the use of lye, and once some of the substance squirted into one eye, blinding him on that side.

Grandpa Nelson possessed one of the most dreaded tempers Jimmy had ever known. "He would fight anyone," says Jimmy. "It didn't matter how big or how young. But, unfailingly, he would get the hell knocked out of him. When he would get belted across the room in some saloon, he would crawl back to his feet and ask the guy if he'd had enough."

But the Captain was always gentle with his family. During the winters, and in later years after their retirement from the barge, the Nelsons lived with the Cagneys. "We didn't count the numbers," says Jimmy. "I slept on the floor with my grandmother, Harry and Ed slept in one bed, and my mother slept with little Bill."

On those occasions when his father would come home it wouldn't be until about seven in the morning, and by then one of the sleeping places would more than likely be free. But on many occasions, according to Jimmy, his father would fall asleep at the piano. "Eventually he would slip off the stool and land on the floor, where he'd sleep it off. He drank sixty shots of rye every day."

Jimmy recalls that his father was very proud that there was a river-barge captain in the family, even though it was on his wife's side. On one occasion he was bragging about it to his drinking buddies, who insisted that he take them to see it all for themselves. He did so and was greeted cordially by the Captain, who had no prejudice against those who enjoyed a drink. He stood by quietly as his son-in-law ushered his cronies around the barge and then took them into the cabin, where he proceeded to bring out the Nelson family photo album as if it were his own.

The happy visitors were leafing through the photographs, until one of the men took aim at a photo of a man posing rigidly in a derby hat. He made a sporting remark that suggested the subject was something of a dandy. Whatever the remark, it was enough to send Captain Nelson into a blind rage. The photo that was singled out was of himself. "Get ashore, you sons-o'-bitches!" he bellowed. "Get ashore!" Jimmy says that the Captain reached for his shotgun and took after the men. "They all shinnied up that ladder," says Jim, "hell bent for the streetcar."

As much as Jimmy loved the barge adventures, there were times of deep loneliness, especially on Sundays, when the barge would be tied up to a dock of some distant town like Port Redding. "Every Sunday I would watch the excursion boats go by," he said, "and imagine that my father would be on one of them, coming to see me. It never happened."

There was never a time that he felt more lonely than on his first day of school. He was taken as far as the principal's office by his mother, and from there he was on his own. "I was crying like hell," he says. "I remember walking up a flight of steps to go to my classroom. I walked in and the teacher called me over and gave me a hug. I didn't know what the hell was going on. She told me to go back and sit down, and I was there from then on."

He remembers himself as being quiet and shy in class, as though he were subconsciously intent on keeping a low profile. "I remember once I stepped in some dog do," he says, "and took it into the classroom with me. There was a terrible stench and I saw the cause of it on the heel of my shoe. I scraped it off on the desk support, and left it there. I didn't want to make a fuss. The smell lingered there for quite a while."

When he refers to his shoes in those early days, it means the single pair he owned at one time. They were his leisure shoes, his school shoes, and his Sunday-go-to-Mass shoes. His other items of apparel included a short peaked cap with a snap, a buttoned blouse with a drawstring at the bottom, and knickers with the buckles always hanging unfastened.

When he was six years old he wasn't the tough kid on the block that he would soon become, and one of his sharpest memories is the time he backed off from a fight. "There was this tough kid—Boo Boo Hayes was his name. He was a big kid and he didn't like me. Maybe it was because I had red hair. I went home and told my mother about it, and she went and got another big kid to go after him. He let me alone after that. A couple of more years and I'd have taken him myself."

In those days, and in that environment, parents didn't reason such matters out with other parents, or appeal to school principals.

Issues were dealt with more expeditiously and directly. If the Cagney boys became involved in a dispute, they were expected to deal with it themselves. If they were unable to, their mother would determine what measure of justice was appropriate and would take action. Jimmy recalls a night watchman doing a crazy dance in the streets to a bullwhip being snapped by his mother. He had given Harry a cuff for allegedly urinating down the stovepipe of his shack, whereas Harry had merely been a spectator to the event.

Another time, a teacher grabbed Ed's hair and boxed his ears for whispering in class. When his mother learned of it she set out in search of the cruel teacher. Carolyn Cagney's reputation had preceded her, and someone warned the teacher, who took off for parts unknown. He didn't return until he was assured that the enraged mother had cooled down.

For every memory involving conflict, however, Jimmy has many others that depict the happy innocence of days long past. He remembers the frequent rides on Blank's butcher wagon. Jimmy Hogan was the delivery man, and when he saw Jimmy walking along the street he would reach down and grab him and hoist him high on the wagon seat. They would ride along the route behind the huge white horse with the biggest rear end Jimmy had ever seen. It was then, at such an early age, that Jimmy established his lifelong love for horses.

There were always girls in Jimmy's life, many of them—for as long as he can remember. His first female fantasy-figure goes back to an age when he was much too young to understand the attraction. The pretty neighborhood girl was named Annie. She was a few years older than Jimmy, and thought enough of him to stop and tie his shoe laces whenever there was the need. Jimmy made sure the need would be there when he saw her approaching.

There was also Marie Cody, who had chosen Jimmy as her fancied beau. The news came to him through a children's game, "Walter Wildflower." Jimmy recalls that the game centered around a song. The children would form a circle around a girl, singing: "Walter, Walter Wildflower, growing up so high. We are all your ladies and we are sure to die. Wildflower, turn your back—turn your back and tell your fellow's name."

Jimmy says that he was walking down the steps of his flat and there was pretty Marie Cody in the center of the ring. "When it came time for her to say who her fella was, she said it was Jimmy

Cagney. Then the song went: 'Jimmy Cagney is a nice young man, comes to the door with his hat in his hand. He is sick and going to die, and that will make little Jimmy cry.'"

That was the extent of his romance with Marie Cody, but it was extremely important to him at the time. He remembers that Marie grew up to be a very beautiful girl but died while still in her teens.

There were other girls of whom he can bring sharp mental images. Rosanna, a little Czech girl, liked to dance on the sidewalk to the tune of a street organ. "Oh, Jesus, was she ever tough," Jimmy recalls, "and Lily Flower was pretty as her name. She would go up to the roof with ten or twelve boys, and they'd stay up there a long time. I was never sure what went on up there, because they'd never let me come along. I figured it out later on though. But I never got in on it."

CHAPTER 2

immy has often said that his family may have been poor, but he never knew it. As a matter of fact, they never did live in squalor. They may have had more than their share of meager meals during tough times, but there was always food, and somehow they always managed to maintain a fairly stable standard of living. Each apartment they lived in consisted of five rooms in more-or-less typical New York brownstone buildings. While some of their homes were more comfortable than others, and in better neighborhoods than others, all were furnished adequately with good, sturdy furniture. Jimmy recalls a time when the family sofa was re-covered with leather, which, even then, was a symbol of luxury. There was an icebox and a coal stove in the kitchen, and the family enjoyed two extra luxuries of the day, a piano and a Victrola.

Many other families were far less fortunate than the Cagneys. Jimmy recalls the humiliation and degradation suffered by the Fitzpatricks when they and their belongings were moved onto the street. Another family never ventured out on Sundays because they owned no dress-up clothes. "They were proud," Jimmy recalls. "They were very proud people."

And Jimmy recalls an incident involving his childhood friend Peter Hessling, known to his friends as Bootah. Jimmy was standing in front of the St. Francis De Sales Church waiting for Communion when Bootah appeared carrying a basket on his arm. "I asked what he was doing, and he said his family didn't have any food. He was on his way to ask the priest if he could give them something. He went up to the house and came back a few minutes later. I said, 'How'd you make out?' He said, 'Wouldn't give me nuttin'.'"

While their father's drinking and gambling habits kept the family in a state of chaos, the Cagneys were not destitute. Carolyn Cagney would never permit it. She somehow saw that they maintained at least a minimal standard of living, and her close relatives were close by to provide pleasant highlights to their struggle. They weren't compelled to live the constant downbeat experience of so many of their impoverished neighbors.

It was the Nelsons who introduced the Cagneys to the wonders of marine travel, and through other relatives of their mother the children had their first taste of rural life. It was Jimmy who was most indelibly impressed by the visit to the faraway home of Aunt Jane and Uncle Nick Nicholson. The Nicholsons were actually the aunt and uncle of Carolyn Cagney, and their distant residence was in the wide-open expanses of a place called Flatbush. To Jimmy it was another land, another world. Everything about the visit was magical, including the mode of transportation that brought them there.

Their father hired a friend to transport the family to Flatbush in a luxurious, horse-drawn barouche. During the earlier stage of the journey, eight-year-old Jimmy was entranced by the four wheeled carriage and by the spirited, high-prancing horse that pulled it. He had ridden in the butcher's wagon, but never before had he been a passenger in such style, and in a vehicle especially hired for him and his family.

Soon the city streets gave way to open spaces, and Jimmy studied the terrain in open-eyed wonder. His senses widened to absorb every exciting particle of it: the brightness of the country sky, the deep greenness of the meadows and treeline, the wildflowers interspersed in natural bouquets. He was entering a world that existed only in storybooks. He could see now that it was real, and he liked what he saw.

At last the cozy, elm-shaded cottage of the Nicholsons was pointed out. It was in this snug, wood-frame house that he and his family would spend the next two weeks. There was a white picket fence around the cottage, and it dripped with a profusion of morning glories. Jimmy couldn't remember ever seeing anything quite so pretty. It was almost at this moment that he was transmuted from city-dweller to country boy. It would take some years for the physical transfer, but the spirit had already made the change.

It was during those glorious two weeks in Flatbush that Jimmy was first shown the real-life people behind the make-believe of Hollywood. Vitagraph Studios was only a block or two from the Nicholsons' home, and through some of their influential studio acquaintances Jimmy was permitted to roam more or less freely around the backlot and soundstages.

His favorite actor at the studio was the comedian John Bunny, but the illusion was soon shattered. One afternoon when Jimmy was near the front gate, he watched the approach of a studio conveyance that was carrying a group of actors out of the studio to a location. "Among them," says Jimmy, "was John Bunny and Flora Finch, who was the other half of the acting team. I moved closer to look at the horses, and John Bunny said, 'Hey you. . . . Get outa the way.' Nobody talked to me that way, even then, so I answered him back. I think I was more respected after that."

Jimmy and his brothers tramped along country trails; savored the special sweetness of tree-ripened cherries, plums, and apples; and skinny-dipped in pristine ponds instead of the polluted murk of the East River. By the time they had become fully acclimated to the good new life, the vacation came to an end. Their father, who had returned to the city, rejoined them now in the barouche. The trip back to the city would not hold the wonders of the outward journey, and Jimmy, for one, was not ready to return.

Once the pangs of disappointment were dissipated, it was back to the Yorkville tough-kid for Jimmy. He tried not to dwell on what he left behind in Flatbush, because he knew it would be a long time before he would have any say in where he lived. In the meantime, it was business as usual.

When Jimmy was close to ten, the family lived for a while on East Ninety-sixth Street. The Nelsons came to live with them there after retiring from the river barge. The old skipper was like a fish out of water, and the doughnuts that Grandma Nelson fixed for them here were never what they had seemed to be on the barge. Not long after their retirement, Grandma Nelson died, leaving the grizzled old seaman more lonely than ever. Jimmy loved both grandparents, and it became apparent to him now that his love remained unexpressed. Somehow there were invisible barriers that held emotions at bay. There had been hugs and words of affection between him and his grandmother on occasion, but never between him and his grandfather.

"I came out of the bedroom one morning," says Jimmy, "and

there he was, just standing there. I had the sudden desire to kiss him, and I did. I gave him a hug and a kiss. I know he had to have been startled, because nothing like that had ever happened before. I don't think he had ever been kissed before. He grabbed me, held on to me, and kissed me back. It was the only time it ever happened." Grandpa Nelson survived his wife and barge-mate by two years. He died in 1912, at seventy-two.

It was at this approximate time that Jimmy's father managed to inveigle his way into saloon proprietorship. The Earets Brewery backed the venture, and Cagney senior, the hail-fellow-well-met, was finally his own man. Over the door was affixed the sedately lettered plaque, JAMES F. CAGNEY. It was a classy establishment with a long bar covering most of the interior space; beer was a nickel, shots were a dime, the lunch was free.

Each day James senior would prepare the free-lunch counter, with its assortment of pickles, frankfurters, bologna, and pig's knuckles, or whatever other delicacies he thought would please the very special patrons of his saloon.

Being of the firm conviction that the successful saloons were those that were generous with gratis rounds, Cagney established the practice. He may have handed out more free drinks than any other barkeep in history, especially when his own sixty were tallied into the day's giveaways.

It was Jimmy's daily task to deliver a hot meal from home. He would carry a plate, insulated by a newspaper, along the streets to the saloon's location at Eighty-first Street and First Avenue. These noontime meals were probably the only home-cooked ones his father had over many months. It was during this time that Cagney senior's visits home became less and less frequent, and that Carolyn Cagney began to suffer from an increasing variety of illnesses. Her recuperation from one illness began a chapter in young Jimmy's life that he would never have dared dream. The family set out to find a home in the country, where the climate might prove better for Carolyn's health. After careful search it was decided that they would move to Ridgewood, Long Island.

Jimmy had readjusted to city life after the summer vacation a couple of years earlier and had had no hopes that his family would actually take up rural residence.

Now, as if the gods were blessing him for breaking clean in the clinches, Jimmy would be returning to his beloved countryside, and it would not be for just a holiday. The plan was to live there permanently.

"Our block was a quarter of a mile long," Jimmy remembers. "And there were only nine houses on the entire street. We played ball on the empty lots—constantly." Ridgewood is one of Jimmy's fondest memories. He had all the open space one could ask for, yet no more than three blocks to walk for a movie or an ice cream soda. He entered sixth grade in the Ridgewood school and, for the first time, earned good grades.

"The teacher was Miss Hendrichson," he says. "One day I answered a question in class that must have been kind of erudite. She said, 'You know, I'm beginning to learn something. This is the only boy in class who knows anything. . . . You understand what I'm saying?' She directed the question to the other members of the class, and emphasized it. I felt pretty important, I guess. The Ridgewood school was an easy school—a good school."

During the year-and-a-half he lived in Ridgewood, Jimmy's father made weekend trips to the island. He had lost his own business but had found a good bartender's job in a saloon at Seventy-sixth and First Avenue. Life seemed very good to Jimmy at this time. His mother was regaining her health, and he was realizing his potential in school for the first time. It seemed to Jimmy that everyone in the family was benefiting from the move out of the city. Just as he was becoming secure about his way of life, it was snatched from his grasp.

Jimmy's father was tired of the weekend trips to Long Island, and now that Carolyn's health was restored he could see no good reason to sustain the inconvenient family separation. He located a pleasant flat for them on East Seventy-eighth Street, and they made the move back to Yorkville. Jimmy recalls the flat as exceptionally nice by previous standards, but he would have preferred to sleep on the floor of a shack in Ridgewood to avoid returning to the city. The next school term he entered P.S. 158, at Seventy-eighth Street and York Avenue, and his grades plummeted.

The monthly rent for the new apartment was eighteen dollars, which was also the elder Cagney's weekly salary. It was on the second-floor of a building whose entrance was enhanced by a wrought-iron railing that framed the stone steps. There would be two other homes for the young Cagneys before they were grown and scattered. A year later they would move to 400 East Seventy-eighth Street, and then a few doors away, to 420. All their homes were in essentially the same neighborhood. It simply meant a few minutes more or less of walking to meet friends. The arena for most of Jimmy's outdoor activities was Central Park, which was never farther than a mile away.

Jimmy insists that he never played stickball, a pastime so many New Yorkers hold dear, but his brother did. He was serious enough about baseball to make daily excursions to the park, where the game could be played properly. The same park served later on as a place to bring girls or meet new ones.

On one occasion, a girl named Nora chose Central Park as the scene for making Jimmy his first sexual offer. He says he was only about twelve at the time, so he had no library of clever retorts to draw from. "I just ignored it," he said. "Just kept on walking."

He said there was a lovely Jewish girl named Sarah with whom he enjoyed long conversations, but it was Annie Mularkey he liked most during his pre-adolescent days. "Her sister was kind of boyish, and always had a red, runny nose. They were both about my age, and are probably gone by now. Too bad we couldn't have kept in touch over the years. But when we moved out of the neighborhood, that was the end of that."

He didn't have real dates, Jimmy says. When he could go to a nickelodeon it would be with his brothers, whenever a spare nickel would come his way. Romance was reserved for walks through the park, stoop-sitting, or, perhaps, for real privacy, a secret tryst on one of the more private rooftops.

On a few occasions Jimmy's father found time to take him fishing, but Jimmy doesn't remember fishing as one of his more favorite pastimes. As his father fished, Jimmy would stroll about the deck of the boat being seasick. As much as Jimmy loved the sea in later years, he was never a good sailor. Seasickness would almost always spoil an otherwise splendid time.

Within about a year-and-a-half after moving back from Ridgewood, Jimmy was given one more chance for adventure. He, his mother, and his brothers were included in a summer camp program sponsored by the Eastside Settlement House. It was a free outing for the poor, for which Jimmy says his family qualified hands down.

Carolyn and a woman named Maggie Horack accompanied their children to the sprawling farm that was set picturesquely near

Stepney, Connecticut. The children at the camp numbered about twenty, and they were housed in a barracks-like arrangement in the barn. The mothers were billeted in what Jimmy describes as a "tent-like concoction." The camp was run by Joe Zizmar and his brother, who, along with a few helpers, slept in a three-story farmhouse. "It was an important house," says Jimmy. "We ate our meals there—at a long, long table.

"It was a good life there. There were cows and swimming, and I boxed for the first time with gloves. There was no stress—no strain." Jimmy and his brothers had a memorable summer, and despite the primitive conditions, his mother enjoyed herself as well. Each Sunday Jimmy hoped that his father would take the time for a visit, but he never came. "I guess he was too busy in New York."

When the time arrived to return home after one of Jimmy's more perfect summers, it came with deep regret. It was somehow easier to readjust to the city after having lived in Ridgewood. This time he must have sensed that his next experience of country life would be a long time in coming. More than a week after their return home, his mother heard Jimmy crying. When she asked what was troubling him, Jimmy responded, "I want to go back to Stepney."

Despite all the family problems, the poverty, and Jimmy's street-fighting habits, he rarely got into trouble with those in authority. His grades could have been much better, but he was never the cause of class disturbances. He says that in all his years of school he was never once called before the principal. And his encounters with the law were limited to a pair of minor incidents. One of them followed a confrontation over a snowball; the other was the result of an extended fight with neighborhood tough-guy, Willie Carney.

A snowball was thrown while Jimmy was an innocent bystander. Someone pelted a passerby squarely in the head, and when he turned around his eyes fixed on Jimmy. He charged into Jimmy with his unjust accusation. Jimmy turned on him so swiftly that the man started to run for his life. "I followed him to where he lived," says Jimmy, "and he tells me to get outa there. That didn't mean anything to me—I was going to brain him. He ran inside and called a cop, and when the cop came and remonstrated with me, I called it off."

There was another occasion when Jimmy was compromised by a snowball, but the police weren't involved. He threw an iceball at someone, but it sailed over the target and smashed through a neighbor's front window. "I ran and hid, but in about an hour the man who owned the window found me. He marched me home to my mother, and the two of them had a coffee klatsch that lasted about an hour. Finally, a settlement was agreed upon. My mother paid for the window, and I had to pay her back in weekly installments. The window cost a small fortune—I think it was a dollar-and-a-half."

The Willie Carney battles grew out of a skirmish that began with Jimmy's brother Ed. Carney spotted Ed bouncing a golf ball against the steps of the family stoop and declared that the ball was his. He grabbed it, and when Ed protested, the bigger boy gave Ed a brutal beating. At the time, Ed was recovering from an illness, which compounded the need for revenge. But Jimmy would have set things straight for his gentle brother under any circumstances.

Jimmy went out looking for Carney but was unable to find him. He returned home, but after less than an hour a neighborhood boy came pounding at the Cagney door. The word was out that Jimmy was spoiling for a fight—and with one of the toughest kids in Yorkville—so there was an immediate contingent of spectators thirsty for blood. The word brought to Jimmy was that at this moment, Carney was at work pulverizing another hapless neighborhood kid—and less than three blocks away. Jimmy took off in pursuit.

As Jimmy strode grimly along, his following increased in numbers. First there were two, then four, then a half-dozen; by the time the distant circle of spectators to Carney's ensuing fight came into range, Jimmy had a Pied Piper's parade at his heels. They arrived just as Carney's unequal opponent abandoned his struggle. He was a pulp of bleeding flesh, hurt and frightened. "Is it all right if I take over for you?" Jimmy asked the beaten lad. It was all right.

Then Jimmy looked Carney over from head to toe. He told Carney who he was and why he was there, but Carney already knew. Jimmy told Carney to take a rest, and then they would have a go at it. When Carney signaled that he was ready, the Cagney calm was broken. Jimmy tore into him with fists ripping at his face and body. With each blow Jimmy conjured up the image of his gentle brother Ed and the beating he had taken only hours earlier. The image made his own punches venomous, and made the blows of his opponent as soft as a girl's caress.

The huge and frenzied crowd moved and swayed in and out of the street following the fight action, but the crowd also attracted the attention of the police. After ten or fifteen minutes of un-diminished slugging, a pair of precinct cops dispersed the crowd and broke up the fight. Before they were too far separated, Jimmy made sure that Carney understood that the fight would resume at the same time the next afternoon, in a different place.

Jimmy had heard of Carney for a long time. He knew of his reputation for toughness and for crazy behavior. Carney was some-body who had to become notorious. It was essential that his name become known on the streets, no matter what was required to achieve it. If he didn't have a grievance to settle, he would make one up. If he failed to stir up anything better, Carney would gather a crowd around him and take dares. One of the more sensational ones was to climb the neighborhood's tallest building and hang by his fingertips from the building's uppermost protrusion.

Jimmy knew all about Carney, all right, and there were many occasions when he wondered how he would fare with him in a fight. But until now he had had no good reason to fight him. Car-ney had avoided him, and he had been content to mind his own businss. But now that had all changed, and Jimmy wondered whether Carney had picked the fight with Ed just to settle the question of who was toughest—once and for all.

The next afternoon Carney was waiting at the appointed time and place, and once more the street-fighters went at it. They fought longer this time, and harder. By the time the police once more arrived, Jimmy's clothes were crimson from Carney's blood. When he went home he cleaned his own wounds with a washcloth and cold water. He had given Carney everything he had, and Car-ney had taken it. Carney had dished out plenty of his punishment too. The third encounter was set for the following afternoon, and Jimmy resolved that this would be the last round of the fight.

The third installment of the fight was no different from the others, except that Carney showed up with one of his eyes swollen shut. The worst damage Jimmy had to show was a pair of lips that looked like twin hotdogs. They had at it with all the gusto of the previous rounds, and in the blur of activity Jimmy heard a Jewish woman plaintively begging for the fight to stop. "Those boys are killing each other," she wailed. "Somebody call their mothers. Why don't their mothers come and stop this bloodshed?" Jimmy kept slugging away, inwardly amused at the irony. One of the most frenetic spectators on Jimmy's side, the one who was cheering him on with the zeal of a young cheerleader, was his mother.

The fight was once more stopped, but this time because it was obvious that Jimmy's right hand was fractured. Carney may have been a bully with an unrelenting streak of cruelty, but he wanted to win the fight with Cagney on the square. It was vowed that the fight would start up again once Jimmy's hand had healed, and it would have, but by that time Carney was no longer around. He got himself into more serious trouble with the police and was sent to reform school. Jimmy never saw Carney again. He would later hear from him, but their paths would never again cross.

CHAPTER 3

immy may have had a reputation as a formidable street-fighter, but if fighting had been his ultimate goal there would have been some variations in the way his life turned out. He was a fighter because it gave him stature in the community, and it was something at which he could excel. He was really more of an athlete than a brawler, and once his energies were directed into the more genteel sport of baseball he could prove his talents. He became so absorbed in baseball, and became so good at it, that for a time he had no doubt at all that he would become a major-league star.

Being small and wiry, he chose catching as his position, and he played it well. He played on a team who called themselves the Jon Jays and on a particular Sunday found themselves opposing the notorious team from Eighty-first Street. The event was anticipated with mixed emotions, because the Eighty-first Street team was composed of some of Manhattan's toughest characters. There was a real possibility that a win on the baseball diamond could result in a loss in the brawl that would inevitably follow the game. The apprehension was wasted energy, however. The Jon Jays did win the game handily, thanks to the pitching of George Mitchell and the expert catching and hitting of Jimmy Cagney, but instead of settling the matter in a postgame brawl, the team from Eighty-first Street simply drafted the winning battery of Mitchell and Cagney.

That was how Jimmy became a member of The Original Nut Club Team of Yorkville, one of the better sandlot groups in the city. "It wasn't a club," Jimmy explains. "It was just a baseball team, and they were good."

He has no recollection of the origin of the team's name, and may never have known it, but his association with the group was one of his teenage coups. The team was important, and while its members were street-hardened punks by reputation, Jimmy says that beneath it all they were "nice guys."

"They were mostly quiet fellas, confident," he says. "No complaints at all. They were guys like Loggerhead Sullivan, Brother O'Mara—all good guys."

The team was good enough to play all around Manhattan and Long Island, and they made several tours to New Jersey. At least two of the players went on to major-league careers. One of them was Jimmy's lifelong friend George Deportsa, who excelled both in baseball and in basketball and became a second baseman for the Boston Red Sox. Another was Neely Finn, who played for the team in Brooklyn. He was also a promising boxer. "He was a tough kid," says Jimmy. "Looked like a girl, pretty Irish face. He knocked out his first two opponents and they called him back to take on a third. He knocked him out too. A quiet kid, never knew he was around, but when he hit 'em, they went down."

Jimmy's own boxing skills were harnessed in the gymnasium ring of a gathering place called the Eastside Settlement House. He soon learned that he was as formidable in the ring as he was on the streets, and the coaches encouraged him to take up boxing as a profession. At the time, Jimmy was holding down three jobs to bring home a few dollars to help support the family, so the vision of great rewards for a few rounds of boxing appealed to him very much.

As a popular little street kid, Jimmy had had the opportunity to get to know many professional fighters. He had learned the rudiments of the game before he passed his tenth birthday. He was taught to jab effectively when he was only six, and this was followed by the skills of hooking and feinting, so when later instruction came at the Eastside Settlement House it was a matter of adding the fine tuning to an already operative machine.

"Irish Patsy Klein and Eddie Fitzsimmons came from my street or the streets nearby," Jimmy explains. "As I saw it at that age, being a fighter was a quick way to easy dough, so when I was sixteen or seventeen, I decided I'd pick up some ready change that way. I began to get ready."

Jimmy was working as a waiter in an uptown restaurant with Harry and Ed, and was also attending Peter Stuyvesant High

School. He would rise at dawn and run a couple of miles, he would shadowbox between classes, and in the hour or so after school, before having to report to work, he would work out at the gym. He was told that he would get ten dollars for going four rounds in a preliminary bout at the new Polo Grounds, and it sounded good to him.

Just when Jimmy was ready to sign for a fight, his mother interfered. She knew something was going on because Jimmy was never home, and when she saw him it was apparent that he was run-down. "She asked me what I was doing to myself," Jimmy said. "I told her I was going to take on a four-round prelim bout for ten dollars. She said, 'Do you think you can lick me?' 'Why?' I asked. 'Because you'll have to lick me first,' she said. That was the end of my quick-money ring career."

It may have been the end of Jimmy's ring career, but the street-fighting never ceased. "Once," he said, "I was walking down Ninety-sixth Street, a tough street. It was about nine o'clock at night, and I thought it would be safe, but I was wrong. A chunk of iron came whizzing past my head, just missing me. I'd have been dead if it had hit its target."

Jimmy's mission into this no-man's-land was to search for burnable material that the gang needed for their Halloween bonfire. There was no such thing as trick-or-treating in those days. On Halloween they would build huge bonfires and would hide as the fire engine raced up the street to douse the flames. The other tradi-tional excitement on that night was to stage sock fights. After stuff-ing the ashes from the fires into socks, they would turn their coats inside out as a guard against excessive dirt and damage, and start out in search of rival gangs. When they met, the fight began. "We would belt the hell out of each other, and some of the guys would put rocks in the socks for good measure. Nice boys."

Yorkville customs were just as different on Christmas. Cagney says that there was never a visit from Santa Claus in his neighbor-hood. "Some of the homes had Christmas trees with lighted can-dles, but we never did, and there were no presents, either. I was happy as could be if I found an orange in my stocking on Christ-mas morning. We weren't that poor really; that's just the way it was. We never observed the holidays the way they do today. On Thanksgiving we would have a turkey dinner maybe, but not on Christmas."

Thanksgiving was the time for dressing up in costumes. "Everyone would dress up as Indians, tramps, whatever, and parade the streets." Then, on general principle, there would more than likely be a street fight before the promenading came to an end. In Jimmy's youth, very little encouragement was required for trouble to erupt.

"There was this fella named Whistle," he recalls, "a tough, tough guy. He was a Czech or Hungarian, or something, sallow skin, big shoulders. I remember him with a club in his hand, whacking guys down. Somebody stole his cap, and you didn't do that to Whistle. He was going to kill the fella. He got a gun, and I remember him walking up Seventy-ninth Street with tears running down his face. His cap was his prized possession, and he would have committed murder for it if he found the guy who stole it. A cop finally showed up, and Whistle blew."

Once Jimmy was doing his homework when news reached him that a marauding gang from Eighty-third Street had invaded his block and were breaking heads with broomsticks. Jimmy answered the call. "As I went in swinging and banging, out of the darkness came a brick, and it caught me in the left side. I dropped to my knees and stayed there. I managed to crawl to the curb and was violently sick. For years those lower ribs would spasm and hurt like hell."

He walked into trouble once when he was in strange territory, in the area of East Sixty-ninth Street. A smaller boy was taking a beating from a big kid, and Jimmy walked into it. "I nailed him. Then he came at me with one of those sticks with a nail on the end—that they use to pick up paper. He stabbed me with it. I was going back at the kid when his brother, about twenty, came into it. He hit me on the mouth and cooled me. My head hit the wall and I went down."

Then, unable to defend himself, he was attacked by as many as twenty punks. He managed to escape with his life, and in so doing made a pledge to return with his own gang from Eighty-second Street. "They knew the Eighty-second Street gang was tough. When I came back with them, there was nobody in the neighborhood. I was never able to square things with the Sixty-ninth Street bunch, because when my mother saw how badly beaten I was, she made me stay at home."

When he was very small Jimmy sold programs for Armory

events, for which he was paid fifty cents a night. Otherwise, he was always sweeping out, delivering, picking up after—performing some sort of menial task for small pay. Every cent of his earnings was handed intact to his mother.

His first regular job came at fourteen, when he was hired by the *New York Sun* as a kind of gofer-office boy. His principal task was to deliver advertising proofs to uptown advertisers, along with copies of the paper. At the time he would have weighed in at about ninety-five pounds, which often made his cargo as heavy as his own weight. The *Sun* job required him to wake up at five-thirty. After completing his uptown delivery run, he would wash up and run to class at Stuyvesant High School. After school there would always be one or more evening jobs awaiting him.

Later on, all the older Cagney brothers worked for the New York Public Library. Jimmy started out at $12.50 a month and was rewarded by a raise to $17.50 after a year. His work title was "book custodian," which meant that his task was to gather up the stray books and return them to their proper places on the shelves. The job, Jimmy says, wasn't as easy as it sounds. On his free nights Jimmy worked at the Lenox East Settlement House, where he would serve in a variety of roles, including bouncer. On Sundays he was a ticket clerk at the Hudson River Day Line.

The boys were prepared to take on the added responsibility of an extra mouth to feed in 1916, when Robert was born. With all of them well on their way to adulthood, the novelty of having a little brother appealed to them, but, sadly, Robert died of tubercular meningitis at the age of thirteen months.

By this time, James senior was spending very little time at home, and Carolyn knew that something had to be done about it. He was a hopeless alcoholic who was drinking himself to death. In those days there was little help available to families with alcoholic problems, and practically no help for those without means. Carolyn's only option was to go to court and sign papers to have her husband committed to a cure in jail. The summons was drawn up, and someone in the family had to deliver it. Jimmy, as the favorite son, drew the ugly assignment.

"I had to serve the papers on him," said Jimmy. "We stood there in the hallway at Eightieth Street and Second Avenue, and he cried when I gave him the papers—we both did. I put my arms around him. 'I'm sorry, Pop,' I said.

"The next morning he appeared in court bright and shiny. Not a sign of booze on him at all. The judge sentenced him to Blackwell's Island for sixty days."

It was a family tragedy for a loved one to be sent away to jail, but it was a personal calamity for Jimmy, because he was the one who took the action that sent his father before the judge.

James senior survived the jail sentence, and no one knew what miseries he endured in his cold-turkey withdrawal. Every family member prayed that the confinement would change his behavior. Then, at least, the act of committing him would not have been in vain. But they were disappointed. He went back to his old self-destructive ways. "He never forgave us for what we did to him," Jimmy says, "at least I don't think he did. But he never said so—he never said a word."

As Jimmy grew up, each passing year would hone away the negative memories of his father. Actually, from his personal viewpoint, there were few of these. Instead, there was the ever-present laughter, the little nonsensical games between the two of them, rides on broad shoulders, his father's praise of all Jimmy's childhood successes, and sarsaparillas served to him grandly as he sat as though in a spotlight on the high bar of his father's saloon. It was easy for Jimmy to remember his father and mother seated together on the family sofa with arms entwined, smiling happily in proud recognition of their children's talents. There were happy times, many of them—there had to be—yet something went tragically wrong.

It is difficult even today for Jimmy to discuss his father without fighting back tears, his memories are so bittersweet. But he laughs in recalling how important it was for his father to sing, though, even as a child, Jimmy knew that there were few persons on earth with less to recommend a vocal solo. "His voice was just awful," Jimmy says. "But he didn't know it. He thought he was very good—especially when he was drinking. He had a very heavy vibrato that could shake the room like an earthquake. His favorite song was 'I Don't Want to Play in Your Yard.' It was almost his trademark. Years later I was given the choice of a song to sing in 'The Oklahoma Kid.' That song was my choice."

In a mid-fifties magazine article Jimmy recounted the morning ritual his father carried out as he prepared to leave for work. "He'd kiss Mom goodbye, then he'd blow a kiss to us kids, put a cap on over his shock of heavy black hair, bless himself, run his hands over his trousers to make sure all the buttons were buttoned, and be off. He did that every morning of his life.

"My father was a nice man, a gentle man. He worked at being a nice guy. As I grew up, and he grew older, he was class going downhill."

Because of the problems their father had, none of the Cagney children would have much to do with drinking. The only one of the five surviving children who imbibed even lightly was the youngest brother, Bill, but, according to Jimmy, he never drank more than he could handle. As for Jimmy, he would have an occasional glass of wine with dinner, but never more than that.

Considering the adversity faced by the Cagney family, it was almost miraculous that Carolyn Cagney was able to keep her sons in school. By the time the United States declared war on Germany in 1914, Harry had already entered Columbia University, Jimmy was about to graduate from high school, Ed was in his second year, and Bill was just entering. They were all attending classes regularly and working constantly to keep food on the table.

There was a government call for volunteers to join the military, and a draft was soon started. It was unthinkable for the Cagney boys to join up, with their heavy family responsibilities, and, fortunately, none was conscripted. Jimmy's mother was encouraging him to pursue an artistic profession. Carolyn had been gifted as an artist, and Jimmy seemed to have inherited her talents. Jimmy didn't reject the idea, but he had a more practical nature. His great love for the outdoors was growing with his own maturity, and he could think of nothing that would please him more as a way of life than farming. He wrote a letter of application to the Farmington School of Agriculture and waited hopefully for their acceptance. He knew that he would have to somehow raise money for tuition, but he would face that obstacle when confronted by it.

The Cagneys were then living in a ground-floor apartment at 420 East Seventy-eighth Street, which, Jimmy concedes, was not exactly a farming area, but he couldn't see how that would matter. The family was surprised one afternoon to be visited by a representative of the Farmington School. "My mother and all my brothers were gathered around," said Jimmy. "The man stayed around for a few minutes and then left. He never came back, and I never heard from him again. Maybe after seeing our house he thought I

wouldn't have enough money for tuition—I don't know—but that
was the end of that."

An artistic career took on an added glow after Jimmy's disappointment with the agricultural school, but he still didn't think the
idea was very practical; and where would he get enough money to
enter art school? Then everything seemed to fall into place, and he
had World War I to thank for it.

Harry, at Columbia, got word that the army was seeking re-
cruits for the Student Army Training Corps on the campus. It was
a World War I version of ROTC, and Jimmy signed up. He was
assigned to the military camouflage unit as an artist. Practically
overnight Jimmy became a college student, an artist, and a soldier.
When he completed the four-year course he would become an
army officer, but he would also earn his college degree.

Jimmy studied diligently, kept all of his jobs going, and even
signed up with the band as a drummer. If the Cagneys had particular problems at the beginning of 1918, they were all too busy to
know it; and the senior Cagney was visiting home now and then as
well. The boys soon learned that they would once more be candi-
dates for big brotherhood. Carolyn Cagney was pregnant with her
seventh baby. Once more the boys were pleased, especially since
they had lost little Robert two years earlier.

There was cause for consternation, however, because as the
pregnancy progressed the tragic influenza pandemic of 1918 was
taking firm, devastating root. Jimmy remembers seeing caskets
piled six or seven high outside the local cemeteries. Few families
escaped the contagion; within a matter of a few months twenty
million people had died around the world, and as many as one
billion had contracted the disease.

The Cagneys considered themselves fortunate to be excep-
tions. It appeared that they would weather the scourge. When
James senior complained of nausea, weakness, and muscle sore-
ness, it was assumed that he was just suffering from another morning hangover. Carolyn wasn't so certain, however, and she was
carrying a baby. When her husband's morning eye-opener failed to
have its desired effect, she insisted that he go to a hospital—just to
be safe. If he did have a touch of the flu, she didn't want to risk
infecting the baby.

Jimmy was at the university when word was sent to him that
his father had been admitted to the hospital. Without delay, he left

school and boarded a streetcar. Forty-five minutes later he was at the registration desk of the specified hospital asking for the number of his father's room.

The nurse looked at him strangely, but there was nothing in her expression to portend the gravity of her next words: "I'm sorry," she said. "Mr. Cagney died this morning."

CHAPTER 4

His father's death in November 1918 came to Jimmy as a stunning blow. He had been only forty-one. The children had all heard the frequent admonitions that he would eventually drink himself to death, but that had been going on for years. Now, he *was* dead, and the cause of death was listed as influenza. There was probably little doubt that his death had been caused at least indirectly by his drinking; his resistance was so low that he was unable to ward off the virus. But he was gone, and it didn't really matter now what had taken him away. All that remained were memories.

Among Jimmy's memories were all the recriminations. There was guilt for words left unsaid, and penitence for actions taken. The hallway encounter that had led to his father's incarceration came back to haunt him. At the time, and over the years, Jimmy often wondered if there had been a better course for him to have taken. He had been conditioned to do what his mother told him without question, but maybe on that one occasion he should have resisted more. Perhaps he should have at least questioned it. But he hadn't, and it was past.

In reminiscing about his father's death, Jimmy says: "He had the charm of a minstrel. He did everything to the tune of laughter. He was totally deficient in a sense of responsibility to his family, yet he always thought he was doing well for us."

When it came to making arrangements for the burial, Jimmy was elected to handle things, or perhaps he volunteered; he doesn't quite remember. He remembers clearly, however, how little money there was in hand for what had to be done. He somehow made arrangements with the undertaker to embalm the body and have it brought back to the house. Then he called the priest and asked him to stop by.

When the priest came to the house Jimmy explained their financial situation, but asked that the priest do the best he could to give his father a decent funeral service. Jimmy handed over his last two dollars, and the priest said he would be on hand for the service. "He never came. There were no services. A carriage took the body off to the cemetery, and that was that."

There had been a wake the night before, but it had not been what the Irish had learned to expect. Several drinking chums of his father's had staggered in and asked for whiskey. "There's none here," Jimmy told them. "Goddamn it, you aren't going to get any!" They stumbled out of the parlor in disbelief. Who ever heard of an Irish wake without whiskey?

When the burial was over, Carolyn Cagney went through her husband's belongings. She would give the boys what they could use and dispose of what remained. In doing this she came across his checkbook, which she inspected closely. There were a series of curious entries. "That was another of Pop's little weaknesses. The horses. In his checkbook my mother found entries as high as one hundred and fifty and two hundred dollars, all made out to his bookmakers. That money would have been a fortune to us—even if we had seen half of it."

The World War I armistice was signed at the time of James senior's death, which meant another change in Jimmy's life. The end of the war meant the end of Jimmy's free education. He remained in school as long as he could but then dropped out entirely. Harry and Ed were both intent on higher education; they planned to become doctors. It made sense to Jimmy that he should work full-time to make their tasks a bit easier. They had practical plans, and he had only a dream of somehow becoming an artist. But there was another compelling reason for bringing in as much money as possible: His mother would soon be giving birth to the last of the Cagney children, and Jimmy wanted to do all he could to see that the last was best.

Harry Cagney was an excellent athlete, always competing in track events, swimming, and diving; somewhat by accident, he also became involved in acting. With their mother's encouragement, all the boys were active at the Lenox Hill Settlement House. There were myriad activities there for people of all ages, and Carolyn

Cagney induced Harry to participate in elocution classes, thinking it would help him in his medical career. The elocution classes involved the producton of amateur plays; Harry became one of the leading men.

Acting held no interest for Jimmy, but he did find himself involved in the production, as a painter of scenery. When the staff saw how good he was, they let him paint dance posters and provide whatever other art was needed.

One night, when Harry was to open in a play, he was taken ill. Panic ran rampant; who would step in to take his place? There were no understudies at the settlement house, but what they had not reckoned on was Jimmy Cagney's photographic memory. He had been hanging around during rehearsals and had learned all his brother's lines. The delighted production staff curled Jimmy's hair for his role and altered the satyr's suit to fit his size, and the curtain was run up on time. Jimmy was sure he would never live down the humiliation of it, but he played the role without so much as a miscue. He was perhaps the last to know it at the time, but his acting career had begun.

Jimmy was not yet hooked as an actor, and he has always insisted that his amateur theatrics at the settlement house had nothing to do with his subsequent career. He does admit, however, that acting became much more interesting to him some months later when Hunter College, the nearby girls' school, started asking the boys at the settlement house to play opposite Hunter girls. Jimmy made himself available and acted in several Hunter productions. It was fun, and he did it all with considerable ease, but his first love was still baseball, and he seldom missed a Sunday playing date with the Nut Club team.

On one of those Sundays, the Mutual Welfare League of Sing Sing Prison invited the Nut Club players to meet the convicts in a game on the prison grounds at Ossining. Jimmy made sure he was on hand for this, because he knew they had a good team, with several solid minor-leaguers on the prison roster. He didn't know, however, that his visit to Sing Sing would play like old home week at Yorkville.

When they arrived on the field, Jimmy took his usual place behind homeplate to warm up the pitcher. As the pitcher started blazing away, Jimmy heard a voice say, "Hello, Red." Jimmy had been admonished, along with the other team members, not to engage in conversations with the inmates, so he ignored the greeting. A moment later: "What's wrong, Red, gettin' stuck up?" Jimmy turned to see his old friend Bootah. During furtive exchanges Jimmy learned how Bootah had ended up in Sing Sing. He and another boy, also a friend of Jimmy's, had been sentenced to five to ten years for wounding a cop in a stickup.

Later, with the game in progress and with the Sing Sing team at bat, Jimmy heard the spectators cheering on the next batter, whose name was Lafferty. When he stepped into the batter's box, Jimmy said, "Are you *Jack* Lafferty?" "That's me," said the con. It was Dirty Neck Jack Lafferty, a name as familiar to Jimmy as Jack Dempsey, but not for similar reasons. Lafferty had been a friend of Jimmy's father whom he had heard discussed dozens of times. It was Cagney senior, in fact, who had helped Lafferty get his sentence reduced to twenty years after killing the man whose car he was in the process of stealing.

Lafferty had started off in the car when the owner managed to catch up in time to jump onto the running board. Lafferty pulled his gun and shot the man dead. The elder Cagney had called on his friends at Tammany Hall in behalf of Lafferty, saying that the lad was only twenty-five, that he was essentially a nice guy, and that he had been a victim of circumstance. The Cagney charm helped keep the sentence to a minimum.

Lafferty had been a regular at Cagney's saloon. After a few drinks he would say, " Someday I'm gonna kill somebody, Jim " "What makes you say that?" Cagney would say. "I don't know— but I'm gonna do it." He did.

Jimmy found Lafferty distinctive because at his youthful age he had snow-white hair. Jimmy's father found him distinctive because he was the first saloon brawler he had seen break a beer mug and use it on someone. At the ballgame, when Jimmy explained who he was, the convict turned to face him. "I'm sorry, kid," he said, almost tearfully. "I'm sorry about what happened to your dad."

At a later inning, another of Jimmy's former friends asked if he still went down to the Eastside Club. Then another spoke of old times. In all, Jimmy had fleeting reunions with a half-dozen guys from the streets. Almost every member of the Nut Club team knew at least one person behind bars. It was a Yorkville class re-union.

Of all his old acquaintances, the only one for whom Jim felt real sympathy was poor old Bootah. He knew him really well, and had always found him to be a quiet, reasonable, and decent human being. Jimmy wondered why some survived and others didn't. Many of the boys from the streets had had brushes with the law, but for minor offenses. Bootah, on the other hand, went all the way. He was in jail this time for wounding a policeman but would be released within a couple of years. It was after returning to the streets that he would commit the ultimate act.

"He was pulling a stickup on East One Hundred and Second Street," said Jimmy. "At that moment a cop came around the corner. The cop's wife had taken sick, and he was excused from his shift to go home and look after their four kids. That was what he was doing when he came upon Bootah holding a gun on this Italian guy. Bootah swung around. . . . Bang! He shot the cop dead."

On July 21, 1927, the night Jack Dempsey fought Jack Sharkey, Jimmy was working as an understudy in *Broadway*. It was also the night that Peter Hessling, known best as "Bootah," was executed in the electric chair at Sing Sing.

Jimmy has often said that there were only three ways a kid from his neighborhood could get ahead: by means of the ring, show business, or crime. To do it any other way was next to miraculous, and the miracle for the Cagney boys was their mother, because all of them fared very well in life. Carolyn Cagney was intrinsically intelligent, had the highest ideals, and instilled a spirit of integrity into her children. She may have come from nothing, but she was never satisfied to stay there. She transferred her high aspirations to her sons, and then, on March 25, 1919, there came another addition to the family for whom she had high hopes: on that date Jeanne Carolyn Cagney was born. As Jimmy would often say of his mother, "She saved the best for last."

Jimmy says the family motto was always "'United we stand, divided we fall.' I can't remember a time when if any of us had three bucks, we didn't throw it immediately into the kitty. Doing things together, as mother drummed into our heads, sharing everything, working for the common end, instead of each going off in separate directions, gave us the feeling we were strong. The trouble with most poor families is that they don't have that community feeling. Alone, they're helpless in a tough world."

The feeling of community was strengthened with the arrival of

Jeanne, and everyone's efforts were intensified to handle the additional responsibility. It was frustrating to Jimmy, however, because there weren't enough hours in the day to bring home an adequate income, certainly not on the salary he earned at Wanamaker's.

Jimmy and a shipping-room colleague would occasionally commiserate with each other about their desire to earn more money, but more often the discussion involved show business. The other boy was a fanatic on the subject, and when Jimmy once demonstrated his ability to dance "The Peabody," he was duly impressed. It was the single step Jimmy had learned at the settlement house, but was not an easy one.

Jimmy's coworker came to him excitedly a few weeks after seeing his skillful rendition of the dance step. A replacement was needed for the chorus line of a revue playing at the Keith's Eighty-sixth Street Theatre, and he said that Jimmy should hurry over and audition. Jimmy considered it a waste of time, but he had to admit that there was nothing to lose. He went to audition.

The show, called *Every Sailor,* was based on a wartime show with a cast of navy personnel. Its original title had been *Every Woman.* The producer, Phil Dunning, had retained most of the navy cast in the show, but one of the chorus boys had had to drop out.

When his turn came, Jimmy demonstrated his dance step and improvised one of the steps he had observed another dancer do while he was waiting. The director halted the routine, and Jimmy was certain he was being dismissed. Instead, he was hired on the spot and began rehearsals immediately.

Much to Jimmy's surprise, he learned that he would be performing as a chorus girl instead of a boy. Since it was a military show, the female characters were played by men in women's costumes. When he learned that the salary would be thirty-five dollars a week, he was ready to wear whatever they told him to. "That was a mountain of money for me in those worrisome days," Jimmy said. "I couldn't dance or sing or do anything, but they needed a boy and needed him badly. I somehow filled the bill. To me, it was just a chance to get a job."

Jimmy's mother had always been proud of him. It pleased her that he had inherited her flaming red hair, and that he had been born with her artistic talents. But after bringing the family to see Jimmy in *Every Sailor,* she would have preferred that his artistic skills be restricted to palette and brush. Her reaction to his performance that night was simply stated: "You'd better get an education."

PART TWO

From Street Fights to Footlights

CHAPTER 5

immy Cagney was a rather brash and confident child, but a curious phenomenon began to set in during his teens. His cockiness turned to shyness. He mentioned this to Burton James, the director of the settlement house, who replied with fixed gaze, "Maybe you're getting some sense."

Jimmy regarded this as a keen observation, but it didn't solve the problem. His shyness would, in fact, follow him relentlessly throughout life, and it was a stroke of luck that he learned early that his self-consciousness could be peeled away when he walked onstage.

"I am not myself up there," he explains. "I am not that fellow James Cagney at all. I lost all consciousness of him when I put on skirts, wig, paint, powder, feathers, and spangles. Besides, that was the time, right after the war, when service acts were still fresh in mind—when female impersonators were in vogue."

Still, he didn't broadcast to the neighborhood that he was doing a "drag" act at the Keith Theatre. Only his closest friends knew about it. As for losing himself in the characters he portrayed onstage, there would be a price to pay. From his very first appearance before an audience, Jimmy would suffer from the severest possible form of stage fright. It didn't manifest in the usual butterflies-in-the-stomach sensation; it was more a sledgehammer in the solar plexus. Almost always the tremors would lead to nausea and vomiting, but his symptoms would disappear immediately upon his first entrance.

Every Sailor ran for eight weeks after Jimmy joined the cast, and when it closed he had no illusions about a theatrical career. He considered it a fluke that he had landed the job in the first place;

having sneaked into the cast, he was able to deliver some much-needed money to the Cagney kitty. When the show closed, he assumed that his career had closed too.

The idea of making the rounds of producers' offices in search of further dancing jobs didn't occur to Jimmy, and if it had he wouldn't have been able to afford the luxury. He pounded the pavement in search of a job and after a few days found one as a runner for a Wall Street brokerage firm. The job entailed dashing from one firm to another to verify stock sales. He had had his share of jobs by this time, but none that was duller than this one. He hated it.

Had Jimmy found a better-paying job that didn't bore him to death, he might never have sought another show business job, but under his current circumstances he fairly leapt at the chance to audition for another show. He had been told that a show scheduled to open at the end of September 1920 needed chorus people. He was standing in line when the auditions were scheduled.

Jimmy let a half-dozen or more dancers slip in ahead of him at the Longacre Theatre. Since he knew so few dance steps, he thought that it might be to his advantage to see what the other boys were doing. When he finally took his turn, he had plotted out a routine that was composed of the better bits he had been watching. It was good enough for Jimmy to get the nod from the director. It was the second time in his life that he had tried out for a professional dance job, and it was the second time he was hired. The show was called *Pitter Patter,* and the pay once more was $35 a week.

The show was a musical version of an old Willie Collier farce called *Hottentot,* and while it would earn little artistic distinction, it was good enough to have an eight-month run. Jimmy milked the job for every cent it was worth.

When Ernest Truex took over the leading role, Jimmy was given the job of being his dresser. He was also the baggage man when the show went on the road. Both jobs increased his income, but another opportunity paid off only in prestige. It was decided to drop the boys' chorus line in favor of a specialty dance number, and it was Jimmy who was chosen for it. At the time, the prestige had about as much value to Jimmy as dance taps without shoes, but he held a job, and his weekly income had risen to $55. When the show was playing in New York he gave all but streetcar fare to his mother. When it went on tour he kept only his minimal road expenses.

Pitter Patter marked the onset of one of America's great show-business careers, but to Jimmy, at the time, it was "just a job." More important to him, even in retrospect, was the key person he met while doing the show. The association began with little flourish, but it grew with the weeks. In due course he became aware that in Frances Willard Vernon, a diminutive chorus girl, he had made an important chemical discovery. She was right for him; the balance between them was perfect; in fact, without their partnership at the beginning of his career, there might never have been a career at all.

Willie, as Jimmy called her (he also calls her Bill, Billie, and any number of assorted names), had been with the play as long as Jimmy, but he didn't particularly notice her at first. When she was pointed out to him, with her long curls, ruffled dress, and hat full of ribbons, Jimmy whispered, "All dressed up and let out for an hour."

Willie noticed Jimmy, with the initial observation that he was a very serious young man. He was constantly studying, rehearsing, reading. He didn't seem to let loose and enjoy himself, as did so many other members of the cast.

She had been born sixteen years earlier in Fairfield, Iowa, and christened Willard Vernon. "My parents had four girls, and I was the last—an accident, I guess. They had a boy's name ready for me, but I was a girl. So they called me Willard anyway. I had to do something about that when I left home, so I chose the name Frances and added it on. I had a book about Frances E. Willard, who knocked down saloons, so I took Frances."

An occasion arose when the cast was invited to a party, and Willie was asked if she planned to attend. She looked across the room at Jimmy, who was busy as usual with some of his chores, and said, "I will if I can go with the red-haired boy." Jimmy was told of this, and started examining the cute little chorine more carefully. By now she had been cued by some of the other girls; she had abandoned most of the ruffles, and her curls had been tied up in a more contemporary style. She was still incongruous because of her obvious innocence, but she no longer carried the trademark of midwestern hick. Jimmy took her to the party, and a relationship took root. But it wasn't a matter of rushing to the altar at once; there were a couple of complications. In the first place, Jimmy already had a girlfriend. Willie wasn't immediately apprised of this, but then neither was Jimmy informed that Willie had a beau impatiently waiting in Iowa for her to "get that show-business thing out of her system."

Jimmy had been dating a girl named Nellie Oliver on a fairly steady basis since he was about sixteen. She was a beautiful blue-eyed blonde with an Irish cop for a father and a well-bred American mother. Jimmy's mother had taken it for granted that Nellie would eventually become her daughter-in-law, and the idea appealed to her. Nellie was right for Jimmy. They were from the same basic background.

Nellie, the prettiest of three daughters, was studying to become a stenographer. She was intelligent, witty, and—of great importance to Jimmy—an outstanding dancer. Their dates were usually limited to a stroll in the park, or an occasional movie, when Jimmy had a few cents to spare, and on special occasions they would go out for a long night of dancing. Each understood the problems of the other; they were compatible, and there was no good reason for Jimmy to break up with her. The only possible reason was Frances Willard Vernon, but that was the dilemma.

Jimmy continued to date Nellie at the early stages of his relationship with Willie, and on one occasion he had a date early in the evening with Nellie and then tried to get a late date with Willie. That was a mistake. Willie learned of it and handled the matter with the usual dignity of a woman betrayed: she flung his photo across the room and tried to bean him with a jumbo-size jar of cold cream. The jar was wide of its target, however, and shattered in a gooey mess against the wall.

The violent outburst from an ordinarily docile person imprinted a message in Jimmy's consciousness: Willie might have been small, but she was not weak, and she would not be satisfied to play second fiddle to Nellie Oliver or anybody else. It was not a difficult decision to make, because by this time Jimmy knew he was in love with Willie. The problem was to let Nellie down easily. He did the best he could the next time he saw her. She was, of course, heartbroken, and Carolyn Cagney was bitterly disappointed that Jimmy had chosen an Iowa farmgirl over Nellie.

The situation with Willie's boyfriend back home almost paralleled Jimmy's, except that she had half a continent of space between her and the problem. That space was reduced by a few blocks when the show went on tour and paused for a run in Chicago. The young suitor showed up from Iowa to surprise the girl he had every intention of marrying. Now it was Willie's turn to break a heart, and as Jimmy paced the floor in apprehension, Willie went out with the young man to gently break the news. Later there were a barrage of telephone calls and backstage notes from the anguished boy. When the show moved out of Chicago the run was nearing its end. There were no further obstacles to their marrying, except one, and that would take some time to overcome: the Cagney family still depended on Jimmy's salary checks for survival, and with the show closing neither he nor Willie knew what lay ahead.

"I knew Jimmy would become a success in show business," Willie said. "I can say that in all honesty. I thought he would succeed mostly as a dancer, or maybe singing in musical comedy. There was this little piece in the paper about *Pitter Patter* that said, 'Watch this boy, he's good.' I was always convinced that he had it."

Whether or not Jimmy had it, at this point in his career, was moot, because his talents weren't negotiable without a job, and work was hard to find. One of his first jobs after the closing of *Pitter Patter* was a dancing and singing role in a vaudeville act called "Midge Miller and Her Boy Friends." The act was a flop, and Jimmy looked further.

After weeks of poverty, Jimmy found a part in a sketch owned by the comedian Hugh Herbert. Jimmy, in fact, replaced Herbert, who had been playing the same role. It was called "Dots My Boy," and Jimmy was called upon to play a Jewish boy with a heavy Yiddish accent. This was a natural for Jimmy, since he had been brought up in a neighborhood where everyone over thirty had some sort of accent, many of them Yiddish. In the act Jimmy would do an intricate specialty dance, and when the applause followed it, his stage mother, Ada Jaffe (Sam Jaffe's mother) would rise up from a mezzanine box and call out, "Dot's my boy." Jimmy would then recite a poem about mothers.

The act was good for a run of several weeks, and when it ended Jimmy began rehearsing another act with the comedian Harry Ormonde. They were scheduled to break it in at the Fox

Star Theatre, but unfortunately for Jimmy, that was where it also closed—the same night.

During the lean months after the closing of *Pitter Patter*, Jimmy and Willie formed their own act, called "Vernon and Nye." The "Nye" was a rearrangement of the last syllable of Jimmy's last name, but the pseudonym brought no magic. The act, which featured mostly Willie, attracted little attention. It wasn't the result of limited skills, because Jimmy had always credited Willie with having more skill as a dancer than he had. It was that the elements of the act failed to meld into a viable entity.

Jimmy and Willie were trying to work out a new approach to the same act when news came from Iowa that changed their plans. Her father had died, and Willie's sister, Jan, sent the rail fare for her to attend the funeral.

After the burial, Willie spent a reasonable time with her mother and then accompanied Jan back to Chicago. Willie had hoped to return to New York, but there was no money. She was given a place to sleep among Jan's children, and then homesickness for Jimmy and for New York started to set in.

The situation was so similar to what she had experienced a few years earlier that Willie became depressed. She had been sent to Chicago to live with her sister and to attend school. Her parents planned that each of the four girls would be educated at the best schools and would then begin careers as schoolteachers. All the sisters acquiesced, except Willie: She took her tuition money and ran away to New York. Now it seemed that she had returned to where it had all begun.

Willie says that she would have returned to New York even if it had required hitchhiking, but it didn't come to that. "One day my sister says to me, 'I have to go into Chicago to do some shopping, and you can go to Loewe's State Theatre.' I went, and I remember that the closing act was two girls who played the piano and sang. When the show ended I was coming out of the theater, and this woman came up behind me and tapped me on the shoulder. She said, 'Are you a dancer?' I said that I was. She asked if I had seen the last act and I said that I had. She told me then that one of the gals had to leave the act, and asked if I wanted to join the show. I said yes right then and there."

The obvious question arises: How did the woman know that Willie was a dancer? Willie doesn't know. The woman, named

Woodsie, became a very close friend of the Cagneys, and even she is unable to explain why she tapped Willie on the shoulder. It is accepted by Willie as something of a miracle, because nothing took precedence over her desire to return to New York. The show worked its way to Milwaukee and points east, until it finally delivered her to New York and to Jimmy.

There would be many other separations for the young couple, but it was work that took them away from each other. It was not as if either was stranded without the means to return. One of their subsequent separations found Willie playing in a show in Philadelphia, and she recalls an incident that makes her shudder. "I was paid sixty dollars," she explained. "On the way back on the train I went to the ladies' room and left my purse there. I ran back in a few minutes, but it was gone. Somebody had stolen it. I hate to think of it even now . . . that money meant so much to us then." At that time, sixty dollars was enough to pay a month's rent and buy food for as many days. It would surely have kept them from eating bread and jelly and calling it a meal, as they had to do so frequently.

Before starvation set in, Jimmy landed a job in an important vaudeville three-acter that had originally been called Parker, Rand, and Leach; Leach wanted to be replaced, so the act became Parker, Rand, and Cagney. The vaudevillian named Leach was Archie Leach, who would later change his name to Cary Grant.

The act was reviewed by *Variety* with less than unbounded praise. "Parker, Rand, and Cagney," the item said, "begin with two boys and a girl in a skit idea that gets nowhere. It is a turn without semblance of a punch. There are no laughs and the songs mean little. One of the boys can dance. Small time is its only chance. Trio gets $275 tops." The boy who could dance was Jimmy, which gave him the only positive words in the writeup.

After a brief run, Jimmy was back on the New York streets making the rounds. Vaudevillians would congregate and compare notes across from the Palace Theatre on Forty-seventh Street, where Seventh Avenue and Broadway intersect. It was a triangular piece of property, known then as "Panic Beach," where out-of-work performers would pick up casting tips or trade dance steps. Many of the same faces would appear each day to await news of openings in their particular specialty and, perhaps, enjoy loafing while waiting. Jimmy was never one of them. He may have stopped by, but never to pass the time of day. And he didn't hold out for openings of his specialty, either, because his "specialty" was whatever they might pay him to do.

"The result was that I worked in a variety of acts that I may never have qualified for," says Jimmy. "I was always taking a chance that I'd get fired, and it happened a few times. But each one of those little jobs built up priceless experience, and a resilience to the tough times that lay ahead." And the tough times were frequent.

Jimmy would become depressed over his career, or lack of it, and would probably have given up had it not been for Willie's encouragement. Her support was more than spiritual. Chorus girls were in much greater demand than boys, so it would be her jobs that would carry them over many of the rough spots; but there was also the constant worry over the survival of his family.

Harry and Ed were working and attending college, and Bill was bringing in his share of earnings, but so much was needed now, especially since the birth of Jeanne. Jimmy's mother did not encourage him to continue in his career; she thought it a waste of time. He was inclined to agree, but Willie's constant affirmation instilled in Jimmy a will to succeed.

Both Jimmy and Willie landed good jobs in *Lew Fields's Ritz Girls of 1922* and toured with it on the Shubert circuit. It played throughout the Midwest, and all seemed well until they hit St. Louis, where the money dried up. Most of the cast members had wondered *when* it would happen, not *if* it would, because it was Fields's reputation to overextend himself. In St. Louis Fields's creditors managed to seize the players salaries legally, and there was every possibility that the company would find themselves stranded there. The actors banded together, however, and refused to leave until they were paid. The Shubert Brothers came through with the money to transport the cast back to New York.

Back in New York, Jimmy returned to his corner of the Cagney apartment and Willie settled in at the midtown rooming house of Madame Pichieu. There were no doubts by now that they would sooner or later become man and wife, but two years had passed since their meeting, and the altar didn't seem to be getting any closer. It was Jimmy's hope to get a good job and do it right, but that possibility seemed remote. Then it occurred to him that this might be as good a time as any to tie the knot. They had managed to save a little money from the tour, so why not?

Jimmy made a very direct and succinct proposal of marriage, and Willie thought it over for at least a second before saying yes. "We went to City Hall, got the license and got married," said Jimmy. "No great to-do about it."

The ceremony took place on September 28, 1922. Willie packed up her belongings and moved them from Madame Pichieu's place to the Cagneys' apartment in Yorkville. It was not the most idyllic of newlywed arrangements, but for the time being it was the way it had to be.

Carolyn Cagney was not overjoyed with her new daughter-in-law, and Willie was no more thrilled with her, but, as Jimmy recalls, "They got along all right together." He says it was understandable that they wouldn't get along too well. "They were poles apart," he says. "She was a girl from a little town in Iowa, and my folks were big-city poor people." Despite their differences, the young Cagneys and the rest of the family managed to live together in unison, if not in harmony, for the next couple of months.

CHAPTER 6

As a residual from the Lew Fields tour, Jimmy managed to get his name listed on the Shubert talent sheet and, as a result, obtained a few vaudeville dancing spots. Whether with or without his bride, he worked the sticks, doing whatever was asked of him.

Then the two of them were hired for a vaudeville road-show called *First Act.* It gave them an unbroken thirty weeks of work and allowed them to save the extraordinary sum of $150. Part was spent for a room of their own. Their next job was with Lew Fields's *Snapshots of 1923,* but that was even less successful than the first. They were soon out of work again.

Jimmy recalls the winter of 1923–24 as the all-time low point of his fledgling career. For the first time he was forced to take a job other than performing. For extremely low wages he signed as assistant property man for the Provincetown Playhouse, in Greenwich Village. His principle function, he soon discovered, was janitorial work, but he had no complaint; it was a job and he desperately needed it. One night, however, the subways were running late, causing Jimmy to be a few minutes late for work. He was greeted by the flush-faced company manager, who demanded to know where he had been. Jimmy did his best to explain the situation, but no excuses were acceptable. The manager thrust a pushbroom into Jimmy's hands and ordered him to get busy sweeping the stage. Jimmy returned the broom with sufficient impact to send the manager sprawling onto the floor. "Sweep it yourself, you son-of-a-bitch!" Jimmy told him. He turned around and walked off his three-dollar-a-night job.

Willie was doing well for a while in a dancing act with Wynne

Gibson, who would later become a Paramount contract player. Whenever possible, Jimmy would try to book himself in acts that would coincide generally with Willie's itinerary, but more often than not it failed to work out. Then would come separations that they both abhorred.

Jimmy says that he would have given up on show business at about this time if he had had anything better to turn to, but as he saw it, he was earning more money being mostly unemployed than he would have on the best paying steady job he had ever held. Good jobs were not easy to find. "I had no idea what my second choice might have been," he says. "Not art, certainly. There was no money there. The most I ever earned doing that was five dollars a week."

Not only did Jimmy have Willie's total support, but there were others who had faith in him. One of them was his closest friend from the old days in Yorkville, Artie Klein. Artie and Jimmy had become pals when they were both about ten. Artie's parents were Jewish immigrants, yet he never learned Yiddish. Jimmy, on the other hand, knew it very well. The two of them played together, dated together, and daydreamed together. Now that Jimmy had broken from the ranks of the street hoods in Yorkville, Artie regarded him as one of the winners of all time. He refused to allow Jimmy to worry about money—at least not while Artie had a job. At the time, Artie was a stock clerk. He frequently visited Jimmy and never failed to ask whether he was short of funds. If Jimmy even hinted that he was, Artie would hand over half his money. For an extended period of time, Artie gave half his weekly paycheck to Jimmy, because he knew that he needed it.

"He was just a straightforward and honest guy," says Jimmy, "and the best friend anyone could ever have." The friendship continued until Artie's death a few years ago, and Jimmy repaid him many times over for the generosity Artie expressed at a time when it really mattered.

Jimmy recalls another significant incident that occurred during those tough times. He was walking with his wife along the city streets, when she recognized a look of longing as Jimmy glanced at a clothing display in a store window. What he had spotted was a handsome winter coat. "Why don't you buy it?" Willie asked him. "Why, I can't afford that," he quickly replied. Willie wanted him to have the coat, and she went in and bought it for him. She said that he could pay her back, a little at a time. The small ledger book remains among their souvenirs today, with entries showing the quarters, half-dollars, and dollars Jimmy repaid.

The luck of the Cagneys improved during 1924, with a string of fairly good jobs. With their memories of near-poverty vivid, they found themselves listening intently to the harebrained scheme of an old friend, a young man named Leonard who had been the press agent for *Pitter Patter*. Leonard, who had always wanted to become an actor, expressed his notion that New York was not the place for launching a big-time career. The place was Hollywood. That was where fortunes were being made. He finally convinced the Cagneys that they should join him on his odyssey westward. He wanted their company badly enough to pay both their fares on the train.

It was Leonard's timing that had the greatest impact on the Cagneys. As it happened, Willie's mother had recently moved to a town called Hawthorne, near Los Angeles, and this was a perfect opportunity for Jimmy and his mother-in-law to meet. Willie felt certain that her mother would welcome all of them at her home, and as for Jimmy, he had nothing to keep him in New York. He had been curious about Hollywood anyway, so why not take a crack at it? They were soon on their way.

It wasn't a belated honeymoon for the Cagneys; a three-thou-sand-mile trip across the country in railroad coach seats didn't afford the privacy or the comfort for that kind of celebration. It was no more than a long, tedious trip.

As it turned out, Hawthorne wasn't exactly within megaphone range of Hollywood; it was a forty-five-minute streetcar ride away. Yet the three of them rented a comfortable furnished house not far from Willie's mother's place for thirty-five dollars a month.

Jimmy and Leonard started making the rounds of the Hollywood studios. They soon learned that it was a different world from New York. In Hollywood, actors needed agents to get them inside the high fences and iron gates of the studio compounds. Jimmy never got his first studio interview, nor did Leonard. They found movies to be a closed society—at least to them. It didn't occur to Willie to make rounds herself. If Jimmy couldn't make it past the studio gates, she could see no purpose in trying.

Jimmy came across a friend from the vaudeville circuit, Harry Gribbon, who was in Hollywood to make it big in movies but who, so far, had remained on the outside looking in. The two of them pieced together what they considered to be a surefire vaudeville routine—by stealing bits of other acts—and made themselves available for booking. They finally managed to get booked in a San Pedro theater, but their high hopes were shattered after their very first performance. The act was a dismal flop, and the Gribbon-Cagney partnership came to a swift close.

Willie managed somehow to keep everyone eating throughout the Southern California drought, but it began to seep into all their minds that they could starve more comfortably in New York, where camaraderie could mollify their misery. "We started getting hints from Willie's family that she had married a hoofer who couldn't earn a dime," Jimmy said. "Then, the question arose in my mind, 'Why don't you go back where you came from? You aren't doing anyone any good in California.'"

Jimmy sent an SOS to one of his dependable friends, Jim Fair, who was then a reporter for *The New York Times*. "He sent us 'Hollywood Medicine.' In other words, he sent us money to get back to New York." Jimmy and Willie said farewell to the West Coast—and to Leonard, who decided to remain—and boarded a Southern Pacific train. After three days, Chicago loomed before them, and they had another dilemma to deal with: Should they transfer to the New York Central when they arrived, or should they stop off to give Chicago a try? Willie's sister still lived there, which would give them a place to stay, and everyone knew that Chicago offered many opportunities for show-business folk. They decided to give it a try.

In Chicago, they cashed in the tickets to New York and took a streetcar to Willie's sister's home. But there were no friendly faces to greet them: Jan had gone on vacation and had subleased her house.

Through their impetuousness, the Cagneys had improvised a major crisis. Here they were in a strange city with neither friends nor relatives. They had only the money from the cashed-in train tickets, and after a frugal meal there was no longer enough to finance their trip to New York. They had no choice but to spend even more of their diminishing funds to rent a cheap hotel room, and to hope for quick employment. Their situation in Chicago was far more bewildering than what they had left behind in Los Angeles.

The team of Vernon and Nye was resurrected for the emergency. It failed them again, but the nickels and dimes the act did generate kept the Cagneys from starvation.

On one of their bookings they spent all but their last ten cents for the fare to Milwaukee, where they could expect only eight dollars for the night's work. Willie dined on a bottle of soda pop with her remaining nickel; Jimmy settled for a nickel's worth of cookies. But he could have saved his money. As he thought about the forthcoming stage appearance, his jitters began. The jitters turned to nausea; the nausea led to vomiting. It didn't particularly matter whether it was for big money or small; Jimmy's stage fright persisted. It was worse if he sensed that a job was beyond his capacities or if it was of special importance. The latter was true in this case, because they so badly needed the eight dollars.

After several weeks of destitution, Jimmy managed to get himself into an act with Victor Kilian that delivered the Cagneys back to New York. There Kilian was cast in a major role in Eugene O'Neill's play *Desire Under the Elms,* and he tried to help Jimmy get a part. Jimmy was given an interview, but the director told him that there was nothing for him in the play. He did say, however, that there was another production coming up in which Jimmy could very possibly be used.

Jimmy dismissed the notion from his mind. These people were talking about legitimate acting, and he was a hoofer. He could hold his own in vaudeville, and maybe even in musical comedy, but in drama? He doubted that he would ever get the call—but he did.

Maxwell Anderson had written a play called *Outside Looking In,* based on a novel by Jim Tully about the lives of hoboes. The lead role, "Oklahoma Red," had been assigned to Charles Bickford, but they were looking for another redhead for the role of "Little Red." Jimmy was called in for a reading.

Jimmy says that there were only a couple of redheads around Broadway at the time, he and an actor named Alan Bunce. "I assume I got the role because my hair was redder than his." But he did get it, and the barrier had been broken. Jimmy was now a bona fide actor and, the critics would declare, he was a good one.

Jimmy was signed for two hundred dollars a week, and the play opened at the Greenwich Village Playhouse in September

1925. After its initial success it moved to the spacious Thirty-ninth Street Theatre, where it had a four-month run.

The drama critic Robert Benchley thought it miraculous that two such perfect redheads could be found for the roles. He praised Bickford highly and said: "Mr. Cagney, in a less spectacular role, makes a few minutes of silence during his mock-trial scene something that many a more established actor might watch with profit."

Burns Mantle said of Bickford and Jimmy: "He and Mr. James Cagney . . . do the most honest acting now to be seen in New York. I believe that Mr. Barrymore's effective performance of Hamlet would be a mere feat of elocution if compared to the characterization of either Mr. Bickford or Mr. Cagney, both of whom are unknown."

It would have been a natural temptation for Jimmy to believe all this praise and limit his future job seeking to legitimate opportunities. Instead, he went out looking for jobs of any kind, wherever he might find them. He was offered membership in the Theatre Guild, which included such esteemed actors as Edward G. Robinson, but, paradoxically, Jimmy turned it down. He was willing to take any kind of performing job, but if he was going to work in the theater, he felt that the pay should be at the best rate available. Since the Theatre Guild offered less money, Jim went elsewhere for work. His stubbornness was born at an early age.

What he came up with was a vaudeville date for him and Willie called "Lonesome Manor," which toured throughout the Midwest and many southern states. The southern leg of the tour wasn't nearly as successful, however, because Jimmy's staccato delivery sounded to the audience like so much gibberish.

Jimmy was playing the role of a substitute New York newsstand boy who sold papers on the corner of Forty-third Street and Broadway. A little girl from Kokomo, Indiana (Willie), happens on the scene to buy a hometown paper. The boy flirts with the girl in his city way, with a series of jokes passing between them. He sells her the paper, and they go into a song-and-dance routine, which is climaxed with the girl singing "There's No Place Like Home." The boy sings an upbeat number that extols the virtues of the city. One of the song's choruses goes: "Oh, there's no doubt about it/And I cannot live without it,/So I simply want to shout it night and day./There's just one place I want to be/And that's the place that's haunting me—taunting me/And that's Broadway."

The act was a hit, and they managed to get a number of other jobs over the next couple of years. "My Bill [Willie] was a fine dancer," Jimmy says, "and I worked very hard to learn my job so we could make it into the better theaters. We worked the bill with people like Van and Schenck, Ken Murray, Buster West, and Bill Robinson."

Jimmy attributes much of his dancing skill to the tutelage of the veteran vaudevillian Harry Boyle, who was willing to spend hours backstage running through routines with him. But Jimmy also stole shamelessly from Bill Robinson and all the other top-notch dancers with whom he shared bills. "I didn't just steal Robinson's dance steps," says Jimmy. "I tried to steal everything. He was the greatest showman of them all. His dancing was simple but very great . . . he had great style."

He recalls Robinson as one of the softest touches in show business. Robinson was always handing out money, whether it was asked for or not, and was one of the most pleasant of show-business personalities to work with.

At about this time, Jimmy had his one and only encounter with George M. Cohan, whom he would later portray in the film *Yankee Doodle Dandy*. He had seen Cohan once on the stage, but their "meeting" was not really a meeting at all. Jimmy came to see the agent Chamberlain Brown for an interview regarding a forthcoming production in which Cohan was involved. "I stepped into the office and saw Cohan leaning against a desk. When he was behind my back he must have given me the thumb, because I was dismissed then and there. Never saw him again. After *Yankee Doodle Dandy*, Cohan said in a magazine interview 'What an act to follow,' but he didn't think much of me back then."

After his return to the vaudeville circuit, Jimmy came back to New York with much more confidence. He and Willie were finally managing to keep their bills paid, and he was vastly improving his performing skills. When the next opportunity presented itself, he was ready.

While Jimmy was still touring, William Brady was preparing to produce a musical play called *Broadway*, and he wanted Jimmy for the leading role, Roy Lane. But in the ensuing months Jed Harris took control of the property, and his choice for the role was

Lee Tracy. The Phil Dunning/George Abbott show opened in the 1926–27 season with Tracy in the role.

The character was described by the authors as "a typical song-and-dance man," so Jimmy thought that he would qualify. "Lee Tracy could act the part perfectly," Jimmy said, "but he was no dancer, and he had no firsthand knowledge of vaudeville. Because both these things were in my bones, I felt I had an approach to the part like a homing pigeon to his coop."

Jimmy had missed out on the New York production, but he was remembered later when it was time to cast the London company. Phil Dunning, who had hired Jimmy for *Every Sailor*, convinced Jed Harris that Jimmy was right for the role. Jimmy would get three hundred dollars a week, and Willie would get one of the chorus parts so that she could travel to London with him.

Jimmy began rehearsals with all his energies unleashed and his creative juices flowing. He had very definite ideas about how the role should be handled, and since he was about a hundred and eighty degrees different from Lee Tracy, he had no compunctions about expressing himself. The suggestions were listened to, but each innovation was turned down. Jimmy was puzzled at first, but then he realized what was happening: They wanted no changes because they had liked Lee Tracy's work, and expected Jimmy to copy Tracy in every detail. This was no simple task for Jimmy; not only was he practically a foot shorter than Tracy, but they were poles apart in personality as well. Jimmy managed finally to blend a little of Tracy and a little of Cagney, and when it was time for dress rehearsal he was confident. He believed that he had done what had been almost impossible—to etch a character acceptable to all.

The dress rehearsal was to be on the night before the company's sailing, and the audience would be composed of the whole hierarchy of New York's theatrical community. Jimmy went through his usual bout of stage fright on the night of the run-through, but all was well once the curtain went up. He glided through his performance with ease, and the series of final curtain calls confirmed his feeling that he had done well.

Everything had been taken care of before the performance. The Cagneys had given up their apartment, and all their luggage was onboard the ocean liner. He and Willie had only to get out of their costumes, remove their makeup, and attend the going-away party that the management had scheduled for the cast. The plan was to spend what then remained of the night aboard the ship, which would sail just after daybreak the next morning.

The party was delightful, as Jimmy recalls, with good food, champagne, and throngs of friendly show-business luminaries. That night Jimmy and Willie met many prominent actors they had only heard of before. One was Robert Montgomery, who would later become one of the Cagney's closest friends.

As the guests began to leave, Jed Harris asked to have a word with Jimmy. Jimmy was anticipating a belated congratulations, since that had been the tenor of the evening, and he supposed that Harris might offer a few last-minute suggestions. Instead, Harris told him that the ship would be leaving without him—he was being replaced.

CHAPTER 7

No matter how often Jimmy suggests that his work through all the years was "just a job," and that he really took none of it too seriously, there can be little doubt that he was shattered by the news from Harris.

He and his wife had said their goodbyes, their apartment was gone, their clothes were in the hold of a ship on which they would not be sailing, and, worst of all, everyone in theater circles knew about the firing almost immediately. It might have been easier to accept had Jimmy's replacement been someone he could admire, but the actor they chose was, according to Jimmy, "a skinny little man who couldn't dance, couldn't sing, couldn't do anything."

Willie Cagney was never known to curse; those around her were amused at her more daring expressions, such as "Oh, bean soup" or "Thundering blue mud!" Whether she uttered more explosive invectives on this occasion isn't remembered, but she remembers her anger very well. "We were both devastated," she recalls. "Jimmy kept saying it was all over. He made up his mind he was going to get a job doing something else."

The producers had Jimmy and Willie on run-of-the-play contracts, which protected the Cagneys as well as the producers. At first they said that Willie could go ahead with the company to London, assuming that she would never leave her husband. In her anger, she led them to believe that she would go with the cast, but finally it was agreed that both she and Jimmy would join the New York company as understudies, Jimmy understudying Lee Tracy. It took a ruling in the Cagneys' favor by the Actor's Equity Association to produce this compromise. At least they could count on a steady income, enough to continue helping Jimmy's mother, as long as the London company played.

There had been other disappointments for Jimmy in regard to his theatrical career, but he and Willie agree that it was during this crisis that he came closest to packing it in. His pride and confidence had been shattered. It required the fiercest determination on Willie's part to buoy Jimmy's spirits during this time.

The Broadway theater was thriving during this period, and it may have served Jimmy best in the long run to remain in New York. There were forty-two plays running, and one of those being cast as he sat out the performances of *Broadway* was the Mary Boland play *Women Go on Forever*. Jimmy had heard there was a part in it that would be right for him, but he did nothing about it. There was another more practical idea taking root.

Soon after his setback a friend offered to back Jimmy in opening a dancing school, and the idea appealed to him. A studio was rented in New Jersey, and Jimmy and Willie bought a small house near the studio, in Scotch Plains. It was a development call Free Acres, where for seven hundred dollars a house could be purchased. A single tax was shared by all the homes in the development, making it a very inexpensive place in which to live.

A few dance students signed up, and the Cagneys started to teach dancing during the day. In the evenings they would race by train, trolley, and bus to Manhattan for the show. When the curtain fell they would return by subway to the Twenty-third Street Ferry, get a train for another leg of the journey, and then walk two-and-a-half miles uphill to get home.

It was a hectic routine, but not impossible when the Cagneys were languishing backstage each night as understudies in *Broadway*. Then the situation changed: *Woman Go on Forever* had opened without Jimmy, and although it was not a hit, it was having a run based on the popularity of Mary Boland, its star. The juvenile, Roy R. Lloyd, had to leave the show, and Jimmy was asked to replace him. It was an offer he couldn't refuse.

The dance studio was not meant to teach neighborhood children basic tap. "The Cagné School of the Dance" was designed to help professionals to expand their skills. The project couldn't be simply abandoned; they had serious students, and a commitment had been made. During the strenuous days of rehearsal for his new show, Jimmy left the teaching responsibilities to Willie, who was certainly as qualified as he. Then, after he opened in the show, it was back to the earlier routine. After a reasonable time the Cagneys halted new enrollment, and eventually they were able to get out from under the unprofitable venture through attrition.

Jimmy's play ran for four months, and when it finally closed he was glad for the rest. As finances stood at this stage of his career he could never be really happy about a layoff, but the double role of dancing teacher and actor had exhausted him.

Jimmy's teaching earned him not a penny in profit, but it may have opened the way to a broader field of theatrical endeavor. Word had circulated about his skills as an innovative teacher, so when he was hired for the lead dancing role in *The Grand Street Follies of 1928* he was also engaged as choreographer.

The show opened to rave reviews. The critics loved Jimmy's dance numbers, especially the tango-tap he created and performed as the show's finale. The cast of the revue was composed of young actors who satirized the performances of Broadway celebrities. Dorothy Sands did a very successful take-off on Mae West, who was appearing at another theater in *Diamond Lil,* and Helen Hayes was mimicked by an actress named Paula Truman. The show had a run of several months. It closed in time for Jimmy to squeeze in a season of summer stock in Cleveland and in Stockbridge, Massachusetts.

Jimmy was on the move now, and Willie was ready to bow out of the act. There had been a time when she had dreamed of a Broadway career, but the glamour had worn thin. All of her aspirations were now channeled into the career of her husband. She had always believed that he would succeed, and now she was sure enough of it to look for a hook on which to hang her size-five tap shoes. From now on, she would limit her activities to those behind the scenes.

Jimmy returned to Manhattan in time to begin rehearsals for a second revue, *The Grand Street Follies of 1929.* He would not be called upon to stage the dances for this show, but he was given several numbers to perform. He had a specialty tap routine with Lily Lubell, was a dancing cop in "The ABC of Traffic," and played a harlequin in another number.

The critics were less favorably impressed with the 1929 version of the *Follies,* and the show closed after only two weeks. But Jimmy's luck was still running high. The timing of the show's closing made it possible for him to segue into another show at the Booth Theatre.

The famous director George Kelly was preparing a play called *Maggie the Magnificent*. Magazine articles later stated that Kelly had spotted Jimmy and Joan Blondell trying out a dance routine backstage, liked what he saw, and hired them on the spot. Jimmy denies the accuracy of the story. He says that he didn't meet Blondell until after rehearsals began and has no idea of the circumstances of her hiring. As for him, he was waiting in the outer office with twenty or thirty other actors. "Kelly came out, and saw me there. He said, 'Send that boy in next.' I went in and he said, 'You're hired—how much do you want?' I told him, 'Three hundred and fifty dollars.' He said, 'Well, we can pay that.' It was that simple. I wasn't asked to do a reading or anything else." Later, Jimmy was told that he was hired because he looked like "a fresh mutt." Kelly said that everything Jimmy was could be seen in his face. "I didn't know what he was talking about," Jimmy says, "But it didn't matter—it was a job."

Jimmy played a street-wise punk named Elwood opposite a gum-chewing, wisecracking blonde played by Joan Blondell. The show opened October 22, 1929, to miserable reviews, but Jimmy and Joan were singled out for unanimous praise. The stock-market crash occurred a week after the opening, but it wasn't blamed for the play's short duration. Its run of thirty-two performances was probably longer than it would have had if someone else had directed it. Kelly's prestige assured a greater audience than the play itself deserved. Important people came to see it, which helped the budding careers of Cagney and Blondell immeasurably.

Jimmy looks back on his roles in *Women Go on Forever* and *Maggie the Magnificent* as significant steps in his career. They gave him the opportunity to work with two great directors, John Cromwell and George Kelly. "I have met few really first-rate directors in my life," Jimmy says, "and those I know, I measure against the very best, George Kelly and John Cromwell. What they share is something so rare among directors as to be virtually nonexistent. They were directors who could play all the parts in the play better than the actors cast for them."

The teaming of Cagney and Blondell in *Maggie the Magnificent* opened the way for another opportunity a few months later, when they were cast together in the Marie Baumer play *Penny*

Arcade. William Keighley was the director and was coproducer with W. P. Tanner. This melodrama, set in a carnival, concerned bootlegging and murder. Jimmy played Harry Delano, the no-good son of the woman who owned the penny arcade in the carnival. Blondell was Cagney's girlfriend, Myrtle.

The play was panned by the critics after its opening on March 11, 1930, but again Cagney and Blondell were singled out. Arthur Rule of the *New York Herald Tribune* said that Jimmy was "all there as the good-for-nothing son." Wrote Brooks Atkinson of *The New York Times,* "The play contains an excellent performance by James Cagney as the weakling." The play failed (it ran for only three weeks), but Cagney and Blondell were again successful.

Jimmy Cagney would have doubts regarding his survival as an actor for many years to come, but after teaming with Joan Blondell he would never see another day of poverty. The confidence his wife had in him was proving to be justified, and she would have no reason to regret her withdrawal from an active show-business career. Willie acted as Jimmy's muse, his mother confessor, his personal cheerleader, and his bookkeeper. She budgeted their money, noting down every expenditure they made, from expensive tap shoes down to a three-cent stamp. Later on, Jimmy would turn his business matters over to his younger brother Bill, but meanwhile no one could watch over him more devotedly than Willie.

As the stock-market crash reverberated around them, Jimmy's income was three hundred dollars to four hundred dollars a week. President Hoover was declaring, "Prosperity is just around the corner," but Jimmy's had already arrived.

Vaudeville was now part of Jimmy's past, but he never minimized its importance to his career. He credits vaudeville with having the single greatest effect on his life, with the obvious exception of his good luck in finding a mate. He says that the learning experience of vaudeville is sorely missing in today's performers, even if they are unaware of it. "In vaudeville, by persistent trial and error and unremitting hard work, the performer learns how to please an audience."

Now that he was a legitimate actor, Jimmy still looked on himself as hoofer, a song-and-dance man, and the fact that he was earning big money held no reality for him. "I never considered it a big thing when I was earning three hundred and fifty dollars a week in those days," he says, "because I knew that the next week I might be earning twenty-five. I would turn it all over to Willie and forget about it. She knew what she had to do. I just wanted to keep working, and that was all."

After *Penny Arcade,* Jimmy would gladly have returned to vaudeville if an opportunity had come along, but there were some surprises awaiting him. Al Jolson, then at the peak of his popularity, had seen *Penny Arcade* and liked it. He didn't change his mind when the play closed early; that simply made what he had planned a bit less expensive. He offered the show's producers twenty thousand dollars for the screen rights, and they accepted. Almost immediately, Jolson sold the rights to Warner Brothers. There was a proviso in the deal that Warners didn't like. Jolson demanded that James Cagney and Joan Blondell be included in the package.

Warner Brothers disliked being told who would play in their movies, but having great respect for Jolson, they agreed. The studio offered the young actors a trip to Hollywood and a three-week contract. Jimmy got five hundred dollars a week and an option for a term contract. Jimmy was wise by now to the ways of Hollywood moguls and had no illusions about future stardom. Five hundred dollars a week was pretty good money, and even if he got nothing but the guaranteed three weeks of work, he would return home with fifteen hundred dollars that he wouldn't have had otherwise.

Even though Al Jolson was instrumental in Jimmy's introduction to the movies, the two of them had never met, and in fact would never meet.

Jimmy made the train trip alone from New York and found no welcoming committee awaiting him at the station. In fact, he had considerable difficulty in finding anyone who would talk to him after he called the studio. Eventually he got through to someone in casting who told him to come to the studio the following day to meet the director John Adolfi. Jimmy was staying in Hollywood with friends from New York, who gave him careful instructions on how to reach the Warner Brothers studios in distant Burbank. He caught the streetcar on Highland Avenue, and after wending its way over the hills and dales of the Cahuenga Pass it delivered him to his designated stop, just a block away from the studio gates.

It was no simple task to get past the guard stationed at the entrance, but Jimmy was finally admitted and, without much difficulty, located the office of the director. The problem was that

Adolfi wasn't expecting him and could not be located. "I waited outside for about a half hour," Jimmy says, "and said to hell with it. I took the streetcar back to Hollywood."

He tried again a few days later and had better luck. Joan Blondell was there at the same time, and they both met Adolfi. They learned then that the studio had decided to test them for the leading roles, instead of the subordinate parts they had originated. It turned out, however, that the leads went to Grant Withers and Evalyn Knapp. That was fine with Jimmy: the agreement was that he and Joan would do their original roles.

After their first meeting with Adolfi, Jimmy and Joan emerged together from the inner offices. The first thing Joan asked was where his car was parked. Jimmy had to confess not only that he did not have a car, but that he didn't know how to drive one. "She was driving a little roadster, and she said, 'Come on, I'll show you how to drive.' Jesus Christ, she showed me."

Jimmy said that the area around Warner Brothers was all wide-open spaces then. Cahuenga Pass was nothing but a winding, two-lane country road, where sixteen lanes of freeway now exist. Joan made him get into the driver's seat, and she sat beside him. "She told me to drive, and I did," says Jimmy. "I went around a corner going about forty-five or fifty, and Joan said, 'OHHHHHH.' The car damn near turned over. I didn't know I was supposed to take my foot off the gas when you turned a corner. That gives you some idea of what a great driver I was. She said, 'Slow down, Cagney.' When I found the brake, I did."

It was only a few days later that shooting began on *Sinners' Holiday*. He was nervous to the point of throwing up, but no one else knew it, and the studio had a preview of the Cagney-to-come in this, his first picture. "There was a line in the show where I was supposed to be crying on my mother's breast. Zanuck had written the line, and I was expected to say it. It was, 'I'm your baby, ain't I?' I refused to say it. Adolfi said, 'Well, I'm going to tell Zanuck.' I said, 'I don't give a shit what you tell him, but I'm not going to say that line.' They took the line out."

Despite Jimmy's display of temperament, the studio heads seemed to like what they saw. Before his three-week contract expired, he was extended for three weeks and then given a seven-year contract at a starting salary of four hundred dollars a week. Jimmy may have felt momentarily elated, but after reading the document he didn't have much feeling of security. It was apparent that all the clauses were to the benefit of Warner Brothers; they could drop him at any time.

Jimmy could count on four hundred dollars a week for a minimum of forty weeks, a total of sixteen thousand dollars. It was more money than he could even imagine, and it would certainly help make life different for a number of people. He had helped his brother Harry during his college years but had always wished he could have done more. Harry was a practicing physician by this time. Now Jimmy was helping Ed as he entered his final years of medical school. Carolyn Cagney had health problems, and with the money Jimmy was earning he could see that she was well taken care of. As for eleven-year-old Jeanne, she would have something none of her brothers had ever had as children: manufactured toys, and a closet full of good clothing. His film career might last for only forty weeks, but while it lasted all the Cagneys would thrive.

PART THREE

Hollywood's "Professional Againster"

CHAPTER 8

Many great stage actors have had limited success in the movies. Alfred Lunt and Lynn Fontanne failed in films even though they were revered in the legitimate theater. But with James Cagney it was almost as if the medium were made for him. He was a natural.

His staccato speech came through clearly, his lithe body movements made even sluggish direction seem the product of a ballet master. He snapped, he cracked, he sneered, he shot, and he slugged, but he was rarely if ever accused of over-acting. Jimmy's delivery and reactions were as natural as if he were in front of the Lenox Hill Settlement House in Yorkville, instead of lights and cameras on a soundstage. "No stress—no strain," as he has said so often. "Just a job." And that was exactly the way he seemed to handle his screen assignments.

The title of Jimmy's first film was changed from *Penny Arcade* to *Sinners' Holiday,* which Jimmy thought typical of his new medium: the latter title made no sense at all, and he couldn't see how it applied to the story in any way. He whizzed through the shooting with Joan Blondell in the fifteen days allotted, and when the fifty-five-minute film opened in October 1930 it was approved by the critics.

Jimmy played Harry Delano, a sniveling, mama's-boy killer. Ma Delano runs the penny arcade and lives above it with Harry; his brother Joe; and his sister, Jennie. Jennie is propositioned by Mitch McKane and rescued by Angel Harrigan, played by Grant Withers. Harrigan, a barker for McKane's concession, quits after the incident and is hired by Ma to work in the arcade. Harry has been involved in bootlegging with McKane, and in the heat of a quarrel he kills him. Harry gets his girlfriend Myrtle (Blondell) to lie for him, and because the earlier quarrel between McKane and Harrigan it is Harrigan who is charged with the murder. Jennie, who is in love with Harrigan, is ultimately responsible for fixing the blame on Harry, her brother.

In a moving scene, Harry breaks down and cries in his mother's lap, and she comforts him. Out of love for her son she conspires to further implicate Harrigan, but Harry finally has to pay for his crime. He is shown to be a rather sympathetic killer: his deceased father had been a worthless alcoholic whose antisocial behavior was unwittingly learned by Harry. This was the first movie about murder to show the roots of criminal behavior, setting a pattern for many Warner Brother films to come.

Jimmy's portrayal of Harry earned these words from the *Exhibitor*'s *Herald-World* critic: "Cagney has by no means an easy role in his portrayal of a highly nervous youth who by nature cannot go straight. It is the type of part which can be spoiled by the slightest shade of overacting, but Cagney carries his characterization in each sequence just far enough."

Mordaunt Hall of *The New York Times* wrote: "The romance of a carnival barker and the daughter of a penny arcade proprietress is well told in the screen version of Marie Baumer's play *Penny Arcade*, now known as *Sinners' Holiday*. Grant Withers as Angel Harrigan and Lucille LaVerne as Ma Delano are well cast, but the most impressive acting is done by James Cagney in the role of Harry Delano. His fretful tenseness during the closing scenes is conveyed with sincerity."

Before Jimmy could catch his breath after the breakneck schedule of *Sinners' Holiday*, he was whisked into *Doorway to Hell*. Lew Ayres was cast in the role of Louis Ricarno, a Mafia-type ganglord; this, according to Jimmy, was the miscasting gem of the decade. Ayres, with his ethereal good looks, would have been better cast in the secondary role, and Jimmy given the ganglord part, but the studio heads prevailed. This was Ayres's sixth picture, his third in 1930. His first that year, *All Quiet on the Western Front*, was soon to be released; Warner's may have thought that casting him as a heavy would broaden his screen image and thus enhance his career. It certainly didn't hurt him, and when the picture was released the critics did not mention the incongruity in the casting. The film was generally approved and became yet another Warner Brothers quickie success.

Jimmy plays Steve Mileway, a lieutenant to Ricarno, who has given up the rackets to live in Florida. Mileway starts collecting the profits for himself, and even takes over the boss's woman. Mileway eventually winds up in jail, and Ricarno is killed by enemy bullets.

The *New York Herald Tribune* called it "an excellent gangster film" and spoke highly of Ayres's acting; Jimmy was hardly mentioned. *Variety* was particularly impressed with Archie Mayo's direction and added, "The supporting cast is uniformly good, with honors going to James Cagney as Mileway."

Jimmy could see that the only permanent people in the film studios were those who worked in the production departments, and he publicly maintained that he felt as though he were in the "big league for con men and frauds." He was learning fast that the only people he could really trust were members of his own family.

He felt confident enough, however, to send for Willie. He told her to sell their modest accumulation of furniture, give up the apartment, and sell the bungalow in Scotch Plains, New Jersey. But, as it turned out, the bungalow had already been sold. Jimmy had leased it to a theatrical acquaintance who had somehow managed to sell it without the Cagneys' knowledge. Jimmy is still unable to explain how this was possible, but since the property was part of a single-tax legal structure, it somehow happened. There seemed to be no legal recourse; the Cagneys' equity was down the drain.

Jimmy had hoped to have a snug little home awaiting Willie when she stepped off the train, but as a contract player at Warner Brothers he felt fortunate to find time for an occasional restroom break. In the days before the Screen Actors Guild, it was common for the studios to work their contractees as much as twelve hours a day, seven days a week, and that was exactly what they were doing with Jimmy. He managed to arrange for him and Willie to stay in the apartment of an old Yorkville friend until they could get the time to find a place of their own.

The friend was assistant manager of the Pig 'n' Whistle Restaurant, next to Grauman's Egyptian Theatre. "He was a boyhood friend," says Jimmy, "who intended at one time to become a priest. He had the damnedest habit. No matter what you said to him, he would say, 'Huh, me?'" Willie soon found a comfortable apartment on Hayworth Avenue, in West Hollywood. It would be home for the next several months, but because of Jimmy's shaky beginnings with the studio, it would never lose its transient status.

Jimmy rented a very used Chevrolet to transport him to and from the studio. Willie remembers it clearly: "It nearly took your head off when you let out the clutch." But the problem could have been Jimmy's questionable driving skills. By a minor miracle, he managed to navigate the hills and dales between West Hollywood and Burbank.

Willie, meanwhile, spent endless hours awaiting Jimmy in their apartment. She would read, sleep, and daydream, but mostly she spent the long hours of loneliness hooking rugs. Jimmy always hoped to get home by seven or eight, but frequently he didn't arrive until well after midnight. He was expected back on the set by eight or nine the next morning. Many of the rare moments of their home life were spent sharing Jimmy's laments about his long day.

"Jimmy would come home mad about something that happened on the set," says Willie, "and he would say, 'Pack the trunks, we're getting out of here.' Finally, I just kept them packed. I thought we'd be leaving any minute." So, in addition to hooking rugs—which, if Jimmy stayed at Warners long enough, could have covered half of Los Angeles—Willie was packing and repacking trunks and suitcases. The early days of Jimmy's film career could not have been the most stable of their marriage.

Jimmy had not been given a single day off between *Sinners' Holiday* and *Doorway to Hell*. He had come on the set after the second picture had started production, and it was made in such haste that no actress had been chosen for the leading female role. Dorothy Mathews was elevated from the extra ranks to play the part.

For Jimmy's third film he was again paired with Joan Blondell. They were assigned small roles in support of Grant Withers, Mary Astor, and Regis Toomey. The film, *Other Men's Women,* was directed by William Wellman, but his more memorable works would come later.

Under his new contract, Jimmy was earning a hundred dollars less every week but working twice as hard. After *Other Men's Women* he was called upon for another supporting role, even smaller than the previous one, but with a vast difference: his services were requested by the eminent actor George Arliss. As one of the very few actors to be given cast approval, Arliss interviewed a number of contract players for the small but important role of Schofield, the insurance salesman, in his next film, *The Millionaire*. Jimmy, as always, was one of the last to be interviewed, but the moment Arliss laid eyes on him he knew that Jimmy was what he wanted.

"He wasn't trying to impress me," said Arliss in his autobiography. "He was just being natural and, I thought, a trifle independent for a bit actor. There was an attitude of 'Here I am; take me or leave me; and hurry up.'" Arliss took Jimmy, and wanted him just the way he was at that moment, wearing exactly what he had on. The role, which played no longer than five minutes on the screen, was a pivotal sequence in the film.

As the insurance agent, Jimmy stimulates the retired millionaire to get out of his easy chair and come back to life. The contrast between the cultured old man and the fast-talking young salesman splashes across the screen like fireworks. Arliss was willing to admit afterward that this was at least one time when a scene was stolen from him. The film was released in 1931. Though only a few reviews mentioned Jimmy's performance, he was noticed by the insiders.

Jimmy looks back on the exchange between him and Arliss with a touch of embarrassment, recalling how he asked the revered artist whether it would be all right to add a few little bits of business to the scene. "I said, 'Mr. Arliss, would you mind if I adjust your shawl, or do a little piece of business here and there?' He said, 'Young man, do anything you please.'" Jimmy would always try to include little bits of action in his movies that would help bring to life the characters he was playing—"something for them to take out of the theater with them," he would say. In this film, for instance, he spoke around a pipe during his hard sell to the old man.

Jimmy had performed in four films in as many months at Warner Brothers, and there was another film awaiting him before he finished his work for 1930. This assignment was to chart the course of much of his early career in films. Although Jimmy was unaware of it, he was being closely observed by several people. One of them was William Wellman, who had directed *Other Men's Women;* two others were the Chicago authors John Bright and

Kubec Glasmon. Bright had written a novel about bootlegging, *Beer and Blood,* and Glasmon was helping him adapt the property into a screenplay. All three wanted Jimmy to play the lead in the film.

Gangster pictures were beginning to work well for the studio, and there was one ready for release that they believed would set trends. It was *Little Caesar,* starring Edward G. Robinson. Production chief Darryl F. Zanuck was ready to proceed with *Beer and Blood,* but wasn't sure he wanted to commit Jimmy to the film.

Zanuck was hoping to lend him to Howard Hughes, who was about to produce *The Front Page.* Lewis Milestone, who would direct the film, agreed that Jimmy would be perfect to play the reporter Hildy Johnson. Milestone tried to sell Hughes on the idea, but it was dismissed summarily. "He's nothing but a little runt," was Hughes's response.

By the time Zanuck had learned that Jimmy had been rejected by Hughes, the leading role in *Beer and Blood* had been assigned. Eddie Woods had been borrowed from First National to play Tom Powers, but Jimmy was given the second lead role, Matt Doyle. In the screenplay for the film, now retitled *The Public Enemy,* Tom Powers was described as tungsten-tough, brash, and ruthless. His pal, Matt Doyle, was supposed to be an easygoing, nice guy. Wellman completed three days of shooting before he had time to view the daily rushes. When he saw what had been shot, he went running to Zanuck. An enormous mistake had been made—Woods and Cagney were playing the wrong roles.

It was not a simple matter to convince Zanuck that the roles should be switched, because Woods was engaged to Louella Parsons's daughter, and even then Parsons was a force to be reckoned with. But Wellman eventually persuaded Zanuck to agree to the change.

Woods was stunned by the sudden edict; Jimmy was baffled. But the next morning he found himself saying all the lines that had been delivered by Woods a few days earlier. It meant little more than a shoulder-shrug to Jimmy—after all, it was "just a job"—but, as it would turn out, *this* job would make it possible for the Cagneys to unpack their trunks and store them away.

CHAPTER 9

It would always be important to Jimmy Cagney to innovate, to extend himself beyond normal limits, to make everything seem real on the screen. The simple process of throwing a punch was as important to him as the most dramatic scene in the film. It could look phony, or it could look like the real thing. Jimmy's perfectionism began with his very first film, *Sinner's Holiday*. Lucille LaVerne, who played his mother, was the recipient of his advice on that occasion. He pointed out that her slap across the face would look authentic only if she hit him full-force with four fingers extended. The secret was that she should keep her thumb doubled under. It would not have given the sharp sting of a five-fingered slap but would give the illusion of one. She agreed, and when the cameras were rolling she let fly. Somehow she caught Jimmy's cheek with the butt of her hand and sent him flying.

A similar situation came up in *Public Enemy,* when he and Donald Cook, playing his brother, were setting up a punch scene. Cook threw the punch, and Jimmy was supposed to duck, but it caught him on the mouth. Filming was held up while Jimmy had a chipped tooth repaired. He often wondered whether the punch could have been a product of William Wellman's own sense of realism. "He's a tough mug," Jimmy suspects him of saying; "give him your best shot."

Before the guilds and unions, the studios spent little time worrying about the welfare of their contractees, and the lack of consideration went beyond the hours they were asked to work. An occasional punch in the face was a hazard of the trade, and could be almost anyone's fault, but there were other practices that were slightly more dangerous. In *Public Enemy* Jimmy became familiar with one of them: the use of real bullets in shooting sequences. Within a few years, special-effects artists would be able to simulate an exploding bullet with relative ease, but back then, if the script called for tommy-gun fire, a real tommy gun was used.

"Warners hired a man named Bailey," said Jimmy, "who had been a machine-gunner in World War One. He sat on a platform above as I skittered along the wall. Just as I passed, Bailey opened up with the machine gun and the wall crumbled to dust. I would have crumbled too, had I been a moment late." Jimmy never complained about the practice, because it didn't occur to him to complain. He assumed that that was the way things were done. It would require a much closer call before he would suggest that an alternative device be used.

Gangster films were enjoying huge successes in Hollywood at this time. In *Little Caesar* the main characters were hard-bitten criminals from the start, but this was not true in Bright and Glasmon's script. The story begins with Tom Powers and Matt Doyle as a pair of high-spirited boys and follows them through the ranks until they achieve full-fledged criminal status.

Tom and Matt are seen growing up in the Chicago slums during the years prior to World War I. Their mischief turns into more serious crime, and eventually Tom shoots a cop in an armed robbery. With the war over, the pals get jobs as truck drivers for a bootlegger and begin to gain status in criminal circles. Tom has battles with his brother (Donald Cook), a war veteran who remains straight, and is adored by his mother (Beryl Mercer), who knows nothing of his criminal ways. Tom has a way with women. The first is Kitty (Mae Clarke), with whom he becomes bored. He then turns to Gwenn (Jean Harlow).

Gang violence follows the killing of Tom and Matt's boss, Nails Nathan (Leslie Fenton), and in a gangland shootout Matt is killed and Tom seriously wounded. Tom, recuperating in the hospital, is reconciled with his brother and vows to go straight. While his family is preparing a gala homecoming for him, he is delivered to their door. The rival gang has kidnapped him from the hospital and killed him. Tom's body, bound like a mummy, falls into the doorway.

The combination of a lively script, effective direction, and Jimmy's charisma made *The Public Enemy* a model for future filmmakers to emulate. The outstanding scenes are: Tom, bored with

Kitty (Mae Clarke), viciously shoves a half-grapefruit into her face; Tom sadistically murders an old pal who has double-crossed him; Tom cold-bloodedly shoots the horse that threw his boss, killing him; Tom stumbles into the gutter in a downpour of rain after he is wounded; in the final scene, Tom's body is propped up in the doorway of his family's home and falls in when the door is opened.

Most memorable will always be the "grapefruit scene." Bosley Crowther of *The New York Times* later wrote, "This was and remains one of the cruelest, most startling acts ever committed on film—not because it is especially painful, except to the woman's smidgen of pride, but because it shows such a hideous debasement of regard for another human being."

For many years afterward, Jimmy would be presented with trays of grapefruit in restaurants. Mae Clarke blames that scene for typecasting that would all but ruin her screen career. Because of the scene's notoriety, almost everyone connected with the film claims credit for it. Darryl Zanuck insisted it was his idea. "I think I thought of it in a script conference," he said. "When I made *The Public Enemy* I was way ahead in thinking. No love story, but loaded with sex and violence." William Wellman claimed it also: "I needed something big at that moment in the picture and, upon seeing the grapefruit on the table, told Jimmy to try socking her with it."

According the the authors, Glasmon and Bright, the actual origin of the device was a real-life interchange between gangster Hymie Weiss and his girlfriend. Weiss, however, slammed his love with a steaming hot omelette, which, for film purposes, would have been a bit too sloppy.

Whatever its origins, the grapefruit scene made film history, and Jimmy's performance turned him into box-office dynamite. The movie was completed in twenty-six days at a cost of $150,000 and was one of the first low-budget films to gross more than one million dollars.

The only other actor to rate attention besides Jimmy and Mae Clarke was Jean Harlow as Jimmy's second mistress. She was already being seen on movie screens in *Hell's Angels,* and many believe that her appearance in *The Public Enemy* assured her status as a star. Her part wasn't very big, but there was a hot seduction scene in which her sensual attire and sultry murmurs brought a new meaning to screen sex.

In a scene with his mother, Jimmy makes a fist and gives her an affectionate mock punch on the shoulder, as though she were one of the boys. That had been one of Jimmy's father's mannerisms. He would put a hand behind his son's head and give him a gentle poke on the chin, saying, "If I thought you meant that . . ." William Wellman's direction would receive the credit due it, but there was always something of Jimmy in all of his pictures.

With *The Public Enemy* completed, Jimmy was one film away from star billing, which he would retain throughout his long career. But status meant little to Cagney; he was much more concerned with the high salaries being enjoyed by so many of his peers. When he signed the contract with Warners he had been promised that there would be salary adjustments if his films were successful. At this point he was watching his pay envelopes expectantly. He somehow knew there would be no adjustment without a battle, but for the first year of his contract there was precious little time for anything but work and a little sleep.

There was no doubt that he was developing a chip on his shoulder, and already—even before any of his notorious salary disputes—he was labeled a "professional againster." He was always soft-spoken and gentle among the ordinary people who surrounded him: the crew, bit players, laborers. But he seemed to have a built-in sensor for smelling out unsavory elements. If he had a first impression that was negative, it would be an impression hard to change.

Once he was ready to pack up and head east as the result of a relatively minor incident. There was a campaign going on at the studio to achieve hundred-percent participation in a charity drive. Anyone who knew Cagney was well aware of his generosity, but those who didn't know him were unaware of his stubbornness. Saying that *everybody* was doing it was not the way to reach Cagney. He refused to sign over the expected portion of his pay.

The overzealous collector was the actor and contract player Douglas Fairbanks, Jr. He was determined that Jimmy acquiesce, and when Jimmy once more refused, Fairbanks remarked, "You won't be around here very long." As it turned out, Fairbanks was soon without a contract, and Jimmy remained "there" for many years to come. During all the subsequent years he gave generously to the annual drive. But no one was going to coerce him.

Cagney would always be an outsider or, as Pat O'Brien would

later say, "a faraway fella." In this role, Jimmy relied on the insulation of close friends and family. The fact that his family was now three thousand miles away was not at all to his liking, and he would not rest until all of them would once more be drawn tightly together. The first family member to break away from New York and come west was his younger brother Bill. He was suffering from a lingering cold and accepted his brother's invitation to come to Los Angeles for the sun. He came, liked what he found, and stayed, much to Jimmy's delight. Bill had always shown keen business insight; he would prove invaluable to Jimmy in all his studio negotiations and, later, in his investments. Bill would have a brief fling at a career of his own, but it was the business end of Hollywood that would make his fortune and increase his brother's.

For Jimmy's first assignment of 1931, he was given the second lead in *Smart Money*, starring Edward G. Robinson. After *Little Caesar* opened in January to a first week's box-office take of fifty thousand dollars, the studio hastened to cash in on the teaming of their two gangster stars. Jimmy was working in two films at the same time. He would do his scenes for *The Public Enemy*, and then dash to another soundstage to do scenes for *Smart Money*. Fortunately, the early part of the new film demanded little of Cagney's time. He made one appearance at the start of the film and was not onscreen again until the second half. Once more he went from one picture to another without so much as a single day's rest.

Smart Money was far from the level of *Little Caesar* or *Public Enemy,* but Bright and Glasmon once more came up with an exciting script that Robinson and Cagney made the most of. Robinson played Nick, a smalltown barber who finds he can win at gambling. He tries his luck in the city and is soon a kingpin in gambling circles, always one step ahead of the law. Jimmy played Jack, a barber in Nick's shop who follows Nick to the city to serve as his right-hand man. All is well until Nick rescues Irene (Evalyn Knapp) from suicide and falls for her. Jack learns that Irene is being used by the police to entrap Nick. When Nick is framed, Jack reveals that Irene has set it up to clear herself of certain police charges. He labels her stool pigeon and gives her a rap in the face. Nick, unable to believe this of Irene, shoots and kills Jack. When Nick is sentenced to ten years in prison he learns that Jack's charges against Irene were true after all. Clinging to his true gambling spirit, Nick bets that he'll be back on the streets in five instead of ten years. The movie earned no critical bouquets, but it made big money for the studio and moved Jimmy one step closer to fame. It also increased his notoriety as an onscreen abuser of women.

In 1930, Will E. Hays, a former U.S. postmaster general and since 1922 the head of Motion Picture Producers and Distributors of America, Inc., was called upon to create the Motion Picture Production Code, the industry's self-censoring organization designed to uphold higher moral standards. The violence and raw sex of many of the Warner Brothers films led to pressure-group influence that resulted in the Code, and Hays was given the authority to tone things down. An example of an early Hays Office action was reported in a 1931 issue of the *Hollywood Reporter,* an industry trade paper: "Will Hays' newest target is the exposure of femme legs in studio photo releases to movie magazines. The cameras are being lifted above the waist."

Sex was the first demon to be exorcised by the Code; violence was next. Warners had no intention of killing their profitable gangster films, but they did agree to add a disclaimer or moral tag to the end of each one, declaring that the evildoers were ultimately punished. Since Cagney was so closely associated with cold-blooded violence, they decided to give him a change of pace. For his first starring role, Jimmy was cast in a comedy, again written by Bright and Glasmon. The original title, *Larceny Lane,* was later changed to *Blonde Crazy.*

Cagney played a larcenous bellhop, Bert Harris, opposite Joan Blondell as a street-wise chambermaid, Ann Roberts. Bert lives by his wits, conning even the con artists, until Dapper Dan Barker (Louis Calhern) dishes out some of Bert's own medicine. Bert and Ann con their way across country to New York, but Anne has had enough of Bert's precarious games. She meets an honest young man named Joe Reynolds (Ray Milland), and when he proposes marriage she accepts. Bert is finally caught and jailed. Later Ann visits him there to explain that the wholesome marriage isn't working. She will divorce Joe and will be waiting for Bert when he is released from jail.

Jimmy's creative contributions had been well received during the filming of his previous pictures, so he didn't hesitate to make suggestions and to put in occasional ad libs when he believed the script would be helped by them. The director of *Blonde Crazy,* Roy Del Ruth, was not accustomed to this much input from the actors, however, and told Jimmy to play the scenes exactly as they were written. "I stopped putting things in, and word came down the next day, after they saw the previous day's shots. Zanuck asked me what was the matter, and I told him that Del Ruth wanted it that way."

Zanuck spoke to the director, who subsequently told Jimmy to do it his way; but Del Ruth wasn't happy about it. To illustrate his contempt, he ignored Jimmy and, for some unknown reason, put the script on the floor and turned the pages with his feet. When Jimmy was ready to rehearse a scene Del Ruth would not so much as look in his direction.

"I called Blondell over," says Jimmy, "and had her sit there. I told her I would play the scene to her, for her approval. He was trying to put me in my place by ignoring me. I don't blame him much. That's a lot for an actor to do—to take on his own direction. So I did the lines as if Joan were the director. I asked her, 'How was it, Joan?' She said, 'Fine,' as if she were the director. He still ignored me."

By the time *Blonde Crazy* was completed, there were long lines of moviegoers waiting to see *The Public Enemy* in New York. Finally the theater had to remain open all night to accommodate the growing throngs. Nobody doubted that Cagney was box-office dynamite by now, but his paychecks were carrying the same old numbers.

Jimmy was further irritated by the studio's demand for public appearances. He had no objection to promoting his own pictures but could see no reason to promote films in which he did not appear. Actors weren't provided with special material for these appearances, and often the only music was provided by the theater's pipe organ. Jimmy could always do a little dance number of some sort, but to a pipe-organ accompaniment? It was bad enough to make a fool of himself for the sake of his own films, but he was not willing to do it for those of other actors.

Jimmy went to Warner Brothers with his grievances and found little sympathy. The studio heads had no recollection of promising salary adjustments as his films increased in popularity. There would be no pay raise, and as for personal appearances, he would

have to make them along with all the other Warner Brothers contract players.

Jimmy faced an ultimatum. He was reminded that no one had
ever won a battle with a major studio; he would either comply with
his contract or go on suspension until he did so, with the period of
suspension then added to his contract.

What they hadn't realized was that Jimmy hadn't been all that
keen on a movie career in the first place. He loved vaudeville and
could work in that medium whenever he wished, and there was
always the legitimate theater. If all else failed, he could follow his
two brothers into medicine, or, for that matter, he could answer
the lifelong call of the soil and become a farmer. Jimmy and Willie
once more packed their trunks and gave Bill Cagney their apartment. They were off to New York.

Even at age one, Jimmy held the glint of pugnacity in his eyes.

Carolyn Nelson would be going to work at the pencil factory soon after this photo was taken at her First Communion.

At the time of her marriage, Carolyn Nelson Cagney was a natural beauty with flaming red hair.

Left: At a very dapper age ten.
Below: Jimmy, second from left in the middle row, poses with his classmates in this 1910 photo.

Above: Dressed in his Sunday best, Jimmy is seen in this 1913 class picture of the eighth grade of P.S. 158. He is third from the left in the front row. *Below:* Jimmy is second from the left in the top row in this team photo of the Yorkville Nut Club.

Left: The Cagney look is clearly evident in this picture of Jimmy, twenty, as a baseball star. *Below:* The gorgeous chorus girl at top left is young Jamon Cagney as he appeared in his first professional stage production, *Every Sailor,* just after the close of World War I.

A dance routine from *Grand Street Follies of 1928*. His partner is Sophia Delza.

Grand Street Follies of 1928.

A scene from *Women Go on Forever*, the 1927 stage production with Osgood Perkins and Mary Law.

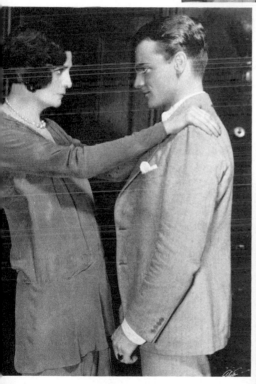

Jimmy and Mary Law in *Women Go on Forever*

Jimmy is cast with Edward G. Robinson for the first and last time in the 1931 picture *Smart Money*.

Left: Jimmy achieves instant stardom by playing Tom Powers in the 1931 film, *The Public Enemy.* *Below:* With Joan Blondell and Eddie Woods in *The Public Enemy.*

Above: The famous grapefruit-in-Mae Clarke's-face from *The Public Enemy.* *Right:* An early Warner Brothers portrait of their rising young star.

Left: Jimmy with his beloved wife "Bill," who, for a time, went platinum. *Below:* With Loretta Young in *Taxi!*

The Cagney smile.

Above: Ruby Keeler leans over Jimmy's shoulder as he holds Joan Blondell. Dick Powell gives the bear hug to Jimmy's off-the-lot buddy, Frank McHugh. The picture: *Footlight Parade. Below:* Allen Jenkins serves as a desk for Jimmy in this scene from *Jimmy the Gent* with Bette Davis. Bette was reluctant to pose with Jimmy, whom she regarded as a "studio roughneck."

Above: With Jimmy McHugh in *Here Comes the Navy.*

Another shot from *Here Comes the Navy.*

Above: An early thirties domestic scene, shot by the studio for the movie fan magazines. *Right:* From *The St. Louis Kid.*

Left: Tennis anyone? Below: Between scenes of *The St. Louis Kid* with Patricia Ellis.

Above: Next to Robert Armstrong in *G-Men.* Jimmy goes on the right side of the law in this 1935 picture. *Right:* Jimmy was Bottom the Tailor in Warner Brothers' ambitious production of *A Midsummer Night's Dream.*

CHAPTER 10

ollywood was soon buzzing with news of Cagney's walk-out. Many of Jimmy's fellow contract players were intrigued with the test of strength; it would help determine their own futures. Others were against the audacity of the upstart actor, who, in their opinion, should have been thankful for what he had. Then there were others who were more or less ambivalent. A column in the *Hollywood Reporter* on the following Monday fell into that category. Publisher Billy Wilkerson devoted his entire "Tradeviews" column that July morning to:

A LETTER TO JAMES CAGNEY

Dear Jimmy,

We heard Saturday that you had walked off the Warner lot to return only when your salary demands were met. Tried to reach you on the phone for confirmation of this but was advised that the number had been disconnected. Not knowing your home address we are using this means to reach you.

Producers, Jimmy, for the most part are a bad lot when it comes to talking salary. They are doing everything they can to trim the weekly paychecks of all employees down to a pretty low basis. We are not for the producers in this wage-cutting war. We are of the opinion that every person has his value and in order for the business to continue, full payment must be made for value received.

Producers are not very appreciative either, Jimmy. They have little respect for contracts when they are put in a financial spot, and care less about services rendered by individuals delivering plenty of value for the money received. This lack of appreciation is very paramount right in your own studio, with New York office cutting the salaries of Darryl Zanuck, William Koenig, Hal Wallace and Lucien Hubbard, the quartet who delivered Warners more hit pictures last year than was shown by all the other studios combined. That's pretty punk treatment.

But let's forget about the Zanucks and the Koenigs—let's talk about Cagney.

Jimmy, we think you are using poor judgment in your present attitude. We don't know the extent of your weekly paycheck—but whatever it is at the present time, we feel you are entitled to more. You are a great bet for pictures as long as the Zanucks continue feeding you material like *Public Enemy* and *Larceny Lane*. Boy-oh-boy, what fat parts! We know a lot of stars who would have been glad to work for nothing—yes, even pay for the privilege of acting the parts that Warners gave you. Those parts made you, Jimmy, or will by the time both pictures have reached a great percentage of theaters throughout the country. They have turned you from an ordinary player with great ability into a great potential star. But, Jimmy, don't forget one thing. You are not a star yet, and you won't be a star unless your studio continues to feed you big fat parts.

The point of this whole thing, Jimmy, is to give you an impartial view of your present condition, even though this condition is now only bringing you in $250 a week (and I'm sure you are getting more). Don't walk out on Warners, that's bad. You are not sufficiently strong at the present time to do that walkout number. Others stronger than you have tried it and have checked in behind the eight ball. Don't get the casting powers at the studio down on you. Don't permit pictures as a whole to look on you as a "walker-outer." You can't stand this kind of talk. Wait until you get another picture or two under your belt; then you won't have to walk out, the studio will have to walk-in to almost any reasonable demand, because they need you. They don't need you so much at the present time. You are not big enough.

So, Jimmy, we want you to know we are in your corner. We think you have a great future that may be spoiled by your present actions. Take what they are giving you at the present and like it. After *Larceny Lane* is released and business gets better in the theatres, drop in on Jack Warner, have a talk with him, thank him for having made it possible for you to jump to the front with two or three pictures, then put the bee on him—gently but firmly—and we will bet a bunch of old United Cigar coupons that you will walk out with a new contract and a chance to get "fatter" parts that are right up your alley.

The rambling message of Billy Wilkerson was almost touching in its sincerity and naiveté. His advice, however, had a certain validity. He thought he was giving thoughtful guidance to a promising newcomer before he got involved in a game that newcomers could only lose. Wilkerson wasn't considering the possibility that Jimmy was sincere when he said, "It's my way or not at all." He probably thought that Jimmy was merely trying to con the con men into coughing up more money; had he known Jimmy, he would have realized that it was no game. Jimmy was perfectly willing to live with any consequences that might result from his walkout. If necessary, he would have left his career high and dry: "no stress— no strain." It would eventually be learned that James Cagney was a very stubborn man—consequences be damned.

There is an unchartered fraternity in Hollywood. Those who belong dance to the studio tune, politic in all the right ways, and sell their very soul to maintain membership in good standing. There are many others who would do almost anything to get on the exclusive membership list but are never invited. Then there are a few others who do not belong, and who thumb their noses at invitations to join. They are the unsocial few who don't care to join groups, or, if they are included in a club function, will refuse participation in the party games; they prefer to sit off to the side and watch. This is the category Jimmy Cagney was in; being a loner made him very difficult to deal with, because the usual rules didn't apply. He couldn't be threatened with ouster from the club, because he didn't even want to be in it. Warner Brothers' frustration with their anomalous young star must have been enormous.

The studio had many stars who were making big money at the box office, but how many showed the promise of James Cagney? For a small investment he was bringing in millions, and it would seem that he could continue to do so for many years to come; yet, what would happen in future contract disputes if an upstart were allowed to win? The studio wanted him back, of course, but they held out in the hope that his return would be on their terms. The studio bosses played the part of the injured father: Where would he be if they hadn't brought him to Hollywood for a movie contract? He would probably be hoofing in some obscure vaudeville theater for three hundred dollars a week. The studio had taken the risks, had provided him with starring material, and had given him membership in the exclusive fraternity of stars. Where was his gratitude?

They were playing to deaf ears. Jimmy knew what his first pictures were earning, and he knew that contract players who were bringing in far less revenue were earning ten times his salary. How could that be fair? He wanted much more money, a little more respect, and a lot less fathering. His brother Bill was assigned to handle the talks with the studio while Jimmy and Willie visited friends and family in New York.

Larceny Lane had opened under its new title, *Blonde Crazy,* and was a hit. *Time* magazine said: "A chipper, hard-boiled, amusing essay on petty thievery. In his first starring performance, James Cagney has a role in which he is more mischievous than wicked. He makes rascality seem both easy and attractive as he did in *The Public Enemy* and *Smart Money.* Wrote *The New York Times:* "Unedifying though the incidents are and feeble as is the attempt at a moral, the greater part of James Cagney's new picture, *Blonde Crazy,* is lively and cleverly acted. . . . Mr. Cageny is alert and pugnacious as Bert Harris as he was in the quick-thinking young gangster of *The Public Enemy.*"

After the success of *Blonde Crazy* Warner Brothers could do little else but write up a new contract for their independent young star. His new salary would be one thousand dollars a week, and this time more of the clauses would be to Jimmy's benefit. Willie packed their trunks for the second move westward.

It was well into 1932 when Jimmy reported on the soundstage for work on *Taxi* Once more the gifted screenwriting team of Glasmon and Bright did the script, and Roy Del Ruth directed.

Now, with big money coming in, the Cagneys began to look for a house to buy. There would be no more court apartments for forty dollars a month; the time had come to reap some of the benefits of Hollywood promises. Jimmy still felt like a transient in the glamour capital, but it was wise in these times even for a transient to buy property—if he could. Prices were low and values high. They found a gleaming villa of stucco and tile at 621 Hillcrest Drive, in Beverly Hills. It was a larger home than the Cagneys would have in the future, but Jimmy wanted one large enough to house his whole family if the occasion arose.

Bill was assigned the task of auto shopping for Jimmy, and came up with a smart and stylish Buick sedan. He also signed Jimmy up for a refresher course in driving, and the daily drives to the studio became a pleasure.

For Jimmy and Willie, it was the first time in nearly ten years of marriage that there was financial solvency, with no need to scrimp and connive to feed everyone, pay tuitions, and handle medical bills. The feeling must have been liberating, yet Jimmy's work days were no easier and leisure was as scarce as before his walkout.

On his return to work he was cast opposite the delicately beautiful Loretta Young in another Glasmon and Bright film, *Taxi!* The film, however, was memorable to Jimmy for other reasons too. In one scene he spoke a few words of Yiddish. As a boy in Yorkville he had easily picked up a variety of languages, and always enjoyed the opportunity to deliver lines in these languages.

Another highlight of the filming was a scene in which, for the first time on the screen, he could display his dancing ability. He was called upon to dance the Peabody in a ballroom competition. This was no problem, since the dance was one of the first he had ever learned, but it was more difficult to find someone to compete against him in the scene. Jimmy knew that George Raft was in town and that Raft was as good at dancing the Peabody as anyone in the world. He suggested that Raft be hired, and he was.

Raft would achieve stardom a few years later, after the public saw him flip quarters in *Scarface,* but meanwhile he and Jimmy played the contest dance scene to perfection in *Taxi!* Jimmy would always feel a warm affinity with Raft, who was also a product of the New York streets.

In the film, there was one more encounter with real weapons. Jimmy was to fire a pistol out of a taxi and then duck as machine-gun bullets rip through the window just over his head. The slugs missed Jimmy's head by a fraction of an inch. It was at this point that he refused to work with any more live ammunition in his movie shootouts.

The film was praised by critics. "We believe Cagney's popularity could equal or overrun Gable's," said the New York *Daily News* reviewer. "He has a grand sense of humor and he's one swell actor. Movie audiences are thrilled. Will hold your attention until the final Cagney wisecrack."

Mordaunt Hall of *The New York Times* wrote: "James Cagney, the terrier of the screen, is to be seen in another belligerent role. This film, which bears the title of *Taxi!*, affords the alert young actor heaps of opportunities for his slang and his short-arm jabs. Mr. Cagney misses no chance to make his characterization tell. Loretta Young is sympathetic and able as Sue."

Warner Brothers could see no reason to break up a winning combination, so Bright and Glasmon were assigned to do the screenplay for Jimmy's next film, *The Crowd Roars,* assisted by a young writer, Niven Busch. The story idea belonged to Howard Hawks, who had been a race driver himself, so he was assigned rather than Roy Del Ruth to direct. In this film, the gangsters were left behind in New York but the blood and guts followed Jimmy to the Indianapolis Speedway. Jimmy portrayed a daring race driver, Joe Greer, who wants his younger brother, Eddie (Eric Linden), to stay out of the race game. Eddie meets Ann (Joan Blondell), but when Joe labels her a racetrack broad, and unworthy of him, the brothers quarrel.

In Joe's overpowering will to win he drives against his pal, Spud (Frank McHugh), and causes his death. Full of remorse, Joe withdraws from racing and becomes a near-derelict. Eddie becomes a full-fledged driver and is hurt in a championship race. Joe shows up and takes over in his brother's car to drive to an exciting win.

Howard Hawks took special care to etch quality into the offering, and the race sequences were authentic and memorable. Several race stars of the day played cameo roles.

The reviewers thought that the dialogue was not up to Glasmon and Bright's usual standard, but the film was well received. The *New York Evening Post* said: "Cagney, as usual, is intensely believable as a racing driver, but it is a shallow part and it permits him little opportunity for the sharpness of characterization which distinguish his earlier roles."

During on-location filming in Indianapolis, Jimmy became close to Frank McHugh, whom he had met on a few previous occasions in New York. Sharing a hotel room, they found that they had so much in common that they spent an entire night talking and worked the next day without sleep. They would remain friends through life.

Jimmy played a prizefighter in his next assignment, *Winner Take All,* which pleased him almost as much as his rare dancing opportunities, because it was something he could do well. He put heart and soul into his fight training, until he felt that he could take on any opponent. He was coached by a former welterweight champion, Harvey Perry, who regarded him as an apt pupil.

Jimmy played Jim Kane, a fighter who has blown his winnings on booze and broads. He is a forlorn figure at the opening of the story, accepting coins tossed into the ring at the request of the ring announcer of another bout. The donations are to enable Jim to go to a health farm in New Mexico. There he meets Peggy (Marian Nixon), who is in worse financial straits than he. In an effort to help her, he takes a winner-take-all fight challenge. He wins big and is once more an important contender, but he has broken his nose in the fight. He returns to the New York ring, is successful, gets his nose fixed, and with his new-found good looks, attracts a society girl, Joan Gibson (Virginia Bruce). Deeply smitten, he attempts to rise to her social heights, but when he again breaks his nose in the ring, she wants no more of him. He delivers her a kick in the scanties and returns to sweet Peggy, who is willing to take him back, bent nose and all.

Warner Brothers rang their cash register once more, and everyone was impressed with Jimmy's performance. Fighters insisted that he had been in the ring as a professional, and it was then that the rumor began that he had indeed had many bouts as a prizefighter. Jimmy, of course, had much experience as a fighter, but little of it was in the ring; it was his background in dance that made the fight scenes so real. The footwork was flawless.

"Like actor Cagney's previous impersonations, this one has a quality of effortless authenticity," *Time* said of his performance. The *New York World Telegram* wrote: "He carries with him a veritable smell of the shower room, of sweating body and sodden leather. He walks like a punch drunk fighter. He does things with his eyes and lips. He gets an inimitable inflection and accent into his voice." Said *The New York Times:* "After having been highly successful in his portrayal as a gangster, a gambler, a taxi-driver, a confidence man and an automobile racer, James Cagney is far more convincing than most players who elect to impersonate pugilists."

Jimmy, however, once more found himself in a real-life battle with the studio. There were two classes of stars at Warner Brothers, said Jimmy—those who were being paid more than $100,000 a picture, and those receiving about 10 percent of that amount. He had recently been among the latter, and although his income had been increased by about three times after his walkout, it still was not enough.

In many eyes, a thousand dollars a week was a king's ransom, and Jimmy was well aware of that; but the point was that the studio was making millions from his work and he was making thousands. There might come a time when his movies would not earn millions, and he was willing to face that situation when it arrived. He said that he would put in writing his pledge to accept a proportionately lower salary if and when his pictures decreased in box-office returns; meanwhile, if they continued to bring in more than ten times what they cost, he wanted a larger share. He could see that it was hopeless to wait for the studio to give him a merit raise, so he did what he considered necessary: he walked out again.

In addition to the monetary dispute, the studio was continuing to demand his participation in extended personal appearance tours, which he wanted no part of. On one such tour, he and a group of other contract players were transported across the Depression-riddled land in luxurious Pullman cars. He had found it embarrassing and in deplorably bad taste.

Then there were the roles the studio wanted him to play. He wanted to portray a wider variety of characters, but they insisted that he remain only a tough guy. He was first assigned to play opposite Mary Brian in *Blessed Event,* but on the first day of shooting, he failed to appear. He was already en route to New York. Lee Tracy took the role that Jimmy had abandoned, in a kind of turnabout of the situation a few years earlier, when Jimmy had understudied Tracy in the play *Broadway.*

In a statement Jimmy made before returning to New York, he said: "I feel that I have given the best years of my life working for inadequate compensation. My employers can't see it my way, so

I'm through. I'm leaving for a tour of America and Europe. . . . After that, I'm turning seriously to the study of medicine."

Needless to say, Jimmy didn't follow his brothers Harry and Ed into medicine. He spent the next five months with his family, enjoying their company while taking periodic trips to the country to shop for a farm. He felt certain by this time that he could earn a living by working the land; if he failed to gain sufficient rewards from acting, which was far less fulfilling to him as a way of life, he would do just that. It was once more up to Warner Brothers. He stubbornly insisted that it didn't make any difference to him one way or the other.

CHAPTER 11

W hile Jimmy was under suspension, another studio offered to buy his contract from Warner Brothers for $150,000; the offer was refused. Jimmy, meanwhile, offered the studio three films without pay if they would release him from the remaining years of the contract: this too was refused.

The director Frank Capra was assigned to arbitrate the Warner Brothers–Cagney dispute by the Academy of Motion Picture Arts and Sciences. He was able to bring a reasonable offer to Cagney, who was holding out for a minimum salary of four thousand dollars a week. The studio would pay him three thousand a week, with annual increases that would bring his salary to forty-five hundred dollars a week by 1935. Jimmy accepted the monetary offer but demanded that the contract state that he was to make no more than four movies a year and receive top billing in all of them. In September 1932 the new contract was signed by both parties. For the first time Jimmy could feel like one of the studio big kids. Dick Powell was drawing six thousand dollars a week; Edward G. Robinson, Douglas Fairbanks, Jr., and Kay Francis were getting four thousand dollars. Jimmy, whose films were the biggest money-makers of all, was at least approaching parity with the other stars.

Jimmy was getting a feel for Hollywood after having been employed there for two years, becoming aware of certain studio practices such as block-booking. Warners owned five hundred theaters that earned half the corporate profits. Ownership of so many theaters gave them tremendous leverage over other chains and independent houses. If a theater-owner wanted to book a hot Cagney movie, for example, he had to accept an arbitrary number of lesser Warner attractions. This practice made it certain that all the studio's products would earn money. The courts later outlawed block-booking, but while it lasted it made the major studios financially invincible. With the Depression firmly entrenched, the studios were pleading poverty. They were cutting salaries, but insiders knew that in most cases the studios were still earning huge profits. Jimmy simply believed in the philosophy of sharing the wealth.

He returned to the studio to report for work in an ironically entitled film, *Bad Boy*. The title was later changed to *Hard to Handle,* but either phrase would have expressed Warner Brothers' opinion of Jimmy at the time.

As work on the picture began, the industry was reeling from the belated effects of the 1929 stock-market crash. On November 22, 1932, one of the Hollywood trade newspapers devoted most of its pages to the plight of the industry. One of the headlines read: WORST WEEK MOTION PICTURE INDUSTRY HAS EVER SEEN.

Box-office receipts were plunging, and there was consternation within the industry; but the major studios would soon learn that even when money was tight, good pictures would still make money, and with block-booking even the bombs could turn a profit.

The irony was that a factory worker who was lucky enough to have a job at this time had an annual income of one-quarter of Jimmy's *weekly* salary. His knowledge of such a disparity may have caused a shiver or two of guilt on Jimmy's part; but, in fact, his own personal depression had lasted for almost thirty of his thirty-three years.

Jimmy had no difficulty remembering his own tough times, and he never divorced himself from past acquaintances. Although he would never admit it, he sent many SOS checks to old friends who asked for help over the years, and those who had helped him during his own lean times were more than amply rewarded.

In the early thirties, for example, Jimmy heard from a York-ville street-battler he remembers clearly—Willie Carney, with whom he had had those three marathon fistfights during his teen-age years. It was Carney who, for a few pennies—or merely for attention—would cling to high-up building ledges by his fingertips. His letter was mailed from the New York Hospital for the Insane. "He had gone crazy," Jimmy says. "He said in the letter, 'Maybe you remember when you and me hooked it up on Seventy-eighth Street and Avenue A. I'm a little nervous now.' He asked if I could send him some cigarettes, money, or clothes. I sent him a whole batch of things, but never heard from him again. It didn't occur to me at the time, but I wondered later if Carney ever got the stuff. It's possible that the keepers took everything. Otherwise, I think I'd have heard from him again."

Hard to Handle was written by Wilson Mizner and Robert Lord; Jimmy was delighted to again work with Mizner, who had also written *Winner Take All.* "Some people are called characters," says Jimmy, "and don't really merit the designation. Wilson Mizner was a genuine character, and a great raconteur. We would go in for a story conference, but there'd be no conference. Everyone would just sit and listen to Wilson—and all of it was delightful." Jimmy was deeply grieved when Mizner died suddenly during the shooting of the picture.

Mervyn LeRoy, fresh from his assignment on *I Am a Fugitive from a Chain Gang,* was the director of the film. Jimmy had been considered for the lead in that film, but since he was on suspension in New York at the time, the part was given to Paul Muni. LeRoy did equally excellent work on *Hard to Handle* and many other films, proving his worth to the industry. It hadn't been easy for him, since he was the son-in-law of Harry Warner.

Jimmy played the role of Lefty Merrill, a fast-talking promoter, who skips from one get-rich scheme to another, until he finds himself enmeshed in a marathon dance event that is more or less on the up and up. Where he made his mistake was in trusting his partner, who absconds with all the ticket receipts. With the money gone, Merrill finds it impossible to pay off the contest winners. He not only has to deal with their collective anger, but he is additionally disturbed because he has fallen in love with the female winner, Ruth Waters, played by Mary Brian. The girl's mother, played expertly by Ruth Donnelly, insists that Jimmy marry her daughter, which, in the end, he is willing to do.

Playing the master of ceremonies in the contest was Allen Jenkins, who became Jimmy's friend when they were both touring with the musical *Pitter Patter.* Their friendship was renewed as they worked together in *Hard to Handle.* Jenkins, who came from a theatrical family, had found that chorus work was no way for him to pry his way into speaking parts, so he enrolled at the American Academy of Dramatic Arts. After graduating he started getting theatrical parts, and he came to Hollywood in 1931. Jenkins became an immediate member of the Jimmy Cagney friendship club and remained one of its charter members.

A typical gathering might be lunch at a fine restaurant or simply a meal at home with a few friends; although Jimmy and Willie had the reputation of being rather reclusive, they did occasionally go out on the town, sometimes in a small group or, more frequently, by themselves. Jimmy says that Willie would usually take refuge behind potted plants at parties: "She would peek through the leaves to see what was going on."

He and Willie liked the Trocadero, the most popular Hollywood nightclub at that time. It was owned by Billy Wilkerson, who, as publisher of the *Hollywood Reporter,* had written that long open letter to Jimmy concerning his first walkout from Warner Brothers. On one occasion, Jimmy and Willie sat near Charlie Chaplin in the fashionable club. They were both fascinated to see Chaplin regaling the other stars with one of the most eccentric dances Jimmy could imagine. "It was one of the funniest things I had ever seen. He was such an eccentric person, it was impossible for him to dance in a conventional way. That night he sent me a note asking me to come to his office and see him. I think I called him, but nothing came of it."

Among Jimmy's recollections of evening entertainment is one that involved the "Mexican Spitfire," Lupe Velez. Jimmy and Willie had just arrived at a party when Lupe showed up in her regal limousine. Also in the entranceway to the Beverly Hills mansion was a well-known socialite who passed herself off as a countess. Lupe was wearing an ankle-length ermine coat, but the countess was adorned with chinchilla. The moment Lupe saw the chinchilla, she knew she must have it. Jimmy says that she lifted up her sleeve to expose a half-dozen jeweled bracelets worth a fortune. "You can have any of these you want," she purportedly said to the countess, "but I want that coat." The countess selected a bracelet or two, and the switch was made then and there. "Lupe put on the chinchilla. She rolled the ermine into a ball and threw it into the trunk of her car."

When Jimmy and Willie attended Hollywood functions, they did so out of the same brand of curiosity that draws people to freak shows: "You would see things you just couldn't believe, yet there it was in front of you." Quieter evenings were shared with friends such as Ralph Bellamy, whom Jimmy got to know during the shooting of his next movie, *Picture Snatcher*. Jimmy played Danny Kean, an ex-con who becomes a photographer for a sensational tabloid edited by McLean (Ralph Bellamy). Kean's job is to snatch revealing photos by any means whatever. The script was based on the true story of a New York photographer who took a forbidden photo of an electrocution at Sing Sing. In the movie's climax, Kean does just that by means of a camera strapped to his leg.

His chicanery earns the scorn of his girlfriend, Patricia (Patricia Ellis), who charges that as a photographer he is as much a crook as when he was in the rackets. By photographing the electrocution he causes Pat's father, a police lieutenant, to be demoted. Kean redeems himself later when he photographs a notorious killer as he is engaged in crime.

The director, Lloyd Bacon, kept the pace tight, and Jimmy was believable as always in his antihero role. It was the same old Cagney film image, but with a newspaper background, which appeased the increasingly inflamed Hays Office. The script was tightened and honed by William Keighley, who had directed Jimmy some years earlier in the Broadway version of *Penny Arcade*.

The favorably received *Picture Snatcher* was another Warner Brothers two-week wonder, and some critics wondered how the quality of Cagney's work could remain high in such hastily concocted productions. Although hesitant to admit it—maybe even to themselves—the studio bosses must have begun to realize that Jimmy was earning his weekly salary—and more.

In one scene, Joe Kean retaliates for a slap in the face by rapping Allison (Alice White) in the mouth. Kean had rebounded to Allison when his affair with Patricia had cooled. Jimmy had carefully coached Alice to hold her head still when he threw the punch. The punch would look real, but he would see that he missed her chin by inches. At the moment of action, however, Alice moved her face forward an inch or so, and Jimmy's wallop connected. "And there was poor little Alice down on the floor, crying her heart out. I was mighty sorry to have hit that cute little kisser."

Jimmy was given his comeuppance in a later scene with Ralph Bellamy. Ralph was directed to slug Jimmy in this scene, and he was worried about it. He had never slugged anyone before, on the screen or off. Jimmy reassured him that everything would be all right. He told Ralph to let his fist fly and said that he would dodge it easily. Ralph put everything into the punch, and Jimmy caught it flush on the jaw. He went flying across the room, landing in a chair that broke under the impact. As had happened once before, Jimmy had to have a chipped tooth fixed. Bellamy was so disturbed by the incident that he swore never to take a poke at anyone again. He says that he has kept his word to this day.

In addition to beginning a long friendship with Bellamy while working on *Picture Snatcher,* Jimmy also started an extended association with Lloyd Bacon and William Keighley. Bacon would direct another half-dozen films with Cagney, and Keighley would direct even more.

Jimmy's third film for 1933 release was *The Mayor of Hell.* Jimmy played Patsy Gargan, a racketeer who works his way into the position of deputy inspector at a reform school. At the institution he is influenced by Dorothy (Madge Evans) to get rid of the cruel superintendant (Dudley Digges) and, through Patsy's influence in high places, manages to assume the role himself. Dorothy's scheme is to introduce a self-governing system for the boys. Patsy can put it over, she is sure, because he speaks the same language as the delinquents.

The new system is just beginning to work out when Patsy finds himself in a conflict with his New York gang that results in his killing a man. He goes into hiding, and the boys at the school believe that they have been abandoned. The former superintendant returns, and his disciplinary measures result in the death of one of the boys. The other boys revolt under the leadership of Jimmy Smith (Frankie Darro). The superintendant falls to his death on a barbed-wire fence. Patsy returns and reinstates his program.

Time said of the film: *"The Mayor of Hell,* far more adroit, far more cleverly invented than *Road to Life,* is propaganda for nothing. Like most of what comes out of Hollywood it is entertaining trash." Jimmy was praised by the reviewer, but he was very nearly upstaged by the crackling performance of sixteen-year-old Frankie Darro as the reform-school ringleader.

To bring in the film under budget, the cast was required to work practically around the clock. This would have been impossible in later years, particularly with so many teenage actors.

Jimmy would often see the director, Archie Mayo, with his head thrown back, sound asleep. Everyone took cat naps whenever possible. Often they had no more than four hours away from the studio overnight. This was a situation that would soon end forever. The Screen Actors Guild was in the process of being formed, with Jimmy active in its genesis. Within another year, the hundred-plus-hour week would be no more than a bad memory to most Hollywood actors.

Strangely, energy was never a factor with Jimmy during those years. He seemed to have Benzedrine in his veins. After the hectic, even brutal schedule of *The Mayor of Hell,* he began rehearsals for an even more demanding film, but this time he made no complaint. As difficult as it was for him to believe, he was actually called upon to do a dancing role in a musical. The movie is now regarded as one of the finest musicals ever made by Warner Brothers.

Cagney broke in a pair of tap shoes, deposited his gat in a safe place, and for the next month devoted himself to the happy-go-lucky life of song and dance. He would play the part of a dance director in this, his first musical, but would do plenty of dancing of his own. His partner would be the lovely new star Ruby Keeler. The picture was called *Footlight Parade.*

PART FOUR

The Dance to an Oscar

CHAPTER 12

A s the Depression tightened its grasp, the Hollywood film studios happened on a medium that was made to order for the times. Their previous escapist products had taken the form of gangster stories or high adventure, but in the early thirties it was discovered that musical productions with plenty of fast-paced dancing and light-hearted romance could be equally appealing to their despondent audiences.

Ground was broken in 1930 with *Whoopee!*, an adaptation of a Broadway musical starring Eddie Cantor. United Artists enjoyed such success with it that other studios decided to try their luck. By 1933 movie musicals had increased in number and in grandiosity. Warner Brothers hired Busby Berkeley, who had directed the lavish dance numbers in *Whoopee!* He was given carte blanche, more or less, and the studio heads sat back to await the results.

Their first musical venture far exceeded the studio's expectations. In *42nd Street* Ruby Keeler and Dick Powell were teamed as dancing sweethearts, and the public fell in love with both of them. They were cast together in *Gold Diggers of 1933,* and, to keep a good thing going, were once more paired in *Footlight Parade.* Cagney had been telling them he could do other things than throwing fists and grinding grapefruits into pretty girl's faces, and now the studio gave him a chance to prove it. He was assigned the leading role, Chester Kent, in *Footlight Parade.*

One reason for the studio's decision to deviate from Cagney's usual casting may have been that Metro-Goldwyn-Mayer was making a film in which Clark Gable and Joan Crawford were singing and dancing. Also in the film, called *Dancing Lady,* was a new screen personality who was causing quite a stir with his seemingly effortless style. His name was Fred Astaire.

In *Footlight Parade,* Chester Kent, a producer and director of movie-palace stage shows, learns that his ideas are being stolen and used by his competitors. In desperation, he rents three rehearsal halls and isolates the casts of three productions long enough to get the finished shows on the road. He races back and forth between the rehearsal halls to keep up with the progress of each cast. He demonstrates a step here and directs a bit of business there—all the while contending with an ex-wife (Renee Whitney), who wants more alimony. He is also caught in the claws of a gold digger (Claire Dodd), while his faithful secretary (Joan Blondell) follows him around trying to protect him. It is she who eventually saves the day by uncovering the chicanery of his partners (Guy Kibee and Arthur Hohl), who are keeping two sets of books to hide the profits.

Hugh Herbert plays an effeminate adviser who has gotten his job through nepotism, and Frank McHugh is a harried choreographer. Lloyd Bacon directed the acting, while Busby Berkeley staged the dance numbers with great flair and originality. Not only were the dances more spectacular than in his previous movies, but he broke cinematic ground by inserting a spectacular water-ballet number.

Also in the cast were Billy Barty, still one of the world's most famous dwarfs, and then-unknown Ann Sothern and Dorothy Lamour as chorus girls. Cast as "sailor behind table" was the youthful John Garfield making his film debut.

The three big dance numbers are shown back-to-back in the last part of the film: "By a Waterfall," which evolves into the water ballet; "Honeymoon Hotel"; and "Shanghai Lil." The first two numbers are performed by Keeler and Powell, but the "Shanghai Lil" sequence is where Jimmy comes in. His lead dancer shows up drunk, so Jimmy has to step in and take his place. For the first time since *Taxi!* Jimmy was issued a pair of tap shoes, and he left no doubt that he could hoof with the best of them.

Busby Berkeley said of him: "He could learn whatever you gave him very quickly. You could count on him to be prepared. And expert mimic that he was, he could pick up on the most subtle inflections of movement. It made his work very exciting."

Of all his movies, the only ones Jimmy ever liked were the

musicals, and, for a time, *Footlight Parade* was his favorite. But today he says, "It was a dog."

Not long before the filming began, Joan Blondell had married the cinematographer George Barnes, and he was behind the cameras on *Footlight Parade*. Two years later she would divorce Barnes and marry Dick Powell.

Cagney says that he didn't become very well acquainted with Ruby Keeler during those early years at Warner Brothers. Like Jimmy, Ruby had been reared in New York. As a teenager she made her debut in the theater, and it was Al Jolson who was responsible for bringing her to the attention of Warner Brothers. That, of course, was how Jimmy had gotten his break in pictures, although he scarcely knew Jolson. Ruby not only got to know him but married him. The relationship didn't help Keeler very much, however, because in a disagreement with Jack Warner over his wife's treatment by the studio, Jolson insisted that she break her contract. She did so in 1937. In 1938 she and Jolson were divorced, and her career came to an end. There were two minor films in her future, but it was really over when she left Warner Brothers. It's possible that the same fate might have befallen Jimmy had his early disputes with the studio resulted in his contract being broken. But he was simply too big a star and moneymaker for the studio to let him go.

Everyone was impressed with his work in *Footlight Parade*, and Jimmy may have imagined that the studio would be giving him one musical assignment after the other. If such hopes were nurtured at all, they didn't last long. His next picture was more of the same: the same that made the biggest bucks. He was cast with grapefruit-recipient Mae Clarke in *Lady Killer*. This time there would be no more Mr. Nice Guy wielding a scalloped grapefruit. Publicity for the film focused on a scene in which Mae was dragged across the floor by her hair.

In the film, later referred to by Jimmy as "just another of those quick ones," he played Dan Quigley, a movie usher, who loses his job and becomes the leader of a gang. Happenstance lands him in Hollywood, where he rises to movie stardom. The old gang shows up, however, and tries to coerce him into robbing celebrities' homes.

One of the redeeming qualities of *Lady Killer* was its abundance of humor. The script was written more for comedy than for melodrama, and Jimmy played it to the hilt. It certainly qualified as just one more Warner Brothers programmer, but the critics liked it. Said *Literary Digest:* "In *Lady Killer* there is a complete and unashamed exploitation of a star. James Cagney, who plays the title role in the motion picture, gives so vigorous, exciting and captivating a performance that one pays scant heed to the episodic and frequently implausible qualities of the narrative. Tough, arrogant and likable, he infuses shopworn material with glamour and makes the work a lively and gusty melodrama."

The critics had fun with the fact that Jimmy was picking on Mae Clarke again and wondered what her fate might be if they were cast together in yet another picture. As for the brutality in this violent sequence, Jimmy was careful to explain: "She knew how to hold on to the wrists. I didn't pull her hair at all."

Jimmy's hectic schedule for 1933 resulted in five completed pictures, and one of them, *Footlight Parade,* he actually liked. One out of five, in his opinion, was not bad at all. "Just doing a job," he would repeat again and again. "Just a job."

His first "job" for 1934 was another crime film with comedic overtones, *Jimmy the Gent.* His leading lady was an up and coming young actress named Bette Davis. It didn't matter to Jimmy whom he played opposite, but he was accustomed to more cordiality from his costars. Bette's contempt for him was made obvious by her reluctance to pose with him for studio stills. According to Jimmy, Bette Davis wanted no part of "roughneck actors."

With the passage of time, Davis became a vocal champion of Jimmy's character and acting ability, but at this time she didn't know him, and she was undergoing professional difficulties. She was feuding with Warner Brothers as much as Jimmy had been, but because she was female her situation was even more difficult. She wanted no part of this quickie film but was forced to make it. She was marking time until a scheduled loanout to RKO, where she would star in the prestigious film *Of Human Bondage,* but Warner Brothers couldn't bear to let her languish for a month before shooting began.

She didn't realize it, but she and Jimmy were on the same wave-length: he wanted better pictures too. As a protest, Jimmy showed up on the set with his hair crudely shaved around the sides, making him look like a scarred pineapple. Hal Wallis had taken over again as studio production head, replacing Darryl Zanuck, who left Warner Brothers to establish Twentieth Century–Fox. Wallis thought that Cagney was directing an insult at him personally. The director, Michael Curtiz, assigned to a Cagney movie for the first time, nearly fainted when he saw Jimmy's hair. In one scene Jimmy turned his head away from the camera to speak on the telephone. The camera picked up what appeared to be a series of ugly scars under the thin hair on the back of his head. The flustered director ordered "Cut!" and wondered how to deal with the dilemma. Jimmy then relented. It was true that his hair was shorn to the quick, but the scars had been affixed by a makeup man. Having made his point, Jimmy took off the scars and proceeded with his work.

Wallis saw no humor in the stunt, and Jimmy's scruffy appearance may have been the reason for Bette Davis' refusal to pose with him. Jimmy's appearance wasn't vastly improved by the removal of the scars, but, if nothing else, he had succeeded once more in giving the audience something to take out of the theater. *Jimmy the Gent* was a box-office and critical success.

In his next film for 1934, Jimmy was cast with Joan Blondell for the last time. It was always a pleasure for him to work with her, but the script of *He Was Her Man* was no pleasure. It was just more of the same. His surprise for the studio brass this time was a mustache. He knew that it would displease Jack Warner, who had forbidden a mustache on a previous occasion because, he said, it detracted from Jimmy's toughness onscreen. Jimmy had just enough time between pictures to cultivate the addition to his countenance, and the mustache stayed.

Jimmy's role was once more that of a hoodlum, and Joan played a former prostitute. With her former profession clearly established, the movie was not shown on television for many years. Jimmy, however, was once more praised for his acting.

Harold Barnes of the *New York Herald Tribune* wrote: "More than any other screen actor today, Mr. Cagney is the exponent of the school of acting of which George M. Cohan is the brilliant dean. Eschewing histrionic fireworks, he is adept at calculated understatement, in which the slightest gesture, the slightest inflection of the voice, is extremely significant. It is possible that you do not care for the disreputable and frequently vicious type of American citizenry he delineates, but you cannot quarrel with the manner in which he recreates them."

In his next movie, *Here Comes the Navy,* Jimmy was paired for the first time with Pat O'Brien, who would become not only his perfect partner onscreen, but his closest friend for the next fifty or so years. They had met briefly in 1926 when Pat came backstage to compliment Jimmy on his performance in *Women Go on Forever,* but their paths had not crossed since then.

Pat was the live-for-today, tomorrow-be-damned type, while Jimmy's philosophy may have been, "I fooled them this time, but next week they're bound to get wise to me." Such differences seemed to bring them closer together, and their common Irish heritage helped them understand each other.

Pat loved partying and nightclubs, and he was consistently gregarious and outgoing. Jimmy was well described by O'Brien as "that faraway fella." Jimmy eschewed nightlife and crowds and he abstained from practically all bad habits. Jimmy admits that he was frequently concerned about Pat's well-being, recalling what booze had done to his father. Pat drank heavily for many years, but never did the barrels of Cutty Sark do him in; he drank more than most, but never became a drunk.

Here Comes the Navy was directed by Lloyd Bacon. Much of the action was filmed in San Diego, aboard the U.S.S. *Arizona.* Seven years later the Japanese would sink the carrier at Pearl Harbor, but in 1934 the peacetime navy welcomed the Warner Brothers company aboard.

Jimmy played Chesty O'Connor, a street tough who has a fistfight in a dance hall with Biff Martin, played by O'Brien. They meet again when Chesty enlists in the navy and finds that his chief petty officer is none other than Martin. Chesty's wise-guy attitude and irreverence toward navy tradition makes him unpopular with the other men and an object of loathing to Martin. The enmity heightens when Chesty starts romancing Martin's sister, Dorothy (Gloria Stuart). Chesty goes AWOL and Martin reports him. In the end Chesty redeems himself through an act of heroism.

Pat O'Brien's initiation into Cagney-type action films was not without incident. In one scene he found himself dependent on Jimmy's superior physical condition and his willingness to demonstrate it. The character played by O'Brien was manning a rope suspended from a dirigible. According to the script, when the aircraft suddenly rose into the air Pat was to be lifted skyward with it. Jimmy was then to climb down the rope from the dirigible's cabin to rescue Pat by securing him with a rope attached to his own body. "This was being shot from the ground up against the sky," Jimmy explains, "giving the illusion that Pat, the rope, and I were well up in the air. As he dangled there and I came down the rope, I put my legs around him. He completely lost his grip. I couldn't support him along with my own weight, so we both went straight down. Somebody said they could see smoke coming from my hands as we slid. Pat's hands were burned, but mine looked like hamburger, because I was hanging on tighter."

There was an abundance of brawling, wisecracking, and fast action in the picture, but it was noticed by some of the critics that Jimmy treated his girlfriends with courtesy and kindness. Although no studio dictums were distributed to the performers, it was obvious that the story had been toned down for the benefit of the Legion of Decency, which had been created just as filming was about to begin. It was the first Warner Brothers film to be modified in this way. The release was enormously successful and would be remembered by many fans and critics as one of the best of the Cagney-O'Brien films.

The fourth and final Cagney film of 1934 was *The St. Louis Kid*, in which Jimmy found himself in the middle of the milk war then making headlines. He played a scab who runs a barricade set up by striking dairymen. When a striker is killed, Jimmy is implicated. His girlfriend (Patricia Ellis) provides an alibi for him but is kidnapped by the opposition. He eventually tracks down the culprits, is reunited with her, and clears his name.

Irritated by the sameness of the plot, Jimmy again tried to come up with a tag that would bring life to the mundane script. "I was so fed up with punching people again and again that I called in a makeup man and had him bandage my hands. At the beginning of the picture I come out of a courtroom with my hands all wrapped up and let it be known to my perennial sidekick, Allen Jenkins, that I am through hitting people for him. Then, a few moments later, some guy is about to poke him for bumping his car, and I have to jump in. I do it, but instead of punching him, I whip around and pop the guy between the eyes with my forehead."

Jimmy used his gimmick throughout the picture, even though his studio superiors would have much preferred that he deal out punishment in the routine way. It may not have mattered much whether Jimmy hit his adversaries with his fists or his forehead, because all Cagney films were making money during these years, but it mattered to Jimmy. His little innovations and improvisations kept him from stagnating completely and provided great personal satisfaction.

The St. Louis Kid, far from a Cagney classic, took two weeks to make, cost $80,000, and brought the studio box-office returns of $1,800,000. These figures and others would later be used by Jimmy in court to illustrate the gap between studio profits and costs, among them actors' salaries.

CHAPTER 13

As a Hollywood misfit, Jimmy would have been perennially miserable in his picture-making routine had it not been for the solid nucleus of good friends he acquired along the way, among them Pat O'Brien, Ralph Bellamy, Frank Morgan, Lynne Overman, and Allen Jenkins. After O'Brien came along, he introduced a new member to the clan, his lifelong pal Spencer Tracy.

The columnist Sidney Skolsky would label the group the "Irish Mafia," although Cagney regarded the term as a misnomer. He points out that there was never anything remotely nefarious in their activities and that only a few of the gang were Irish. There was no Irish blood at all in the veins of Bellamy, Overman, and Morgan, and while there was no denying the ancestry of O'Brien, McHugh, and Tracy, Jimmy made a point of declaring the Norwegian part of his own lineage.

"Our purpose," Jimmy says, "was to meet, talk, find out what was happening with one another, and have a night out. Some people accused us of plotting to help the Irish American Army, and we were also charged with being anti-this and anti-that. One of the most fantastic ideas that got around was that our conversation was profound. In the beginning we ate at such gourmet gardens as Chasen's or Romanoff's, but some drunk would usually come and beat our brains out with his yakking, so at last we decided to have our dinners at our own homes."

To expand the boundaries of private entertainment, Jimmy bought himself a boat in 1934. He kept the *Martha*, a sixty-nine-foot schooner built in 1907, moored at Newport Beach, about fifty miles south of Los Angeles. The boat was used frequently to traverse the Southern California coastline or to travel thirty miles to Catalina Island for overnight outings. "I'm the worst sailor in America," Jimmy admits, "but it never stopped me from going to sea. I was sick most of the time, but it didn't bother me."

The clan, or the "Boy's Club," as it came to be known, would usually be present on the sailing excursions, at least some of them, and the most enthusiastic sailor of all was Spencer Tracy. He had owned a boat of his own but had made the mistake of selling it, so he "adopted" the *Martha* during the years Jimmy owned it.

Time for recreation really became possible only after the establishment of the Screen Actors Guild in 1933. When it grew large enough in membership to force changes in studio practices, Sunday filming became a thing of the past. The new weekend breaks from the rush and turmoil of picture-making were welcomed by all contract players. Jimmy's current contract stipulated that he make only four films each year, which allowed him much more leisure time, but the studio didn't honor the clause. There were only four films in 1934, but he was made to do six the following year. Jimmy would lock horns with the studio at the end of 1935 for this and other breaches of contract.

Jimmy considered his first picture for 1935 a waste of time and film. In *Devil Dogs of the Air,* honoring the Marine Air Corps, he was teamed with Pat O'Brien and Frank McHugh. Once again he and Pat were fighting it out for the hand of a pretty girl, this time played by Margaret Lindsay. The film took eight weeks to shoot and cost $350,000. The box-office returns were huge, proving that the combination of Cagney and O'Brien was good for more than just one picture.

Jimmy, only five years into his film career, reached a milestone in 1935. He became one of the "Top Ten Moneymakers" in Hollywood. Every one of his films of the previous year had earned in excess of one million dollars. It was a year that was significant also because he was given roles other than those of hoodlums. He wasn't exactly converted into a lace-handkerchief Lothario, but he was given a chance to play a Shakespearean role. In the same year, he played a role on the right side of the law. In *G-Men,* the film a number of critics regarded as containing his best performance since *Public Enemy,* he was given an FBI badge.

In *G-Men* Jimmy played Brick Davis, a lawyer who joins the FBI to avenge the gangland murder of his best friend, an FBI agent killed as he made an arrest. In pursuit of the suspect, Brick is directed to the hideout by a former girlfriend who has since married one of the gangsters. The man behind the crimes is a racketeer who befriended and helped to educate Brick when he was young. It is Brick's intention to quit the agency after he kills the racketeer, but he stays on to extricate the girl from the gang; she is saved in a shootout.

By Warner Brothers' standards the budget of $450,000 was astronomical, and a seemingly interminable six weeks were allotted in which to make the film. Jimmy's salary by this time was $4,500, or 10 percent of the budget for one week's shooting. This may have made him feel important for the moment, but he found himself confronted with problems similar to those he had encountered in the low-budget quickies. They still fired real machine-gun bullets into a cord of firewood near where Jimmy crouched, and he wondered whether it would be any consolation if his death occurred in a big-budget movie instead of a programmer. The director, William Keighley, promised that Jimmy would not be injured and he wasn't. But he felt lucky to survive the scene.

The press made a big issue of Jimmy's going onto the side of the law—helped, of course, by the studio press agents—but Jimmy can recall feeling no elation about the changeover. "Didn't mean a thing," he says. "Just a job to do. No stress, no strain."

This was the third film in which Jimmy worked opposite Margaret Lindsay. He didn't especially care for her; she had a quality that kind of rubbed him the wrong way. Jimmy liked regular Joes, and Margaret Lindsay had a phony way of speaking. Born in Dubuque, Iowa, she had bluffed her way into the 1932 Universal film *Cavalcade* by pretending to be British. Her broad A's persisted from that time forward. "She spoke so veddy, veddy affectedly," says Jimmy. "Hahvard, Cahlton . . . that sort of thing. They needed leading women that looked like her . . . pretty, that's all."

Jimmy had a similar feeling about the director, William Keighley, who had been elevated just a year earlier from dialogue director to director. "He and his wife, Genevieve Tobin, studied French and learned to speak it fluently. He was fed up with us American actors and moved to France. . . . Phooey. His mother was a real down-to-earth type, and would shame him in front of everyone. 'Now, Willie,' she would say, 'don't tell all these lies. You know your father ran a grocery store.'"

After the high-budgeted *G-Men* the studio allowed Jim no time to think big. He was immediately assigned to *The Irish in Us,* which teamed him again with Pat O'Brien in a story of amiable enmity; Frank McHugh was also in the film. This time they all played brothers: O'Brien a cop, McHugh a fireman, and Jimmy— too high-toned for mundane chores—a sometime fight promoter. Inevitably, he and Pat compete for the same girl. When a fighter of his fails to show up for a big fight, Jimmy substitutes for the drunken pug. He wins the fight and the girl. The girl was played by Olivia De Havilland, with whom Jimmy was working for the first time; for many years she would be his choice as most beautiful leading lady.

Some of the reviewers suggested that the deft directorial touches of Lloyd Bacon lifted the film above the ordinary but it was agreed that the three principal actors made the picture what it was.

"We called them cuff operas," says Jimmy, referring to the off-the-cuff dialogue they all contributed. "I recall a scene where Frank McHugh comes back from a formal affair. He was wearing a full dress suit with a white cap. Pat looks him over and says, 'You didn't wear that cap to the ball, did you?' Frank ad-libbed the reply: 'Oh, I know—it should have been black.'"

Jimmy's next assignment was the role of Bottom in the Warner Brothers production of Shakespeare's *A Midsummer Night's Dream.*

In the studio's desire to go classical, they hired the famous stage director Max Reinhardt and permitted him the incredible luxury of full cast rehearsals for several weeks before the beginning of production.

When Jimmy was given the role much of the industry was skeptical, but it was Reinhardt himself who had requested him for the job. "I did not want to play Bottom," Jimmy said in a 1936 magazine interview. "I fought against it. The first news that I was cast for the role came to me accidentally. Somebody told me Mr. Reinhardt had seen me in *Lady Killer* ages ago and remembered my performance. From that, he wanted me to do Bottom."

Today Jimmy says: "It didn't matter to me. The studio planned to make it a crusher, with all those stars. Dieterle was supposed to do most of the directing, but Reinhardt was telling him what to do. Reinhardt looked at me and said, 'Ein guter

Schauspieler!': 'A good actor!' He was really a nice man. No temperament at all with Reinhardt."

Despite Reinhardt's confidence in Jimmy, his work in the film was not universally appreciated. He had his share of good reviews, but some were caustic. The *Times* of London said: "The most lamentable mistake in the cast was the Bottom of James Cagney. He seemed to me to misconceive the character, and only became tolerable in the scene where he discovers the ass's head on his shoulders."

"The only thing I was going by," says Jimmy, "is that Bottom was the greatest ham that Shakespeare had ever written. He wanted to play all the parts. The keynote was that the son-of-a-bitch was a ham. I don't know what the hell they wanted." Reinhardt also defended Jimmy's characterization: "The part of Bottom has always been played by a stout, middle-aged man. Why? James Cagney's type is perfect, and his performance delights me."

In a cast that included Dick Powell, Joe E. Brown, Hugh Herbert, Frank McHugh, Victory Jory, Olivia De Havilland, and Anita Louise, Mickey Rooney received the highest praise for his portrayal of Puck. "I was pleased to work with Mickey," says Jimmy. "He was fourteen or fifteen at the time, and very talented. During the filming he broke a leg skiing and showed up Monday morning in a wheelchair. He was being pushed by one of the most beautiful young girls you can imagine. A short time later, he had an affair with a very famous actress. I was surprised to hear it, but Mickey took it all in stride. He always had beautiful girls around."

With his Shakespearean venture behind him, Jimmy had to make the transition from Elizabethan England to the nineteenth-century Barbary Coast of California for his next assignment, *Frisco Kid*. Perhaps it was the wing collar and waistcoat that bothered some of the critics, but Jimmy was accused by at least one of them of "something he's never been guilty of before, and that's the tendency to go beyond the necessary histrionics to 'ham' it."

Jimmy was better appreciated by most of the reviewers, but they were generally bothered by the movie's likeness to the successful Howard Hawks film, distributed earlier in the year, *The Barbary Coast. Frisco Kid* was considered a poor imitation of the original.

Jimmy worked for the *lahst* time with Margaret Lindsay in this film. In a secondary role was the French-born beauty Lili Damita, who was about to marry Errol Flynn and abandon her budding film career. (She would bear Flynn's first child, Sean, who, as a photographer, was reported missing in Cambodia during the Vietnam war.)

The next film to be released in 1935 was Jimmy's last in his current contract, and it became a battlefield on which he and Warner Brothers staged a do-or-die conflict. *Ceiling Zero,* directed by Howard Hawks, would be remembered as one of the finest aviation pictures of the time by many critics, but the studio and Jimmy would recall it as a turning point in studio-actor relations.

The screenplay was adapted from a Broadway drama by the author, navy pilot Frank Weed. It depicted early mail pilots who risked life and limb flying mail routes out of fog-shrouded airfields; thus the term "ceiling zero." Jimmy played the wisecracking, womanizing aviator Dizzy Davis, who, to keep a date with a girl named Tommy Thomas (June Travis), feigns illness and scratches his assigned flight. His pal, Texas Clark (Stuart Irwin), takes the run and is killed. Dizzy is conscience-striken after his friend's death and volunteers for a flight into a storm to test a de-icing device. He plummets to his death as a reformed man.

Jimmy says today that he recalls very little of his leading lady, June Travis, but she remembered him vividly. Many years later she confessed that she had a terrific crush on her first prominent leading man, "but he didn't give me a tumble. He was a very quiet, introspective man . . . even-tempered, somewhat withdrawn. Definitely not the stereotype of the big star who plays prima donna, and has frequent temper tantrums. He was very easy to work with and, as far as I knew, never gave any of his directors a bad time."

It was flattering to Jimmy to belatedly learn of her admiration for him, but as far as he was concerned her crush went unnoticed. He was so staunchly married through all his acting years that he insists he was oblivious to such admiration. What he remembered most about the picture, in fact, was his third partnership with Pat O'Brien, and how the billing appeared on the marquee on the Warner Brothers Theatre in Hollywood.

CHAPTER 14

Jimmy, ever watchful for false moves on the part of his bosses, caught them dead to rights when *Ceiling Zero* opened in Hollywood. A friend of his, a newspaperman, spotted the billing on the marquee of the Warner Theatre that said PAT O'BRIEN IN "CEILING ZERO." He immediately called Jimmy to ask when he had started getting second billing.

Jimmy moved at once. He had a photograph made of the marquee and he hired a lawyer. His contract stated in no uncertain terms that he was to have top billing on all his pictures. This was only one breach of contract. He had been assigned five pictures during the previous year, when four was the limit under the terms of his contract. To compound his grievances, Jimmy was then ordered to appear in another convict role in *Over the Wall*. Instead of reporting for work on a film he wanted no part of, he walked off the lot for the third time in five years and started legal proceedings.

The studio heads had always considered Jimmy a rebel, but never had they expected him to go this far. Never in the history of motion pictures had an actor dared to lock legal horns with a film studio. It was generally believed that any studio, with its limitless resources, would certain prevail over any individual. It may have been naiveté on Jimmy's part, or unmitigated gall, but all the king's horses frightened him not a whit.

He did, however, place full trust in his lawyer and felt that he had little choice when the lawyer insisted that Jimmy fire his current agent, George Frank. "Now, these are orders from the man who's handling my business, so I write Frank a letter saying that I was sorry but from then on I would no longer be needing his services. Well, Jesus, the roof came in on him. He called to ask if I was going through with it, and I told him I had to. The man said I should, and he was the one handling the case. I was terribly sorry about it because I really liked the guy. I had been with William Morris before, and they did nothing. I was happy with the Frank and Dunlap agency."

This remains Jimmy's only regret about the litigation. In fact, soon after the agent's firing, the lawyer dropped Jimmy's case. His practice involved studio dealings, and pressure or simple apprehension must have been behind his action. Jimmy didn't think it would be proper to rehire the agent he had just fired, so his brother Bill handled all of his agenting from that time forward. Jimmy hired a second lawyer—one whose income did not depend on the studios—and the suit proceeded. He made two or three personal appearances at early court hearings but then returned to New York with Willie. Bill represented Jimmy during his long absence.

During the months of litigation, Bill had calls from David Selznick and Sam Goldwyn regarding possible movie deals with Jimmy, but no concrete offers were made. There wasn't a studio in Hollywood that would not have welcomed a deal with a top moneymaker such as Cagney, but it soon became apparent that a kind of blacklist was in effect. The other studios were afraid to risk a lawsuit with Warner Brothers; besides, it was against their interests to hire a known troublemaker.

As for Jimmy, he took it all in stride—no stress, no strain. The Cagneys stayed at the Gramercy Park Hotel, and each day Jimmy would walk the few blocks to the Players' Club, where he would visit with close friends of long standing. One afternoon he was visiting with Ed McNamara, who suggested that the two of them go to Martha's Vineyard to see their mutual friend Denny Wortman, the cartoonist who drew "Mopey Dick and the Duke."

"When we reached the Vineyard," Jimmy says, "I looked around and said, 'This is for me!' I had been everywhere looking for acreage to buy, but in all the places there were concrete roads that led in all directions. But when I came to Chilmark in 1936, the roads were dirt. I liked that. I found a wonderful hundred-acre farm with an old house on it and a deed going back to 1728. I fell in love with it. I wrote out a check for seventy-five hundred dollars and the place was mine."

Willie didn't rejoice at the idea of a farm, and for some time she refused to leave the city to take a look at it. Jimmy eventually enticed her to the Vineyard, where her original misgivings were confirmed. The house was a shambles. It had walls of seashell plaster so damp they fairly dripped, and there was no furniture. After a cursory examination she was ready to return to Manhattan, with its summer heat and humidity. But then Jimmy introduced her to the attic.

"She found a newspaper that announced Lincoln's second Civil War draft, and she found some jelly that had been made in 1898. She came across old whaling-days souvenirs, such as a ladle made of bone. There were letters from sailors who had jumped ship in San Francisco to go to the California gold fields. She was so fascinated by all this stuff that she decided to stay."

Word traveled that the Cagneys had bought the farm, and one day when Jimmy was away for a few hours Willie was accosted by movie fans who demanded to see him. Insisting she was only the cook, she eventually shooed off the intruders, but when Jimmy learned of the incident he was furious. He sent word out through the grapevine that he had a shotgun on the premises, along with a hired hand who was instructed to use it. The fanciful news flash had a far-reaching effect.

"We were looking out of the window one day when Willie said, 'There's a man coming across the field.' I looked too, and said, 'It looks like Tracy, only it can't be. Spence doesn't even like to walk out the front door to get the paper.'"

But it was Tracy. He had decided to pay the Cagneys one of his surprise visits and had hired a taxi to drive him to the farm. As they neared the property the driver stopped and opened the car door. "This is as far as I go," he told Tracy. "I hear they shoot."

While Jimmy was playing the role of fledgling farmer, Bill was holding discussions with an independent production firm named Grand National Pictures. A man named Alperson, the president, had been in the sales department of Warner Brothers but had pulled together enough money to make his own movies, and he hoped to start things off with a Cagney attraction. He offered Jimmy $100,000 a picture and 10 percent of the earnings. Jimmy had been idle for more than a year by this time, which was fine with him, but the offer seemed too good to refuse.

Jimmy agreed to make two films for Grand National. In the first, *Great Guy,* he played an ex-prizefighter who becomes a chief deputy for the Bureau of Weights and Measures. Mae Clarke played his leading lady.

The script stuck with Cagney's tough-guy image, but, as in *G-Men,* Jimmy was on the side of the law. The film was well received by the critics, who were delighted with Jimmy's return to the movies, but the absence of big-studio quality in sets and production was noticeable. Warner Brothers may have turned out Jimmy's pictures for a pittance, but after years of movie-making it had all the requisites for movie furbishings close at hand. Grand National was starting from scratch, and it showed.

Jimmy's second film for the independent company was a musical called *Something to Sing About.* He played a bandleader who lands a movie contract but, in the end, returns to his band and his old girlfriend. For this one, Jimmy called in his dancing mentor, Johnny Boyle, and they did the best they could with what they had.

As with *Great Guy,* Jimmy received good reviews, but once more it was noticed that the production values were low. The dance routines were regarded as so-so, and Jimmy's singing brought no glowing compliments. Jimmy's absence from the screen, and his two independent ventures, removed him from the list of the top ten box-office attractions, but it was hoped that a third Grand National picture might be good enough to restore his popularity. Jimmy agreed to star in a film called *Dynamite,* but suddenly the money dried up. This was just as well, because at this point his lawsuit against Warner Brothers was decided in his favor. Jimmy had done the impossible: he had crossed swords with the ruling powers and had actually emerged victorious. He was free from Warner Brothers. The studio had failed to adhere to the rules of the contract, and the contract was nullified. There would be repercussions from his triumph. Bette Davis was standing in the wings awaiting the outcome of the case, and other contract players would challenge Warners in the future. It was a bitter defeat for the studio, and they could have been angry enough to ostracize Jimmy forever, or perhaps to conspire in an industrywide blacklist. But they didn't. Pride was one thing, money another. The smoke had scarcely cleared from the legal battle before Warner Brothers representatives approached Jimmy. The studio heads were willing to forgive and forget. They wanted Jimmy back on the lot, and he could dictate the terms.

If Grand National had not exhausted its resources, and if the Cagney–Warner Brothers litigation had lasted a bit longer, there is no question that Jimmy's career would have followed a far different course. For one thing, he would never have played another hoodlum. In *Great Guy* he was a nice leading man who would never have considered roughing up his lady friend; he even permitted her to advise him. In *Something to Sing About* he was a romantic lead in a musical. It was clear that Jimmy was looking for properties that would alter his screen image. This might have continued, for better or for worse, but when Warner Brothers offered $150,000 a picture plus a percentage of the profits, he signed on again for five years. He would do only two films a year and could refuse any script he didn't like.

With his new contract, Jimmy would be earning over a quarter of a million dollars a year, which in the days of modest income taxes and low prices was a king's ransom; yet he never developed a feeling of financial security. A few years earlier, when Jimmy and Pat O'Brien were in San Diego making *Here Comes the Navy,* they took a drive up the coast to Rancho Santa Fe to take a look at Bing Crosby's magnificent second home. As they inspected the adobe palace, Jimmy confessed that he preferred to live more simply. "This," he told Pat, "will be a whole lot harder to give up."

Pat, who couldn't conceive of his own well drying up, shrugged it off, as though Jimmy were speaking a foreign language. But Jimmy always had the feeling that sooner or later the red carpet would be rudely snatched from beneath his feet. His uncertainty may have contributed to the consistent quality of his performances. The rush of adrenaline was always there because he had to be good; he didn't dare rest on his laurels.

Jimmy expressed his belief that a good actor cannot be too relaxed, that talent is nourished by a certain degree of emotional imbalance. He uses his brother Bill as an example. Bill acted in several movies between 1933 and 1935, but an acting career was not for him. Jimmy says that Bill was a lousy actor because he had too much poise. He believes that a person who is cool and self-assured cannot reach in and draw up the emotion necessary to lose himself in a part. It is his contention that most really good actors are never very sure of themselves and are always stoking the internal fires to prepare for their roles.

Although he doesn't apply this to himself—he is far too modest to see himself as that good—the description certainly fits, because no matter how calm and cool Jimmy may appear on the surface, he was always a bundle of diffidence underneath. It is easy for him to say that an actor need only stand up, plant his feet, and speak the truth, but in practice he did his share of throwing up, before he ever got to the point of standing up.

His uncertainty was part of the compelling force that made him invest his money in property. He loved the fresh air and natural surroundings, but he also believed that he would one day depend on the land to eke out a living. He bought a second farm in Martha's Vineyard, at Tashmu, a few miles closer to the sea, and picked up a choice twelve-acre parcel in Coldwater Canyon, in Beverly Hills. Over the years he has bought and sold many pieces of property that appealed to him at the time, and, while he has never been compelled to scratch a livelihood out of the soil, he has always been fairly sure that he could.

While Jimmy was in so many ways frugal, no one every labeled him stingy. His generosity toward his family has always been common knowledge, but his giving ways extended far beyond the family fold. Ralph Bellamy remembers that Jimmy was constantly sending off checks to less fortunate friends from the old days, and he could never turn his back on needy acquaintances and charities. In the latter instance, his generosity on occasion came back to haunt him.

Jimmy made headlines in 1935 when Ella Winter, wife of the journalist Lincoln Steffens, said that she had received donations from him to back a left-wing cause. Jimmy had, in fact, contributed to a fund to aid striking cotton-pickers in the San Joaquin Valley. He admitted being acquainted with Steffens but insisted that he was unaware of his political affiliations. From then on Jimmy was labeled a political radical.

He was further smeared by the press when his 1936 donation to the defense of the Scottsboro boys became known. The case involved nine young black men accused of raping two white women in an Alabama freight car and sentenced to death. Eventually, all of the defendants were set free, after the women admitted that their testimony was perjured. The funds raised by non-Communist organizations were generally responsible for the successful defense. The Communists, however took credit for it, and somehow Jimmy's check ended up framed and displayed on the wall of the Communist party office in San Francisco.

Jimmy always championed the underdog, having been among them for so many years of his life. It was with this motivation that he involved himself so heavily in the organizing of the Screen Actors Guild. His own working conditions had been bad enough, but he was appalled by what most other actors were forced to put up with. They were treated like animals. The less aggressive stars were also pushed as far as they would go. A case in point was Boris Karloff, whose screen image belied his gentle nature. "He told me it took him more than three hours to get into his make-up each morning," says Jimmy, "and another hour getting it off after a twelve- or fourteen-hour day. One day I said to him: "Don't go. Go in when you feel like it. They won't do anything.' He tried it and it worked. He was surprised."

What Jimmy wanted was a fair shake for everybody He felt guilty enjoying his own good fortune while others around him were hurting. He helped those who came to him, and his charitable contributions persisted even after further repercussions. Jimmy, along with many other Hollywood stars, donated ambulances to the Abraham Lincoln Brigade, an American unit that fought for the Loyalist side in the Spanish Civil War. His support resulted in a summons to appear in Washington, D.C., before the Dies Committee, forerunner of the House Committee on Un-American Activities. The hearing cleared him once and for all of all Communist charges. Other liberal actors given clean bills of health were Humphrey Bogart, Fredric March, and Franchot Tone. (Jimmy's trip to Washington, by the way, was his first experience with air travel. He didn't like it then, and never has.)

It was 1938 before Jimmy made his next film. He was again teamed with Pat O'Brien. It was almost as if he had returned from a week's vacation to find everything pretty much the same as before. To complete the homecoming, Ralph Bellamy and Frank McHugh were also in the cast. The picture was *Boy Meets Girl,* an adaptation of a Broadway comedy. The property had been acquired for Marion Davies, but when her demands for rewriting went too far she was replaced by Hollywood's newest dizzy blonde, Marie Wilson, and the script was adapted to fit Cagney and O'Brien. There were two other relative unknowns in the cast in addition: a seductive beauty named Carole Landis played the cashier, and a smiling juvenile named Ronald Reagan was cast as "the announcer."

Cagney and O'Brien played a pair of zany Hollywood screenwriters who were kept on the run from the opening credits to the last frame. They had completed several days of shooting when word came from Hal Wallis to do it again and make it "louder, faster and funnier." The director, Lloyd Bacon, thought that he had already paced the action too fast, but apparently it was too slow for Wallis. So they did it all over again. Out of curiosity, Jimmy did something he almost never did; he watched one of the daily rushes. He was with Ralph Bellamy, and on the way out Jimmy asked him: "Would you tell me what I just said? I couldn't understand a word."

When the movie was released, the reviews were mixed. Some critics labeled it the farcical gem of the year; others suggested that Jimmy was out of his element doing comedy. Nobody suggested that the movie was slow-paced, and all thought that the script was funny.

Those who preferred Jimmy's tough-guy characterizations didn't have to wait long. The studio had allowed him a change of pace, but in *Angels with Dirty Faces* he was back in "his element." The script, by Rowland Brown, was one that he had hoped to do with Grand National before the money ran out. He had sensed that it was a winner, and he was right: it led to his first Academy Award nomination.

Jimmy played Rocky Sullivan, an infamous hoodlum who, returning to his old neighborhood, finds himself a youngster's idol. The street kids emulate their hero in every detail, which undermines the work being done with them by Father Jerry Connelly, played by Pat O'Brien. The hoodlum and the priest grew up together on these streets, and a strong affinity remains between them even though they are on opposite sides of the law. Connelly pleads with Rocky to change his ways, but to no avail. Eventually there is a shootout between Rocky and his ex-partner and lawyer, Steve Frazier (Humphrey Bogart). Rocky kills Frazier and is sentenced to die in the electric chair. As the day of execution approaches, Connelly tries to persuade Rocky to die as a coward so as to break his spell over the street kids. Rocky rejects the idea.

The hour of execution arrives, and Rocky begins his last mile, cocky, cynical. Then, when the electric chair comes into view with all its grim starkness, Rocky breaks. He is reduced to a pitiful and sniveling coward, too repulsive to win anyone's respect. With Rocky's breakdown comes the compelling question: Did he really break, or was he doing it for Father Connelly and the neighborhood? The question is unanswered in the script and has remained unanswered through the years. It is the audience's choice to make.

This was Jimmy's first movie with Bogart. It was also the only time he was to work with the scene-stealing Dead End Kids. He tells of his first encounter with the gang: In one scene, Leo Gorcey kept ad-libbing phrases that broke continuity and distracted the other players. Jimmy had had enough, but he waited for the next take. When Gorcey interjected an ad-lib, Jimmy gave him a stiff arm above the nose, snapping his head back sharply. "Now listen," he said, poking a finger into Gorcey's chest. "We've got work to do, and there'll be no more of this goddamn nonsense. We're going to do it the way we were told to do it . . . understand?" Gorcey understood. It was a language familiar to him.

One of the other kids asked Gorcey whether he thought he was dealing with Bogart instead of Cagney. During the filming of the movie *Dead End,* Bogart had done something that rubbed the gang the wrong way. They proceeded to divest him of his pants, and got away with it. Bogart may have looked tough and acted tough, but Cagney *was* tough. There was no further trouble with them on the set.

Jimmy worked with Ann Sheridan for the first time in this film. She was twenty-three at the time, and he recalls her heavy smoking, which would cause her death from cancer at fifty-two. This was the second Cagney film that Michael Curtiz had directed. Jimmy had great respect for the feisty little Hungarian, and it was mutual, apparently; Jimmy says that he and Curtiz never had a clash of temperaments, even though Curtiz was well known for his tantrums.

On one occasion the calm was ruffled, however. Once again, Jimmy was told that he would play a scene amid live machine-gun bullets. "I was up at a window, firing down at the police. I was supposed to be in the opening as machine-gun bullets took out the window around my head. I said to Curtiz, 'Do it in process.' He assured me I wouldn't be hurt, but I repeated that they should superimpose the shot. I said I wouldn't be in that window when the machine gun went off. That was the way they did it, and sure enough, one of the bullets hit right where my head would have been." He was never again asked to do a scene with live ammunition.

Rocky Sullivan is the character most impressionists mimic when they do Jimmy Cagney. Jimmy says that he modeled his portrayal on a hophead-pimp who once worked out of a First Avenue rathskeller in Yorkville. "He wore an expensive straw hat and an electric blue suit, and all day he would stand on that corner. He would hitch up his trousers, twist his neck and move his necktie, lift his shoulders, snap his fingers, then bring his palms together in a soft smack. His invariable greeting was 'Whaddya hear? Whaddya say?' I did those gestures maybe six times in the picture, and the impressionists have been doing me doing him ever since."

When *Angels with Dirty Faces* was released it was an instant hit. Jimmy received an Academy Award nomination as Best Actor, but he lost the Oscar to his friend Spencer Tracy for his performance in *Boys' Town*. Jimmy did win the New York Film Critics' Award, however, as Best Actor of 1938.

It was an excellent year for Jimmy. He was once more growing in box-office popularity. The Securities and Exchange Commission let it be known that Jimmy headed the list at Warner Brothers for income that year, with earnings of $234,000.

CHAPTER 15

uccessful writers of pulp fiction in the thirties knew that one of the secrets of seizing the reader's interest was the use of "narrative hooks"— tags hung on key characters to help the reader distinguish one from the other. Jimmy Cagney never wrote a word of fiction, but he knew intuitively that the characters he portrayed on the screen should have distinguishing features, or, as he often put it, "something for the audience to take out of the theater with them."

This accounted for his talking around a pipe in *The Millionaire,* the bound fists and head-butting in *The St. Louis Kid,* the outrageous haircut in *Jimmy the Gent,* and the many other touches he added to his characterizations.

In Jimmy's next picture, *The Oklahoma Kid,* the tag was something he imagined a Western gunslinger might do—blow into the barrel of his six-gun after he fired it. This was Jimmy's first picture for 1939, and his first Western role ever. His adversary was once more Humphrey Bogart, and by Warner Brothers standards the production was given big-budget treatment, with Lloyd Bacon directing and James Wong Howe at the camera. The music was by Max Steiner.

Jimmy owned a number of horses by this time. He had loved them all his life, but when it came to riding he remained a novice. He recalls sitting on his studio horse with a leg wrapped around the saddle horn. He was on a distant hill taking a brief respite between takes. The horse, a veteran of Western films, heard the sound of the assistant director's clapper, which to him meant action. He took off at a dead run toward the distant camera. "I grabbed his neck and held on. He came to a declivity and jumped it—about six or seven feet. I don't know how the hell I stayed on, but I did. We worked well together after that, once the horse found out I could hang on."

In the film Jimmy played Jim Kincaid, who turned outlaw after his father was convicted and hanged on a trumped-up murder charge by a bought jury. He avenges the injustice when he finally kills the principal bad buy, Whip McCord (Bogart). His girlfriend in the picture was played by Rosemary Lane, and amid all the action Jimmy manages to sing two songs: "Rockabye Baby"—in both English and Spanish—and his father's favorite song, "I Don't Want to Play in Your Yard."

Although Jimmy and Bogart were on the same lot, they never became friends. There was no particular enmity between them; they just didn't hit it off. Jimmy can recall only one occasion when he was with Bogart off the movie set. Once, at Chasen's restaurant, Jimmy found himself in the company of Dave Chasen, Bogart, and the writer John Steinbeck. "It was after hours, and the place was locked up. Suddenly there was a loud banging at the back door. Chasen went there and it was Mayo Methot, Bogart's wife at the time. Bogart excused himself and went back to talk with her. He returned a few minutes later. From what I had heard about their fights, I expected him to be torn and bloody, but he was unscathed and was laughing. What amused him was her parting line, which was, 'You and your goddamned drunken friends.' The funny part was that all of us were sober. Nobody had a single drink."

Jimmy said that Bogart didn't have many friends. "Not many people liked him, and he knew it. He said, 'I beat 'em to it. . . . I don't like them first.' He hated just about everybody, but that was his aim—to hate them first. When it came to fighting, he was about as tough as Shirley Temple."

Bogart was also the inspiration for one of Jimmy's many poems. Jimmy was driving along Coldwater Canyon Drive one afternoon, and as he stopped for a traffic light he spotted Bogart in the sleek sports car next to him, busily picking his nose as he waited for the light to change. Jimmy's commemorative poem read:

> In this silly town of ours,
> One sees odd primps and poses;

But movie stars in fancy cars,
Shouldn't pick their fancy noses.

Jimmy sent the poem to Bogart with an accompanying note but received no acknowledgment. Bogart's reaction to Jimmy's appearance in *The Oklahoma Kid:* "In that ten-gallon hat, he looked like a mushroom."

The original intention had been to make the film a serious documentary-type Western about the mountain men, but when the Warners brass were finished with it, according to Jimmy, it turned out to be no more than another programmer—this time with oats.

Jimmy inserted several bits that the audience "could take out of the theater with them." In one scene there was the line: "Feel the air—just feel it." What Jimmy did was actually reach up with his fingers and go through the motions of feeling it. The detail was remembered years later. In the final scene, Jimmy was to give his girl a kiss after her father (Donald Crisp) had congratulated him on winning his daughter's hand. Instead of embracing her as was scripted, "I looked at him, looked at her, took off my hat, handed it to Donald, and said, 'Hold that.' Clinch and fadeout." Much later, the director Lewis Milestone saw the scene and commented to Jimmy, "I was wondering how you were going to get out of that one."

Although Jimmy didn't think much of the picture, it was appreciated by audiences and critics. *The New York Times* said: "Mr. Cagney is on a horse at the Strand. It is almost the only thing that distinguishes this picture from any one of five other past Cagney films. . . . There is something entirely disarming about the way he has tackled horse opera, not pretending for a moment to be anything but New York's James Cagney all dressed up for a dude ranch. He cheerfully pranks through every outrageous assignment his script writer and director have given him. . . . He's just enjoying himself, and if you want to trail along so much the better for you. The rest of the cast plays it with almost as straight a face, but not quite the same jauntiness."

In Jimmy's next picture, *Each Dawn I Die,* it was back to the big house. He was paired with another Hollywood tough-guy in this film, George Raft. Raft was new to Warner Brothers, having been drawn away from MGM by Jack Warner to round out his stable of hoodlums. With the problems the studio had been having with Cagney and Edward G. Robinson, they considered it wise to keep as many substitute tough-guys on contract as possible.

Jimmy has always prided himself on his ability to discern raw toughness in other men, and he had no doubts at all regarding Raft. "He was the only really tough man I knew in the business," said Jimmy. "He was genuinely tough without meaning to be. He dropped one on Eddie Robinson's chin one time and knocked him assways. As I remember the story, Robinson had the reputation of taking over on the set. He'd say, 'You stand here and do this, and then move over here. . . .' As he was doing this with George, he grabbed his arm and kind of ushered him. Raft said, 'Don't grab my arm.' Eddie failed to heed the warning, and the next time he grabbed him. . . . bang! Robinson was on the floor."

Jimmy regarded Raft as one of Hollywood's finest dancers, even though he was rarely called upon to dance in films. He ranked him with Fred Astaire and was pleased when the occasion arose to introduce the two of them. Astaire visited Jimmy on the set one day and was quickly ushered over to meet Raft. Astaire had been appearing in the New York theater when Raft was working in nightclubs, and he had expressed admiration for Raft's work. "It was interesting to watch their meeting after all those years," says Jimmy. "They were very shy of each other, self-conscious. I could see that very little would be said unless I played straight man for them, so I did. Finally George unwound and started to tell some wonderful, wonderful stories about his early days."

Jimmy and Astaire were close friends over the years, and they hoped to make a movie together one day. It didn't come about, of course, and today Jimmy says that it is just as well: "I could never have kept up with Freddie—not ever."

The review of *Each Dawn I Die* by Howard Barnes of the *New York Herald Tribune* sums up the critical consensus fairly well: "There are few actors who can touch James Cagney for that subtle combination of personality and artifice which constitutes motion-picture make-believe. Moreover, in a particular field of melodrama, it seems to me that he has no peers. . . . In *Each Dawn I Die* he has several scenes to play, such as the one in which he is brought out of solitary on the verge of being stir crazy, when the temptations to indulge in pyrotechnics must have been very strong indeed. Nevertheless, he holds each scene in its proper focus so far as plot and character are concerned, adding a unity to the production which it badly needed. He could easily have been far more showy, but he was wise enough to know that flamboyant performing would have destroyed the slim dramatic continuity which this film boasts."

In his third and final film of 1939, *The Roaring Twenties*, Jimmy worked with the director Raoul Walsh for the first time and with Bogart for the last time. Adapted from a story by Mark Hellinger, the script used the flashback technique and a narrator.

Jimmy played Eddie Bartlett, a World War I vet who returns home to hard times. He falls in love with Jean Sherman (Priscilla Lane), but she loves Jimmy's wartime pal Lloyd Hart (Jeffrey Lynn), who has become a lawyer. Eddie gets involved in bootlegging, as do two other war buddies, George Halley (Bogart) and Danny Green (Frank McHugh). For a while Eddie is riding high, but then a series of events causes his downfall, and he is reduced to driving a cab.

He picks up a fare who turns out to be Jean, now Lloyd's wife. She tearfully tells him that George is still a rackets boss, and is out to kill her husband, who, by now, has become a district attorney. Eddie and George have a confrontation, with Eddie imploring his ex-partner to ease off on the district attorney. The disagreement escalates into a shootout. Eddie mows down the stooges and then gets George, but is himself mortally wounded. He staggers from the apartment and reaches the entrance of a nearby church, where he crumples onto the steps, dead.

Jimmy and Raoul Walsh seemed to get along fine. Walsh even elicited his suggestions for script improvements, and, of course, got them. One of Jimmy's innovations was his two-for-one gimmick: He pops one thug on the chin, and his head snaps back and conks his confederate on the forehead. They both go down unconscious. Another improvisation occurred in a scene where Eddie goes to the nightclub where Jean works to ask her for a date. She refuses. He then asks whether he can stop by for a visit, to which she also says no. Eventually he gets the idea and asks, "Is it all right if I blow my horn as I drive by?" The routine, Jimmy says, was based on an actual incident involving a studio grip.

With *The Roaring Twenties* Jimmy completed his first decade of film-making. Jimmy would never have believed it if someone had said it, but he had also completed his last gangster film for ten years. At the end of 1939 he ranked second only to Gary Cooper among the country's highest wage-earners for the previous twelve months. His earnings: $368,333.

CHAPTER 16

When the Cagneys bought ten acres of land in Coldwater Canyon in 1936, the winding road that crossed the Santa Monica mountains from Beverly Hills to the San Fernando Valley traversed a sparsely populated woodland. Their place was within a mile of the Beverly Hills Hotel but had the ambience of remote farmland. It seemed made to order for Jimmy. Almost at once he sat down with architects to help design a house that would match the roll of the hills. In 1939 the sturdy New England-style home, with stone walls and shake roof, was complete. The Cagneys lost no time in moving in.

It was a small house with only six snug rooms. The polished paneling was rich, the exposed beams heavy and hand-hewn. Two walls of the den were devoted to built-in bookcases, and a mammoth fieldstone fireplace occupied most of another wall.

All of Cagney's homes were to be on the small side, and the tone was rustic, never grand. Jimmy didn't criticize the baronial mansions occupied by so many of his movie-colony peers; if that was what they wanted, it was fine. But he couldn't imagine living in a museum. His penchant was always for warmth and hominess. Relaxation was the preeminent requisite; a table strewn with random books or a chair with a discarded sweater did not look discordant. His home was for living, not for showing. If he wanted to show something, he had his Morgan horses and Highland cattle.

One of the features Jimmy installed on the Coldwater property was a fully functional racing oval. There he would exercise his sulky-trained Morgans and would train others. Later he transferred this activity to the farm he purchased from Louella Parsons in Northridge.

Ralph Bellamy tells a story about Jimmy's compelling desire to "have a country home in the city with everything that goes with it." Jimmy had the riding ring and stables, he had ducks, geese, goats, and dogs, but there was something that didn't seem quite right. Bellamy says that Jimmy counted his hens, and there were twenty-six, but he had only four roosters. He promptly ordered twenty-two more roosters to pair off the colony. "In no time at all," Bellamy insists, "there were feathers all over Coldwater Canyon. All the hens were trembling on top of the chicken coop with twenty-six roosters flying at them."

"Not a word of truth in it," says Jimmy. "Ralph has been telling that story so long I think he believes it, but it isn't true. Don't tell him I said so, though—that's one of his favorite stories."

The tale of the rampaging roosters may be apocryphal, but Jimmy's rural haven in the heart of the city is true enough. The lower property along the road has long since been sold and is now occupied by a dozen homes, but the upper expanse of land remains around the snug little home, with only its gated entranceway visible from the road.

Jimmy suspects that his taste for small rooms dates from his childhood. "When I was little, I would climb up into the space under my mom's sewing machine—the place where the treadle was—and would hide there from anybody and anything that might be bothering me. A writer friend of mine, Harlan Ware, swears that it's my memory of the hours I spent in that safe space beneath the sewing machine that makes me feel comfortable only in small homes. I guess I like to wrap rooms around me like a blanket."

With his new shorter work schedule at the studio, Jimmy had plenty of time to putter around his house, and to spend some time with easel and brush. Between films he would go to Martha's Vineyard to oversee the measures being instituted to make the farmland productive.

He made only two films in 1940, which suited him perfectly. *The Fighting 69th* was a fictional account of the heroics of the famed World War I Irish regiment. In *Torrid Zone* he played a foreman on a Central American banana plantation. Both films were directed by William Keighley and costarred Pat O'Brien. Just about every Irishman on the lot, and elsewhere, was in *The Fighting 69th,* with Frank McHugh and George Brent among the first. A part was written for Priscilla Lane, on the assumption that there must be at least one pretty girl somewhere in the cast to make a picture saleable, but later the role was eliminated.

Jimmy played Jerry Plunkett, a sneering, jeering rebel who mocks military tradition and disdains all authority. He is brash and cocky during training, but in his first battle he shows his cowardice. His cries of fear result in a shelling that kills a number of his comrades. O'Brien was cast as Father Duffy, the fighting priest of the actual "Fighting Irish" regiment. In the film, Father Duffy helps Jerry to redeem himself, and Jerry becomes a hero.

The spectacular battle scenes inflated the film's budget to *Gone with the Wind* proportions, at least from the Warner Brothers point of view. An extensive promotional tour culminated in New York City's Times Square, where the real Father Duffy greeted the cast. He shook hands with Cagney and O'Brien as thousands of fans cheered. Tens of thousands more went to see the film, which made it one of the most successful Warner Brothers films in years.

When Jimmy reported for work on *Torrid Zone,* he was wearing a false mustache, which once more infuriated the brass. Mark Hellinger, the producer, was ordered to get him to remove it before the cameras rolled, but of course he failed. Jimmy saw his character as being mustached, and that was that. Or, as Jimmy put it, "Just for variety . . . that was all." The fact that he had pasted on a mustache instead of growing one did not make it any easier for the studio to get it off.

In the film Jimmy worked for the second time opposite Ann Sheridan, whom he liked very much. (She was married then to George Brent, who had worked with Jimmy in *The Fighting 69th.*) Her convincing portrayal of a hardboiled torch singer in *Torrid Zone* did much to enhance her career.

The reviews were good, and once more Warner Brothers had a winner at the box office. The New York *Daily News* said: "If you want to forget the European situation completely for an hour and a half, go see *Torrid Zone,* Jimmy Cagney's new picture. Its accelerated pace, tough performance and rough humor are a combined guarantee against boredom."

With the completion of the picture, the onscreen team of Cagney and O'Brien ended for over forty years—but their friendship was only beginning. By this time the "Boys' Club" was firmly established, and the weekly meetings rarely failed to occur.

For a person who was essentially a teetotaler, Jimmy managed to surround himself with some big-league imbibers. One of the most obvious revelers was Pat O'Brien, and he was exactly that. He drank heavily, enjoyed it, and was usually well in control of his behavior. Frank Morgan had a reputation for a bottle-a-day consumption, and most of Jimmy's other friends had periods of alcohol abuse. The renegade drinker in the group was Spencer Tracy. He was probably the only one who was really self-destructive, the only one who could be called an alcoholic.

"When Spence was off the sauce, he was kind of a sour guy," says Jimmy. "He would shun company, so I would have dinner with him alone. I think he was a very sad man. I made no demands on him. It was just small talk mostly. Tracy would bring his wife, Louise, with him to gatherings of couples, at which he seemed at ease. But he was always a quiet fella. He could express himself, but in his own way, and I never asked." Jimmy says that he and Tracy never discussed his relationship with Katharine Hepburn, but he does recall Tracy saying that his staying married to Louise had nothing to do with religion. "He was an unhappy man," Jimmy repeats. "He would go on benders . . . whew!" Many times Tracy would show up at Jimmy's house at dawn and demand ham and eggs. None of the group was surprised when he appeared at odd hours seeking camaraderie or nourishment; it was his way.

Ralph Bellamy remembers an incident that occurred in the mid-thirties. "We were playing cops in a picture at Twentieth," Bellamy recalls. "Tracy came into my dressing room and wanted a drink. My God, he looked awful. I gave him the drink, and somehow he managed to get some more, I guess, because when it came time to shoot he wasn't around. I finally found him passed out in his dressing room. In order to cover for him, I had a doctor friend say he was ill."

Tracy came out of it late in the day. To make sure that he was driving all right, Bellamy asked that Tracy follow him in his car. "He was still in the police uniform. In the rear-view mirror I saw him stop, so I turned around and went back. He had pulled over another car, and when I got there he was standing next to it in that uniform, bawling the hell out of a woman driver."

Tracy may have been the only bona fide alcoholic in the club, but it was a fringe member of the group, Allen Jenkins, who took the prize for unpredictability. "He would really turn it loose," says

Jimmy. "Any time he did anything, he did it, by Jesus, he did it. One morning he and Buck Jones got drunk together, and as they were driving, Buck said something to someone in passing that upset Allen. 'I don't like the way you talked to that fella,' Jenkins said. Jones said, 'What are you going to do about it? Do you want to get out right here?' Jenkins said that he did, so they got out and started whaling away at each other. After a while Jenkins says, 'Bucky, I'm getting awful tired.' Buck says, 'So am I.' With that, they get back in the car and drive off.

"About two days later I was in Jones's home in Beverly Hills. We hear, 'Bucky . . . Bucky!' being called from outside. We look out and see Jenkins, still drunk after three days. He had a long raincoat on. Where the hell he got it, we didn't know. He had bottles of booze in each pocket. We didn't make a sound and waited until he finally went away. Jenkins was a wild man . . . always getting into barroom scrapes, and every punch seemed to land against the side of his nose, which gave it its distinctive contour."

As for other members of the clan, Jimmy says that Frank McHugh was not at all what one would expect. He was a very quiet man, and never the life of the party. Ralph Bellamy was a good storyteller, and quite temperate. Lynne Overman was also an outstanding storyteller who could drink and hold it well. The liveliest member was always O'Brien, in Jimmy's estimation. "He was always ready with a story, a quip or a song, and no matter what had gone down the night before, Pat was always bright the next morning. He kept working and always knew every line he had to say.

"Pat drinks very little now because it agitates his arthritis. Can't smoke either. The pain in his legs is terrible, and he got bleeding ulcers from the medication he had to take. He was writhing in pain off-camera in *Ragtime,* but when he got his cue, his pain was forgotten. He's an amazing man."

During his heavy drinking days, O'Brien was able to conduct business as usual, unlike some of the others, such as Allen Jenkins. On a morning when Jenkins's drinking had followed him to the studio, he got into a violent quarrel with Jack Warner. As Jimmy recalls it, Jenkins was laying into Warner about a salary dispute. "If you're going to hold that contract over my head, you can shove it up your ass, you son-of-a-bitch," Jenkins is said to have yelled.

"And that goes for Pat O'Brien, too." Pat, who had just signed a contract for four thousand dollars a week, stood nearby feeling faint.

Of all of his friends, Jimmy considers Spencer Tracy to have been the most talented. He says that he recognized Tracy's talent long before he ever met him, when he saw him in an insignificant 1935 film called *Murder Man.* As for actresses, in 1932 Jimmy saw Bette Davis in something called *The Rich Are Always with Us* and knew that she was special.

"They were both so remarkably alive when they walked into a picture," he says. "They were both incipient thyroid cases. Early in life, Spencer had had a serious thyroid problem, and anyone with a thyroid problem is in trouble. He was a good companion, told stories beautifully, but there was always the tension about him that was intangible. You can feel the stress in such people."

For the year 1940 Jimmy was once again the highest-paid actor at Warner Brothers, but his wealth would soon grow in a way that had nothing to do with income. The Cagneys adopted a baby boy that year and named him James. Soon Cathleen would be added, to round out the family.

CHAPTER 17

Nothing in Jimmy's life ever took precedence over his family. He devoted his life to them. He had enticed his mother to Martha's Vineyard, where he hoped to install her in his spacious and comfortable new home. When he acquired the home, his idea was to have a summer place where the entire family could congregate. It was a lovely place near the sea, with a wraparound porch that he visualized as perfect for his mother. He was mistaken. It was perfect for his tastes, but not for hers.

She explained to Jimmy that her idea of perfection would be an apartment on the corner of Forty-second Street and Broadway, with a big window through which she could watch the passing parade. Jimmy understood but was disappointed. She left the Vineyard after two weeks and never returned.

Later in the thirties, when his mother did finally move to the West Coast, Jimmy once more acted on his conception of what would please her. He bought a charming home on Palm Drive, in the heart of Beverly Hills, and stood beaming as she made her inspection. It wasn't that she was hard to please; just the opposite. She told him that she would rather have an apartment closer to the action. Jimmy had his brother Ed locate a court apartment in the very heart of Hollywood. That was perfect, and it was where Carolyn Cagney would stay for the remaining years of her life.

The family was as close together as they would ever be by the year 1941. Jeanne had graduated Phi Beta Kappa from Hunter College at nineteen, and she came to the Pasadena Playhouse to study acting. An acting career was the last thing Jimmy wanted for his sister, but since she had reasoned it out and made her decision, he gave his full support. Jimmy had envisioned an academic career for his sister, because of her proficiency in French and German, but when she indicated her acting aspirations, he suggested that she devote herself as diligently to learning the performing craft as she had to her studies in language. He considered body control very important and suggested that she enroll in a gymnasium and study dancing. She did exactly that. Totally on her own, Jeanne landed several radio acting jobs and acted in three low-budget movies at RKO. She would later have roles in her brother's films, but Jimmy was always proud that his sister had done so well on her own.

When Jimmy's mother moved to California, his brother Ed came with her. At first he continued his medical practice, but later he gave up medicine to work with Jimmy behind the scenes. He was involved in Jimmy's business affairs and later on as a story editor. The last member of the family to abandon the East Coast was Harry, who waited until his retirement from medicine in 1945 to join the other Cagneys.

Bill Cagney had been in Hollywood for nearly as many years as Jimmy, and was firmly entrenched in Jimmy's business life as well as his personal life. There was never any question in the mind of those who knew the Cagneys as to Bill's ability. He not only earned his share of Jimmy's salary as his manager and agent but augmented Jimmy's earnings by careful investment. It has been suggested that Bill may have been even more successful than Jimmy financially, principally through his shrewd real-estate investments.

His new contract with Warner Brothers gave Jimmy much more leverage in his film work, including the right to have his brother Bill involved in production. On Jimmy's next movie, *City for Conquest,* Bill was associate producer. In this adaptation of the Aben Kandel novel, Jimmy played the role of a prizefighter. To get into condition for the rigorous assignment, he subjected himself to twelve weeks of heavy training that resulted in the loss of thirty-five pounds. He had reached the age of forty-two by now, and his love of food had brought his weight up to a hefty 180 pounds. Jimmy loved the screenplay, written by John Wexley, and his enthusiasm helped motivate him during the excruciating weight loss. He primed himself for the assignment in every way and expected the movie to be something special.

Raoul Walsh was assigned as director but was replaced by

Anatole Litvak by the time shooting began. Litvak later said that this was the only time in his long career that he had had problems with an actor. Jimmy, he said, argued almost every point in the story's interpretation. This was one of the times that Jimmy saw a film he had just completed, and he hated it. Many of the scenes he had liked best had been cut out. He swore then never to watch another of his movies, and he even wrote a letter of apology to the author of the novel. Most of his pictures meant little to Jimmy, but those in which he danced were of interest. This was a fight picture, and he was always proud of his boxing abilities; but the footwork in the ring, the choreographed fight sequences, amounted to dancing in Jimmy's mind.

Jimmy played Danny Kenny, a truck driver whose ambitious girlfriend Peggy (Ann Sheridan) encourages him to enter the fight game. He is successful, but her career as a dancer separates them when she goes on tour with her partner, Murray Burns (Anthony Quinn). Danny's brother, Eddy (Arthur Kennedy), composes a symphony but sells out for the fast money of popular music. Danny is beaten for the championship and blinded in the ring. Reduced to selling newspapers, he is overjoyed to hear a radio broadcast of his brother's symphony. He and Peggy are finally reunited.

Jimmy must have been just about the only person who was unhappy with *City for Conquest*. The *Daily News*: "Cagney's characterization of the prizefighter who is beaten blind in an unequal contest is one of his greatest contributions to the screen and Ann Sheridan is better than she has ever been before." The *New York Post*: "It's like something he was born to do and no one else in the world could ever touch it." The *New York Herald Tribune*: "James Cagney . . . gives one of his finest performances as a mug from the Lower East Side who goes places with his fists."

At the time that *City for Conquest* was made, Jimmy was an inveterate prizefight fan. Although the negative side of the game was clearly illustrated in the film, it was some time before he changed his own opinion of the sport. But a change did occur. "I went to the fights one night with Jim Richardson of the *L.A. Examiner*. I saw this boy get knocked out. His legs were twitching. I said, 'Jim, you just saw a boy die.' He didn't believe it, but I could tell. The boy had a brain hemorrhage and was dead the next morning. I never forgot that."

In interviews, Jimmy frequently advocated going back to bare-fisted fighting, and he was serious about it. He believed that there would be far fewer injuries if boxing gloves were eliminated. He blames the constant thudding of padded gloves for the frequency of brain damage in prizefighting.

He insists that anyone who fights for any length of time will come out of the ring "a little dinghy." "There are little things to watch for. You may not notice the shades of damage, but it's there. One ex-fighter I knew would mimic every small gesture he saw someone else do. If you scratched your eyebrow, he would do it too."

During his work in *City for Conquest,* Jimmy took some hard punches from his ring opponent, who was a professional boxer. "He threw one that caught me right on the chin . . . a dandy. With my face off-camera, I said, 'You son-of-a-bitch,' and let go with a punch of my own. His knees buckled." That started a behind-the-scenes competition that made Jimmy aware that he was working hard for a living. It was a challenge for the makeup man to keep his face photogenic for closeups.

During the filming Jimmy's mother was hospitalized with a slight stroke. After one of his tougher days in the ring, he paid her a visit. When she saw the cuts on his eye and lip, she let out a moan. Jimmy quickly explained that the lacerations had resulted from a movie sequence, and that set her mind at ease. When he told her that he had gotten in plenty of licks, she smiled.

Jimmy's next role was in a remake of a 1933 Gary Cooper movie, *One Sunday Afternoon.* Warner Brothers would do it once more under its original title in 1948, but the 1941 version was called *The Strawberry Blonde.* The 1948 version would be a musical, but this one wasn't, even though it is often recalled as one because of the title song. It is also erroneously recalled as being in color, perhaps because of the suggestion of color in the title.

Jimmy played Biff Grimes, a turn-of-the-century correspondence-school dentist. He loses his girlfriend, Virginia (Rita Hayworth), the "strawberry blonde," to the town shrewdy, Hugo Barnstead (Jack Carson). On the rebound, Jimmy marries Virginia's best friend, Amy (Olivia De Havilland). Biff finds himself working for Hugo, whose shady contracting deals result in Biff's arrest and jailing.

Later Biff is pleased to receive Hugo as an emergency dental patient. He considers doing Hugo in with anesthetic gas but he thinks better of it. What changes his mind is the carping he hears coming from Hugo's wife, the strawberry blonde. It occurs to him that Hugo has suffered enough, and that he himself is better off than he realized. To even things up, however, Biff pulls Hugo's tooth without anesthetic.

Ann Sheridan was originally scheduled for the role of Amy, but because she was feuding with the studio Rita Hayworth was substituted. The casting of the "Love Goddess" rather than the "Oomph Girl" may have paid off in added box-office revenue. The fast-paced comedy-drama, directed by Raoul Walsh, won the critics' approval.

Jimmy's personal touch was a repeated phrase that was certainly something the audience could take out of the theater with them. "That's the kind of hairpin I am," Biff would reply, whenever an explanation of his behavior became necessary. After the release of the film, it became a catchphrase. Jimmy says that he picked it up from his grandfather Nelson but has no idea where the Captain got it.

Jimmy, realizing that the period in which the story was set would be particularly significant to his mother, brought her to visit the set while she was recuperating from her illness. Carolyn had been a young woman at the turn of the century and was herself a strawberry blonde. She watched the filming attentively, and after a particular scene was finished, Jimmy went over to her to get her reaction. "I just want you to know, son," she told him, "they didn't have pretzels in those times."

It must have been clear to Jack Warner that the concessions made to their "professional againster" were paying off in unimagined dividends; since Jimmy's re-signing, each Cagney film was more successful than the last. As a reward for his good work, Jimmy was given another chance at comedy. He was co-starred with Bette Davis in *The Bride Came C.O.D.*

Jimmy played Steve Collins, a pilot for a charter flight service who is hired by Winfield, an oil tycoon (Eugene Pallette), to bring his tempestuous daughter, Joan, home to Texas, in order to keep her from marrying Allen Brice, a bandleader (Jack Carson). For the fee of ten dollars a pound, Steve abducts Joan, but en route to Texas she manages to make him crash the plane in the desert. While police and reporters are tracking them down, Steve and Joan spar with each other and fall in love.

The ingredients were all there, but the critics agreed that the comedy just didn't jell. The too-swift direction of William Keighley may have been partly at fault, and it was suggested also that the bombastic nature of the stars was too much for such a flimsy script. Archer Winston of the *New York Post* wrote: "Okay, Jimmy and Bette. You've had your fling. Now go back to work."

This was the third film on which Bill Cagney served as associate producer and the second time that he worked under Hal Wallis. Bill would work under Wallis on two later occasions, and at some point they had an explosive confrontation. "Wallis was a double-crosser," Jimmy says. "He would say one thing and mean another. He said something about one of us, and Bill confronted him on it. 'You said so and so,' Bill said to him. 'Did I?' Wallis said. Bill said, 'Yeah, you did, you son-of-a-bitch,' and took after him around the desk. He didn't catch up with him or I'd have heard about it, because Bill could hit like the kick of a mule."

In his autobiography, *Star-Maker,* Wallis acknowledged that he and the Cagneys were never best friends, and says of Jimmy: "He was cold to me, and I wasn't particularly fond of him. Nevertheless, he was very talented and few could equal his energy and drive." In the book Wallis also recalled the monumental production problems that arose during the shooting of Jimmy's next film.

The studio had bought a magazine story by Arthur Horman that depicted the courage shown by Canadian bush pilots in World War II. The title was changed from *Bush Pilot* to *Captain of the Clouds,* and Jimmy was offered the lead. He wasn't excited about the script but agreed to do the part as an anti-Nazi gesture.

Wallis described how, after the cast and crew were transported to northern Canada, they were unable to find a satisfactory trading post as a location and had to construct one. Between adverse weather, huge logistic snares, and lack of adequate housing, they never experienced an easy day. Even the beavers were uncooperative, causing floods with their upstream dams.

"Jimmy Cagney," Wallis said, "insisted on being his own double in a scene in which he was knocked into the water by a seaplane propellor. The scene was so realistic that he suffered a slight concussion. After it was all over, our technical adviser informed us that the propeller would normally be off long before the plane drew up alongside the pier, and that we had gone through this experience for nothing."

Supporting roles were played by Alan Hale, George Tobias, Dennis Morgan, and Brenda Marshall. The picture was made in 1941 but released the following year.

Captain of the Clouds was Jimmy's thirty-eighth movie, and his first in color. As it turned out, the spectacular photography received more praise than Jimmy did. Said *Time:* "*Captain of the Clouds* is virtually a documentary of Canada's large part in the British Commonwealth Air Training Plan. Although Cagney is much better than his thankless role, the real heroes are director Michael Curtiz and his five cameramen who caught the matchless greens and browns of Canada's infinite north-country."

Not only was Jimmy upstaged by the scenery, but in several reviews he took second place to a nonprofessional playing himself: Canada's air marshal, William Avery (Billy) Bishop. Archer Winston of the *New York Post* wrote: "No one can match James Cagney, except, oddly, a stoutish man who is not a professional actor at all. Air Marshal Billy Bishop, Canada's flying ace in the last war, makes a speech to the air cadets who are about to receive their wings. It has a ring of iron to it, although the manner is not forced."

At the end of 1941 Jimmy's earnings were $362,500, which ranked him second in the United States in annual salary (first place was held by the head of Metro-Goldwyn-Mayer, Louis B. Mayer). Not bad for a freckle-faced, redheaded street-fighter and hoofer from Yorkville.

CHAPTER 18

The actress Rosemary DeCamp, in her autobiography, wrote:

The camera and the crew were standing still with grave faces. Jeanne Cagney, Walter Huston and I, made up and elaborately costumed, were standing at a little radio emitting the sound of President Roosevelt's voice along with a lot of static. Mike Curtiz, the director, and Jimmy Cagney came in through the freight dock, and walked toward us. When they reached the set, Mike started to speak, but Walter held up his hands. The president finished with the grave news that we were now at war with Japan and Germany. Then, the National Anthem blared forth. Some of us got to our feet and sang the words hesitantly. At the end, Jimmy said, clearing his throat, "I think a prayer goes in here . . . turn that thing off." Someone did.

We stood in silence for a full minute, and Jeanne and I dabbed our madeup eyes. Mike bowed, and with his inimitable accent, said, "Now boys and girls, we have work to do. We have had bad news, but we have a wonderful story to tell the world. So let's put away sad things and begin."

That began our first day on the film, *Yankee Doodle Dandy*, the day after Pearl Harbor, December 8, 1941.

Throughout that picture we all worked in a kind of patriotic frenzy, as though we feared we may be sending a last message from the free world, because the news was very bad indeed during those months in the Winter of 1941–42. We had three weeks of dance rehearsals, during which Jimmy was a great example for all of us. He came through the main gate every morning at six-thirty in his modest old car, wearing his sweatsuit, with his lunch in a paper bag. He worked out dancing, creating most of his own choreography, until noon. He took a half hour to eat, a half hour to rest, and then was back dancing tirelessly until five. We all tried to live up to him.

To Hal Wallis, the producer of *Yankee Doodle Dandy,* it was his favorite picture as an independent producer. He had seen George M. Cohan in *I'd Rather Be Right* and says that he never considered anyone other than Cagney to play Cohan. Jimmy contends, however, that he was chosen only after the part was refused by Fred Astaire.

Wallis says that he didn't even try to call Jimmy about the role but went instead to Bill Cagney, his manager. Bill told him that he would discuss the matter with Jimmy. A call came some days later telling Wallis that Jimmy had turned down the role. "He said he was going into independent production," says Wallis, "and had absolutely no interest in Cohan."

Wallis asked Bill to keep things in abeyance until he could present Jimmy with a script. He then had Robert Buckner write a treatment, which he rushed to Jimmy in Martha's Vineyard. When there was no reply, he had Buckner write the entire script, which he also submitted to Jimmy. By this time, Cohan, terminally ill with cancer, had appealed to Jimmy to accept the role, and Wallis believes that this was the impetus that caused Jimmy to reconsider.

Jimmy doesn't recall all the details of his taking on the assignment, but he is quite sure that the circumstances were other than those described by Wallis. He recalls that Cohan had script approval but says that he refused to play the role unless he could rework the script from beginning to end. The studio bosses were not at all keen about this, but they agreed because they believed that Jimmy was the only actor who could handle the role. Jimmy also insisted that Bill be assigned as associate producer. His sister, Jeanne, was given the part of Cohan's sister, Josie, but without Jimmy's intervention: the director, Michael Curtiz, after meeting Jeanne, selected her.

Jimmy says that Jeanne practiced dancing for six months before the picture went into production. He was astounded at the results. "She was doing cramp rolls, wings, and just about everything else. She was a natural."

There was little question that Jimmy was perfect for the role of Cohan. Cohan was five-feet-six, Jimmy was about five-eight, and they both weighed about 150. Cohan was blond, Jimmy red-haired, but in black-and-white Jimmy photographed blond. They both had Irish features, with jutting jaws, freckles, and blue eyes. Even their careers had some parallels.

While rehearsals were in progress, Jimmy and Bill, with Julius and Philip Epstein, polished the script and rewrote large portions of it. Cohan had approved the original script and declared that it was to be filmed "as is," but that didn't discourage Jimmy. He knew what he wanted, and the original screenplay simply didn't have it. Humor was added, along with emotional impact, and the song "Mary" inspired a major alteration in the true story. The writers made "Mary" the name of Cohan's wife, although neither of his wives actually had that name (one was Ethel, the other Agnes). To make Cohan's true love the inspiration for the fine old song seemed a good idea, and since Jimmy couldn't change the song's title to "Ethel" or "Agnes," the script was changed.

There was no getting around the clause in Cohan's contract that the movie have no love scenes, but Jimmy handled that by having Cohan recite the words of "Mary" to his bride. It played as the most tender of love scenes without a passionate embrace or even a kiss. Jimmy learned much later that when Cohan's second wife, Agnes, saw the scene, she embraced Cohan lovingly. "Oh, George," she said, "I knew you were thinking of me when you wrote 'Mary.'"

Cohan was confined to his New York apartment while the film was being made, but he had a representative, Ed Raftrey, on the set to protect his interests. When the time came for the final cut of the movie to be shown to Raftrey, the Cagneys sat with fingers crossed. "During the showing," says Jimmy, "not a sound came from Raftrey. Then, as the story came to a close, the lounge started to shake. Big Ed Raftrey was sobbing." Cohan was given a private screening a short time before his death, and he was deeply moved. He sent Jimmy a telegram thanking him "for a wonderful job."

To capture Cohan's unique dance mannerisms, Jimmy once more engaged his dancing mentor, Johnny Boyle. Boyle had been featured in *The Cohan Review of 1916* and had staged Cohan's dances. "From Johnny I learned the Cohan stiff-legged technique," says Jimmy, "and his run up the side of the proscenium arch."

Jimmy had seen only one Cohan performance, many years earlier. "He was quite a guy and a fine, fine actor. I was impressed when I saw him on the stage. Some of the things I saw him do, I did when I was impersonating him. I did my best to imitate Cohan when I was on, but offstage I was straight. The studio agreed this was the best way to do it."

Cohan had written and produced forty plays, and participated in many others. Jimmy says that there were nearly one thousand songs to choose from for the movie. Among the songs chosen, and performed so memorably, were "The Yankee Doodle Boy;" "Forty-Five Minutes from Broadway;" "So Long, Mary;" "Mary's a Grand Old Name;" "You're a Grand Old Flag;" "Give My Regards to Broadway," and "Harrigan." Another Cohan song, "You Remind Me of My Mother," was chosen too, but it had to be eliminated. "It was a hell of a song," Jimmy says, "but I couldn't sing it. It was too much for me, for some reason."

Joan Leslie, who played Mary in the film, recalls one of the songs with which Jimmy had no difficulty whatever. "It was the scene in the publisher's office when we sang 'Harrigan.' On most occasions we were given the script before the movie began, but on this picture we would get a new script every day. Jimmy would make the changes. We would get on the set, and he might say, 'This isn't quite right.' Mike Curtiz would say, 'Whatever you say, Jimmy.' Then Jimmy might say, 'I think the girl should say this . . . and turn up her nose, and turn around . . . then we'll go on singing.' Then he would turn to me: 'Joan, now you say this to me, and I'll say. . . .' The script girl was taking all this down, and a new script would be forthcoming.

"Finally, the set was being lighted, and we had a piano player to run through it. Jimmy said, 'Suppose I do the first four or five of the verse, and you do the second, and then we go into the chorus, start out together. When we come to this line, I'll take it. You do the second line.' With that, we would go into it, and do it.

"It gave me such confidence. He made me feel as though I could do whatever he said, which was an extreme compliment. He was asking a great deal of me, but he believed I could do it. He put it all together in about fifteen minutes before we shot it. There was no Le Roy Prinz [the choreographer] there. I felt as though I had rehearsed the routine a hundred times, because he made me feel so secure. I don't remember more than one take on anything with him. We just did it. Then, Mr. Curtiz came over to hug Jimmy and tell him how wonderful it was, and I, of course, basked in that kind of approval, because I was part of it."

Joan also remembers a scene between Jimmy and Walter Huston in which Huston, playing the elder Cohan, is about to die. "Jimmy and I were aged to about fifty. Jimmy goes to the bed, and his father gives him advice as though he were about ten years old. As he starts to talk to Jimmy, who is sitting on the edge of the bed, tears begin to well up in his eyes. You just think his heart is going to break. I was in the anteroom and heard muffled sobs. I came out then and saw all the set-ups: two-shots, long-shots, close-ups, and medium shots. Each time, Jimmy would cry right on cue as if he was heartbroken. Tears like huge dollops would be rolling down his cheeks as he nestled his head on Huston's chest. Mike Curtiz spoiled one take, because he was weeping so loudly. Another scene was ruined by a script girl who couldn't restrain her sobs."

In addition to Jimmy's superlative performance in *Yankee Doodle Dandy*, Joan Leslie was deeply impressed by his demeanor on the set. "The kleig-light operator way up high would call down, 'Hiya, Jimmy.' Jimmy would call back: 'How ya doin', Fred? How's the family.' Another would call to him, 'Hey, Jim, you gonna dance today. . . . I'll come down and watch you.' Jimmy would always visit with them. If he was busy, or preoccupied, he would send them back a wink and a grin, and lift a finger as though to let them know he would get back to them later. He was always thoughtful enough to acknowledge their presence. He would always stand up and swap jokes with every one of them, big or small."

Joan, whose seventeenth birthday was celebrated on the set of *Yankee Doodle Dandy,* worked in a number of other fine movies, including *Sergeant York* and *High Sierra,* but remembers this experience with Jimmy as the highlight of her career.

It was, of course, the highlight of Jimmy's career as well, and is definitely his favorite among all his movies. The scene he liked best was the very last one. "It was when I did the wings coming down the stairs at the White House. Didn't think of it until five minutes before I went on. I didn't consult with the director or anything . . . I just did it."

Jimmy's portrayal of such a patriotic character laid to rest for the remainder of his career the many charges that he was a "pinko." The sincerity of his performance left no doubt as to his political allegiance. It also resulted in his first Academy Award, for Best Actor of 1942.

The film received three other Oscars and eight nominations. Nathan Levinson was honored for Sound, and Heinz Roemheld and Ray Heindorf won awards for Scoring of a Musical. The film received a nomination for Best Picture, but the award went to *Mrs. Miniver*. Walter Huston lost out, as Best Supporting Actor, to Van Heflin, who won for *Johnny Eager*. Robert Buckner's original story was nominated, and so was Michael Curtiz's direction.

A war bond benefit premiere was held in New York City, with the least expensive seat selling for $25 and the most expensive for $25,000. A check of $5,750,000 was donated to the U.S. Treasury Fund.

The reviews were enthusiastic. *Time*'s was typical:

Yankee Doodle Dandy is possibly the most genial screen biography ever made. Few films have bestowed such loving care on any hero as this one does on beaming, buoyant, wry-mouthed George M. Cohan. Canny showman Cohan knew what he was doing when he insisted that Irish Jimmy Cagney was the cinemactor who could play him. Smart, alert, hard-headed, Cagney is as typically American as Cohan himself. Like Cohan, he has a transparent personal honesty, a basic audience appeal. Like Cohan, he was once a hoofer.

With these attributes, Cagney manages to suggest George M. Cohan without carbon copying the classic trouper. He has the Cohan trick of nodding and winking to express approval, the outthrust jaw, stiff-legged stride, bantam dance routines, side-of-the-mouth singing, the air of likable conceit. For the rest, he remains plain James Cagney. It was a remarkable performance, probably Cagney's best, and it makes Yankee Doodle a dandy.

PART FIVE

"Made It, Ma! Top of the World!"

CHAPTER 19

Remembering Jimmy Cagney's uncanny ability to summon tears on cue, Joan Leslie suggested that whether he would admit it or not, he was probably employing the Stanislavski technique of acting. Jimmy steadfastly maintains that all he does is to stand up and say the words. But when it comes to crying onstage or before the cameras he does indeed use a Method-type exercise: he brings back a sad memory to trigger the emotion, and it always works. One might assume that this memory would be his father's early death, especially since he can hardly mention his father without becoming tearful. But there was an earlier death in the Cagney family.

"When I was seventeen Robert Cagney was born, and, as a late child, we were all crazy about him. He was a beautiful boy." Jimmy recalls coming home one afternoon and holding the baby in his arms. He was crying and refused to stop. Finally, in frustration, Jimmy returned him to his crib.

The crying persisted, and it became obvious that something was troubling the baby. He appeared feverish and the doctor was called. As the family waited for the doctor, they were aghast at what they witnessed. They saw the little boy's spine begin to twist backward. The muscles contracted until the body was bent back like the blade of a sickle. They attempted to straighten the body, with the child screaming in pain, but it was impossible. Then the doctor arrived, and he seemed to know at once what was wrong. Robert had contracted tubercular meningitis, and there was nothing the doctor could do to help him. He was doomed.

"My poor mother," Jimmy said. "Jees, that was something. She fell to the floor in a fit, and started to froth at the mouth. We got her out of it somehow, and we could see that the baby was on his way. We were all home the next day when Robert died. I remember a friend of mine, Frank Tassig, came in and saw all the long faces. He said, 'What's up?' We just pointed to the crib where Robert lay dead. He was only thirteen months old."

It was the memory of this tragedy that Jimmy brought forth whenever he needed tears. To this day he cannot think of the incident without great sadness. He recalls it as the most calamitous event of his life. Only four years earlier, his sister Gracie had died of pneumonia after having lived less than three weeks. This too was a tragedy, but Gracie was still an infant, and her death was far less violent. Jimmy can't explain why Robert's death affected him so strongly. It may be because of the frustration and helplessness he felt as the body became contorted in pain, or perhaps he feels guilty for having been annoyed at first when the baby refused to stop crying.

Jimmy's mother had another seizure sometime after Robert's death, and he still feels guilt about the incident. "My mother was in bed. I was standing at the foot of the bed talking to her. I don't know what the hell I said, but I remember she was upset by it. Then she fell into one of these fits. I know it was something I said, but I can't remember what it was. As far as I know she had only those two seizures, and I don't know to this day what caused them, actually. The doctor said they were caused by nervous tension."

It is easy for Jimmy to call forth his misdeeds, as though to examine them and adjust his course. He still remembers the only time he mistreated his little sister, Jeanne. There was great concern about Jeanne's health when she was born, because of the deaths of the two earlier children and of their father. When she turned out to be healthy and robust, the family rejoiced. Little Jeannie was always treated like a princess.

"I'll never forget," Jimmy says. "She was crying and holding open the ice-box door. I gave her a gentle kick in the behind, and told her to close the door. It should never have happened to her. She looked at me with those big eyes, tears streaming down her face. I wanted to cut my throat. I took her in my arms, and swore to myself I would never do anything like that again."

Jimmy, so obviously sentimental, has tears for all occasions and needs no special memories to summon them. Once, during a very quiet moment in a vaudeville dance program, he let out an impromptu sob that rattled half the theater audience. He was watching Harriet Hoctor, a famous dancer of the era. "She did ballet, the whole thing," says Jimmy. "She would go up in the air and she didn't land . . . she settled. Every time she would settle, I couldn't help letting out a sob. Everyone was looking at me. I'm sure they thought I was crazy, but I couldn't help it."

Beautiful things evoke his tears, compliments make him weepy; and, when he was transported from the stone jungle of Yorkville to Hollywood success, he was filled with compassion for those he had left behind. This certainly accounted for the liberal sympathies of his youth. He had been back there in the quagmire of despair, and it had been recent. He could hardly bear to see those who were less fortunate as they scratched for survival. He always championed the struggling man's cause; it was his nature.

An incident occurred during the making of *Yankee Doodle Dandy* that infuriated him. "It was in the scene where that black baritone sang 'Glory, Glory Hallelujah,' Jimmy recalls. "Jesus, he had a voice. I was next to Leo Forbstein, the musical director, and I mentioned how good the singer was. All Forbstein said was, 'I don't know why the hell he wants to have himself photographed anyway.' They were making stills, and the baritone wanted to get in the picture, and this guy couldn't understand that. Jesus, this man was the head guy in the scene, and they didn't want to take his picture. I couldn't believe it."

This experience reminded him of another one that had taken place earlier, in vaudeville. "I played a bill with a black team. We were standing around on a Monday morning. When they called out that it was time to rehearse, these men backed away. I said, 'No, go ahead, you were first.' They looked at me as if something was wrong, and I didn't understand it. Afterwards, one of them said to me, 'You don't know what you did.' I asked what he meant, and he told me how it was with them . . . like they would have to walk twelve miles out of town to find a place to live. I said, 'Jesus, that's awful.' I didn't know. Hadn't thought about it at all."

Jimmy recalls that there was little mixing of colors back in his Yorkville days. The blacks lived above Ninety-ninth Street. "One time a fella named Jimmy Barley had a bright idea. He was maybe fifteen, and I was about ten. He said he would suck the colored guys onto our streets, and there'd be a gang here waiting to jump them. He did it, and at a given signal, the gang started throwing rocks at the colored guys. I remember seeing a big, pointed rock going right into the head of a colored boy who was trying to get away. I never forgot it."

There was also anti-Semitism in Yorkville, despite the large Jewish population in the area. "Gangs would go around and pillage Jewish shops," he said. "They'd call them dirty Christ-killers, or worse. Once, they called this old lady that, and she turned and saw this little Jewish kid among the members of the gang. He was so conformist he was among the ones who were denigrating his own people. She went straight for him. 'Goddamnit,' she said, 'I'll kill you!' He didn't know what the hell was going on."

"Some of my best friends are Jews" is a defensive phrase used by a person accused of anti-Semitism, but if Jimmy Cagney said it, he would simply be telling the truth. Throughout his childhood Jewish boys were truly his closest friends, and he didn't consider for a moment that it should be otherwise. He wanted to see no one abused or humiliated, and he was constantly astounded by the lack of such sensitivity on the part of so many.

It was Jimmy's extreme sensitivity that made his film career so difficult. It has never been a business for the timid or the weak. He learned at once he must assume a tough facade to survive. If Humphrey Bogart chose to hate them before they could hate him, Jimmy Cagney put a chip on his shoulder and dared them to knock it off. It took some time, but his defensive stance worked. They no longer took his threats lightly; when the chip was knocked off, he was really willing to fight.

By the time *Yankee Doodle Dandy* was released, Jimmy was pretty much in control of his career, and this film established his stardom firmly. He could now dictate his terms to Warner Brothers and they would have to agree—with grins on their faces. But that was not what Jimmy wanted. He was determined to be his own man completely, to go it alone. He wasn't pleased with the image he had established on the screen and believed that only he could change it. He was thinking in terms of independent production.

Jimmy had lost several choice roles as a result of his hoodlum image. One was the role of Father Flanagan in *Boys' Town*. The producers had wanted him, but the orphanage officials rejected him because of the parts he had played, and Spencer Tracy played the role.

A few years later, an actor was being sought to play Knute

Rockne. Hal Wallis, in his autobiography, says the studio wanted Jimmy to play the role, but that Mrs. Rockne and everyone associated with Notre Dame turned him down because of his association with gangster films. The studio tried to point out that a good actor could play any kind of role, but they were adamant. Their second choice was Spencer Tracy, but MGM refused to make the loan-out. Pat O'Brien was finally selected, and the role changed his life: it made him a star, and nothing could have pleased Jimmy more. Yet it must have been difficult for Jimmy to swallow such rejections, when his image was not one he had chosen.

Having just completed a movie of which he could feel genuinely proud, Jimmy decided that it was time to break all ties with Warner Brothers. His contract was due for renewal, and the studio tried every possible means to keep him, but his mind was made up. He charged that the studio bosses had lied repeatedly about forthcoming film projects, and there were also some questions regarding the arithmetic they were using to compute his share of movie earnings.

It was announced on March 30, 1942, that Jimmy and his brother Bill would establish Cagney Productions, whose pictures would be released through United Artists. Ed would join his brothers as the studio business manager, and financing for the independent venture was to be assumed by Bankers Trust Company of New York. The agreement with United Artists was for five pictures over five years.

With business out of the way, Jimmy now had time to do what he had been wanting to do for many months; he spent several soothing weeks on his farm in Martha's Vineyard. Then he did something else that he had been wanting to do: he volunteered his services to the USO and related organizations. He traveled throughout the United States for several weeks in 1942, entertaining servicemen with the Irish jig and other dances, and as *Yankee Doodle Dandy* became widely distributed he included the proscenium dance from the picture. When Jimmy touched home base, he and his colleagues discussed production details of the first Cagney film *Johnny Come Lately,* based on a Louis Bromfield novel entitled *McCloud's Folly.*

In September 1942 Jimmy was elected president of the Screen Actors Guild. It had come a long way since its formative days in 1933, and Jimmy was proud to accept the presidency.

On March 4, 1943, while his first independent movie was in production, Jimmy attended the fifteenth Academy Award ceremonies at the Coconut Grove, in Los Angeles. It was an event reflecting wartime austerity, and many industry servicemen were on hand. Marine Private Tyrone Power and Air Force Private Alan Ladd unfurled an industry flag, revealing that there were now 27,677 members of the studio unions in uniform.

The acceptance speeches were more than usually long and tedious, for some reason, and the Oscars were of wartime plaster instead of gold-plated bronze. When it came time for the announcement of the Best Actor award, the audience was a bit weary and restless, but they came to life when Gary Cooper opened the envelope to read the winner. When he announced that James Cagney had won, for his performance in *Yankee Doodle Dandy,* there was a tumultuous ovation. Then everyone settled back for another interminable speech. It failed to materialize.

Oscar in hand, Jimmy leaned toward the microphone. "I've always maintained," he said, "that in this business you are only as good as the other fellow thinks you are. It's nice to know that you people thought I did a good job. And don't forget that it was a good part, too. Thank you very much." That was it, sweet and simple and Cagney-brief.

No stress, no strain.

CHAPTER 20

As president of the Screen Actors Guild (SAG), Jimmy was not playing a titular role. He entered the office when strong leadership was needed, and he assumed active control. Many right-wing politicians were concerned, with some justification, about left-wing influence in the film industry, but there was a more immediate threat that wasn't as widely known: organized crime had arrived in town for a slice of the pie.

The mob sent men from Chicago to infiltrate the unions, and one of them succeeded in gaining control of the Projectionists Guild. The federal government started legal actions that soon resulted in the ousting and conviction of certain gang members. The investigation also resulted in the jailing of Joseph M. Schenck, who, as one of the heads of Twentieth Century–Fox, was found guilty of union payoffs and tax evasion.

SAG played an instrumental role in pressing the case against the mob, and Cagney, as its president, became a prime target for reprisals. There were several incidents of harrassment, including threatening telephone calls. On one occasion, Willie was told that Jimmy had been killed in an auto crash. Since the call was only one of many, she didn't panic. Instead, she placed a call to where she expected Jimmy to be and found that he was there.

"There were other surprises," says Jimmy. "The mob made arrangements for a heavy kleig light to be dropped on me on the set. That was when George Raft entered the picture. When he got wind of it, he made a call to the right man, and the 'surprise' was called off. He may have saved my life."

As president of SAG, Jimmy was automatically chairman of the Hollywood Victory Committee, which organized all the war bond tours during World War II. He, along with many other stars, made tours to military bases throughout the country and staged bond rallies in cities and whistle-stops across the land.

In addition to the tours, Jimmy made several patriotic film shorts, including one for the Department of War Information entitled *You, John Jones.* Jimmy played an air-raid warden who suggested to the audience what might happen to his wife, played by Ann Sothern, and his daughter (Margaret O'Brien) if America should lose the war. The eight-minute short was nationally acclaimed.

The major studios were retooling their machinery to produce war epics, but the first presentation of Cagney Productions was far from that. *Johnny Come Lately* was set in turn-of-the-century smalltown America. Jimmy played Tom Richards, a vagabond who was once a newspaperman. Tom finds himself in a midwestern town where tramps are unwelcome, and he is arrested for vagrancy. The town's newspaper publisher, Vinnie McLeod, played by Grace George, senses an intrinsic goodness that causes her to take responsibility for him, thus keeping him out of jail.

W. W. Dougherty (Edward McNamara) runs the town and holds the mortgage on the newspaper. He orders the widowed publisher to print editorials favorable to him after she has attacked him in her previous articles. She refuses. His son, Pete (Bill Henry) is engaged to Mary Jane (Marjorie Lord), the daughter of the publisher. Tom is attracted to Mary Jane, but when he sees she is in love with Pete, he backs off.

After a series of trials and tribulations, Tom Richards squares off against the political villains and, with the help of the local madam (Marjory Main), is able to prove that Dougherty has been pocketing money raised for the orphans' fund. To avoid prosecution, Dougherty promises to leave town and hand over the mortgage for the newspaper. With everything back on an even keel, Tom sets out once more for the open road.

Jimmy had plenty of opportunity to use his magic fists in the film, but the story is a folksy, nostalgic mood-piece different from anything he had ever done on the screen. It illustrated Jimmy's determination to dissociate himself from his thug roles, and many reviewers approved the attempt. *Time* applauded the production and directed attention to the facet of the picture of which Jimmy was most proud: the good use of strong supporting players: "James

Cagney, who in his time had to plant fists or a grapefruit on young ladies' faces and shoes on young ladies' behinds, here develops his tenderest relationships with middle-aged ladies (the Misses George, Main, and [Hattie] McDaniel), and each of them is worth a dozen average love scenes. . . . Bit players who have tried creditably for years to walk in shoes that pinched them show themselves in this picture as the very competent actors they always were: there has seldom been as good a cinematic gallery of U.S. smalltown types."

Some reviews were far less generous, however. The New York newspaper *PM* said: "*Johnny Come Lately* is so palpably amateurish in production and direction, so hopelessly stagey, uneven and teamless in performance and so utterly pointless that it is bound to cause raised eyebrows wherever it is shown." But the good reviews outnumbered the bad, and with the passage of time the film has been accepted as a minor classic in its capture of the mood and tone of the times in which it was set.

There are Cagney touches throughout the picture. For example, Tom shaves dry with a straight-edged razor, a bit Jimmy borrowed from his pal Frank McHugh, whose brother always shaved that way. Most notable is the use of Jimmy's own sketches when Tom's cartoons are shown in the film.

"It made money," says Jimmy, "but it was no great winner. The director, William K. Howard, was a drunk. After he had ten days or two weeks to dry out he was fine, but then two weeks later he was gone again. It was a shame. We knew about him when we hired him, but we thought he would try to hang onto this thing. It was the first chance he was given in a long time. He could work when he was drunk, but not very well. We finally had to turn him loose and got another guy . . . I've forgotten who it was." (Howard was credited as director.)

With his company's first production completed, Jimmy accepted an invitation to tour American military bases in England for the USO. Before leaving Hollywood, he rehearsed for six weeks with Johnny Boyle to put professional polish on the act he called "The American Cavalcade of Dance." It was a history of dance styles beginning with the early days and ending with Fred Astaire. The climax of the show was Jimmy's number from *Yankee Doodle Dandy*.

The Army Signal Corps did a film of his rehearsals to show the troops overseas. They wanted them to know that this was no slipshod amateur contest, like many USO shows of the past. The GIs were tiring of movie stars who pretended to entertain when all they really did was to stand around and look awkward.

Upon Jimmy's arrival in London in February 1944, the British press attempted to interview him, but he had little to say. He pointed out that he was there for one reason, to entertain troops. He refused to discuss movies or Hollywood in general. "I'm here to dance a few jigs, sing a few songs, say hello to the boys, and that's all."

A reporter for the *Sunday Dispatch* wrote: "He arrived during the weekend to entertain American troops, and expects to be here three months. He is short and slight with blue eyes in a determined face. He seems nervous and shy." Another reporter said: "His physical appearance would have been a surprise to film-goers. He wore a brand-new uniform as smart as a staff officer's. His eyebrows were so faint you could scarcely see them, and his reddish hair was smooth and shining. Completely unlike the tousled 'tough guy' of the pictures."

Jimmy worked harder than he had ever worked in his life, giving several shows a day and then visiting hospital wards, where he happily drew charcoal caricatures of the patients on their casts. When no music was available to accompany his act, Jimmy would plunk a guitar to accompany himself.

During one show exhaustion momentarily caught up with him, and he found himself faltering in one of his more difficult and strenuous dances. A soldier called out that Jimmy was getting old, and the audience howled with laughter. Jimmy took the jibe good-naturedly but couldn't resist challenging the young man. He brought him onstage and instructed him to simply hop on one foot and then the other as Jimmy danced. The GI was game enough, but after a few minutes he became too tired to keep hopping. Jimmy danced on.

Before Jimmy left for overseas he had been reelected to a second term as president of SAG. While he was gone, Bill Cagney was negotiating to buy the rights to the hit Broadway show *Oklahoma!* for a film in which Jimmy would star. For several months Cagney Productions was the frontrunner to produce the movie in association with The Theatre Guild. It would ultimately take seven years before anyone acquired the film rights to the musical, and by that time Cagney Productions was no longer in business.

The top box-office stars for 1943 were announced while Jimmy was away, and he was ranked eighth, having dropped from the sixth spot the year before. It was Betty Grable who was the top moneymaker.

As Jimmy toured the military bases in England, *Johnny Vagabond,* the British title for *Johnny Come Lately,* was playing to standing-room crowds. One London critic gave the film his personal nomination as best picture of the year.

After a quick trip to Ireland to see the land of his forebears, Jimmy returned to Hollywood in mid-May. He began production on his second independent film, *Blood on the Sun,* set in Japan in the nineteen-twenties.

He had returned from the tour in excellent condition, which was fortunate, because his role in the new film called for skills that would prove even more strenuous than dancing. He would have to show expertise in judo, and with Jimmy's policy of doing all his own stunts, that meant becoming a real expert. He went into training under the tutelege of Ken Kuniyuki, a fifth-degree judo expert, and Jack Halloran, an ex-policeman.

The script called for a Eurasian girl as the female lead, and Jimmy thought of Sylvia Sidney. She had rather Oriental features, and Hollywood makeup expertise could turn her into a believable Eurasian. (In fact, she had played the Japanese Madame Butterfly in a 1933 nonmusical film version of the opera.) Jimmy was especially pleased to have Sylvia on the set, because it had been a long while since he had been able to practice his Yiddish, and Sylvia spoke it well.

Jimmy played Nick Condon, the head of a Tokyo news agency, who is roused to action after the mysterious death of a fellow reporter and his wife. Nick learns of the existence of the Tanaka Plan for World Conquest, and he becomes determined to gain access to the plan and spirit it from Japan to the U.S. The Cagneys had hoped that this reversion to a more typical Cagney action film would win back some of the fans he had lost over the last year, but though the reviews were favorable enough, *Blood on the Sun* did worse at the box office than *Johnny Come Lately.*

Toward the end of World War II, a young soldier was receiving wide attention for his brilliant fighting record. Audie Murphy, the son of Texas sharecroppers, had enlisted in the army at fifteen and had won the Congressional Medal of Honor and just about every other honor available to a fighting man. When Jimmy saw his photo in a newspaper, he suggested to Bill that they sign him to a movie contract. So he was brought to Hollywood.

"The kid photographed from every angle," says Jimmy, "and we thought he had a chance to make it. I thought it would be kind of nice to keep him like family, so we put him up in a house I owned next door to us on Coldwater." Murphy didn't like being alone, so Jimmy put his old friend Charlie Leonard in the house with him. But that didn't work out too well. Murphy was high-strung and would wake in the middle of the night screaming; Leonard, who wasn't all that secure himself, would wake in alarm and charge through the house with a gun. On one occasion, Audie woke just in time to keep Leonard from shooting him.

"We tried to work with Audie," Jimmy says. "Tried to teach him how to dance. I showed him the waltz clog, and you should have seen him. You wouldn't believe it. He had a real hayshaker walk, you know, so when I showed him the waltz clog his feet went flying. It was really something. We eventually loaned him out for something, and then sold his contract. It turned out we had no use for him really. He couldn't act."

Charlie Leonard was one of many old friends given sanctuary by Jimmy, and for a time they were close. Then something happened that jeopardized the friendship. The incident serves to illustrate the tenuous ground shared by a have and a have-not. "He was an old friend of mine from before show business. Just a guy around. He broke a trust, and I never forgave him for it." Jimmy, easygoing and generous, didn't lay down conditions for a friendship, but there were certain unspoken assumptions. Leonard had been doing some publicity for Samuel Goldwyn Productions. He was hoping to promote a deal with Goldwyn based on his influence with Cagney. Jimmy wasn't averse to being used for a mutually beneficial arrangement of some kind. It would, after all, be subject to his approval. But he told Leonard to hold off on this particular matter. Jimmy didn't want to state it prematurely, but he was already in contact with the Goldwyn people about a possible project. Leonard ignored Jimmy's request. In the end, Leonard ruined any chance he might have had to become a producer, and Jimmy's own discussions were placed in jeopardy. "It was the first time he ever did anything like that," says Jimmy, "but I never spoke to him again. He wasn't a friend . . . friends don't do that."

This incident points up a problem faced by a person who is a celebrity. It can be dangerous for him to establish friendships. It is a temptation for the other person to use the more important one. Often it is enough for an ordinary person to simply rub elbows with a winner, but sometimes he can't seem to resist manipulating the more influential person for his own benefit.

Jimmy was asked in an interview whether he often found himself closing the door to new friendships. "Um hmm," he replied. "You put out your left hand."

"Do you always have to be on guard?"

"Always."

"It must be difficult always wondering whether you are liked because of yourself or what you represent."

"That's right."

It was doubly difficult for a man like Jimmy, who is basically such a friendly man. His first inclination is to always open himself to others. It would probably have been less difficult for someone like Bogart, who was never as trusting. Jimmy would always be warm toward the ordinary people, because that was what he always considered himself, but of necessity there were few in that category who were invited into his fold. Unless they could somehow prove their allegiances, the risks were too great.

Since this was the way things were, the Boys' Club was very important to Jimmy. Because its membership remained so exclusive, each member could unequivocally trust every other member, and that made for a totally relaxed atmosphere when they got together.

Ralph Bellamy recalls a time when he, Pat O'Brien, Jimmy, Frank Morgan and Lynne Overman were at a table at Romanoff's and they were approached by the actor Zachary Scott. "Morgan and O'Brien were doing a little grog sampling," he said, "and a shadow fell across the table. It was Zachary Scott, wearing a single earring. 'How do you get to join this Irish Mafia of yours?' he asked. Frank Morgan replied acidly, 'You don't get to, you are *asked*. It was Overman who served the coup de grace: 'And we have run out of asks.'"

Jimmy's favorite sanctuary was, naturally, his farm on Martha's Vineyard, where he felt in control of everything. He worked hard doing physical work on the land and the buildings, and took great enjoyment in building his horse population. His first horse was Ashley, with the highest percent of Morgan blood in the country. With Ashley as sire, Jimmy built his stable to nineteen. In the forties, he transported the whole string to California and installed them on the farm he purchased from Louella Parsons in the San Fernando Valley.

Actually, it was Jimmy's plan to move everybody and everything to the new farm. By the time he was doing his own film production, the children were attending school, and he feared for their safety as they stood along the increasingly busy Coldwater Canyon Boulevard boarding and unboarding their school bus. Jimmy was offered forty thousand dollars for the Coldwater place, and he agreed to sell. The family prepared to move to the farm.

Ralph Bellamy explains: "While living at the Louella Parsons place, the deal was made to sell the Coldwater property. Jimmy received the down payment, but the would-be buyers couldn't keep up the payments. Jimmy returned their equity and took back the property, which he owns today." With the street-front property sold, Jimmy's land, consisting of about ten acres on top of the hill, it is estimated today to be worth more than three million dollars.

Jimmy was always active in real-estate speculation, with some of his transactions long forgotten. He bought one parcel of land on Sunset Boulevard during the Depression years. "It was a poinsettia patch when Jimmy bought it," says Bellamy. It sold a few years ago for a million and a half." On the former poinsettia patch are the two high-rise office buildings on the Sunset Strip, at the eastern boundary of Beverly Hills. Its value has quadrupled since its sale about ten years ago.

Jimmy no longer had financial worries, yet the old insecurity remained. At one of the Boys' Club meetings he lamented: "We are all in a precarious business. What if some unforeseen tragedy happened? How would you go about gaining admission to the Motion Picture Country Home?" Spencer Tracy leaned forward. "Buy it, you bum," he said. "Then we can all get in."

CHAPTER 21

immy was no stranger to the White House during his long career. During one of the star studded Victory Caravan tours, which included Bob Hope, Groucho Marx, and many others, the troupe was greeted by the First Lady, Eleanor Roosevelt, on the White House lawn.

Jimmy recalls the occasion but has forgotten many of the details. The screenwriter and producer Jack Rose, who was then a publicist, made the trip in the company of Bob Hope. Rose says that one of the show's highlights was Jimmy's act. "It was 1943, and the Victory Caravan toured all over. Jimmy did his marvelous dance, that thing against the proscenium. Fantastic!"

Rose also remembers a moment involving Groucho Marx. Mrs. Roosevelt received the performers cordially but rather formally, and was introduced to each of them separately. "Then she came to Charlotte Greenwood," says Rose. "Charlotte knew that Mrs. Roosevelt wouldn't recognize her face, so she did one of those big kicks she was famous for. She did those comic dances and was able to kick those long legs high over her head, almost a contortionist's feat. As she let go with this, Groucho leaned over to the First Lady. 'That's what you could do,' said Groucho, 'if you just put your mind to it.'" The entertainers froze in embarrassment as Mrs. Roosevelt moved along the line without comment.

Jimmy would never have been embarrassed by someone else's behavior, but he can recall a few occasions when his own actions left him chagrined. The first incident that comes to mind was a "rich man's dinner" he attended many years ago in Denver. After the main course, a waiter approached him carrying a tray loaded with pieces of pie. He lifted one of the plates from the tray and handed it to Jimmy, who tried to signal that he didn't want dessert. The waiter took the gesture as a signal that Jimmy was reaching out to accept the plate. The waiter let go of the pie, but Jimmy didn't grasp it. The plate fell to the floor with a clatter and a squish, and the waiter kept walking. Jimmy was mortified. For the rest of the evening, he could think of nothing but the lump of pie and the broken plate on the floor next to his chair.

Another dining incident involved his brother Bill. "We were eating in this fancy bistro. I was trying to eat my salad when my fork slipped. And bing! a big piece of lettuce went flying across the table and plastered itself on Bill's forehead. God, how I laughed. I told him I didn't mean to laugh, but, Jesus, it was funny."

The subject of dining transported Jimmy even farther back in time, to when he attended a command luncheon set up by Jack Warner to welcome the movie censor Will Hays to his new post. "They were doing their usual playing up to the politicians. Every contract player had to attend. Warner introduced the actors, and after he finished he said, 'Well, I guess now you've met all of our best artesians.' He meant to say 'artisans,' I suppose, but that was how it came out."

Despite Jimmy's efforts to keep a low profile, he says that he has never felt especially self-conscious in public, even though he has been as recognizable as any person on earth for most of his life. He is usually oblivious to the stares of fans. "I've never been one of the crowd. I was always off there somewhere. My wife complained about that for years, and I can understand it."

He says that he is never aware of recognition by fans unless he is approached by them, and that doesn't occur as frequently as one might suspect. He insists also that unpleasant incidents with fans can be counted on the fingers of one hand. They are, for the most part, courteous and respectful of his desire for privacy. He thinks that they may realize he doesn't belong in that crowded restaurant or theater foyer, that he is not the social animal that many of his colleagues are. He knows that in most instances he would rather be grooming a horse, or building a wall, or sailing, or painting a picture, and perhaps his fans sense that.

Painting became a perfect outlet for Jimmy in the mid-thirties. He had done pencil sketches all his life, but he became intrigued with oil painting when he started to dabble in it. One of his first real endeavors in oil was a portrait of his mother painted from memory. It turned out well, and he was proud of it, but it has since disappeared.

His mother finally succumbed to her illnesses in 1945. The day came when all the children were summoned to her hospital bed to await the final moment. Ed had been the first to know that the end was coming, because he had shared his mother's apartment. He called Jimmy on the set and then reached Harry at his home. They all met at the hospital, and Jeanne joined them some hours later, on her return from New York.

Multiple strokes had robbed Carolyn Cagney of speech, and only her eyes and one hand remained mobile. When Jeanne arrived she went to the bed to hug her mother. Carolyn uttered an unintelligible sound that, according to Jimmy, "spoke volumes of love."

She used her functional hand to point to the fingers of the hand that lay paralyzed. "She indicated Harry by pointing to the index finger," Jimmy says. "The second finger referred to me, Eddie was the third finger, and the fourth finger indicated Bill. Then she moved her thumb to the middle of her palm and clasped the thumb tightly under the fingers. She patted the fist with her good hand and made a single wordless sound. We understood at once that Jeanne was the thumb and that we four boys were to take care of our girl. It was a simple movement, totally eloquent, totally beautiful."

Their mother died shortly thereafter. She was sixty-seven. "There was hardly a day of those years," said Jimmy, "she had not spent in giving." Her death was no small loss to her children. It was their good fortune, however, to have recognized and appreciated her gifts while she still lived—and her gifts were many.

Life had never been easy for this courageous lady, from her childhood days in a pencil factory to her continual illness as an adult. She never weakened, though. With each chapter of adversity she seemed to gain strength, and she passed her strength on to her children. She gave them a strong will to survive and an unflaggingly optimistic outlook on life. However small her material gifts, her gift of love came in giant measure.

Her choice of a husband contributed greatly to her life of hardship, but he was her choice and she loved him always. He tried his best to be a good father, but it was not his calling. But he did make a contribution, and it was of great value. What he left his children was the ability to laugh in spite of misfortune.

The Cagneys were very poor during the early years, but as Jimmy has so often said, "We didn't know we were poor." This attitude alone is an estate to be treasured. They were taught to waste neither time nor energy on self-pity, to focus always on the road ahead.

The Cagney and Nelson genes blended magically to produce five very special beings of whom any parent would be proud. But it was the determination and wisdom of Carolyn Cagney that guided her offspring to their ultimate achievements. In reviewing the life-work of this most special of all strawberry blondes, it seems that she was a worker of miracles. One can only hope that in death she is housed somewhere in a location of her choosing, that her easy chair is wide and comfortable and the glass on her picture window is sparkling clean. No one would want Carolyn Cagney to miss any of the action that was so important to her in life.

CHAPTER 22

The contract between Cagney Productions and United Artists was for five films with a total budget of six million dollars. Now, with two films released and no assurance that either of them would make money, the Cagneys wanted their third effort to be foolproof. Dozens of movie scripts were read, but the property Jimmy found most interesting was a currently running Broadway play, William Saroyan's *The Time of Your Life.* They began negotiations to buy the rights.

While the deal was taking shape, Jimmy had an offer to star in a spy thriller, *13 Rue Madeleine,* at Twentieth Century–Fox. At first he rejected the proposal, but Fox was willing to pay him $300,000 for two months of work, and that was too good to pass up.

Jimmy played Bob Sharkey, a businessman turned espionage agent who is dropped behind enemy lines to find a German rocket site in France. His mission is to pinpoint the site so that the Allies can bomb it in preparation for the D-Day invasion. One of the members of his group, however, is a German agent.

Costarring Annabella, Richard Conte, and Frank Latimore, the film was done with the documentary-style narration so popular at the time. It follows the characters from their induction into the OSS until the climax, when Sharkey is blown to smithereens in the Nazi headquarters at 13 Rue Madeleine.

The film was shot in a number of New England locations and in Quebec. Despite some complaints that Jimmy's New York accent made Sharkey's French proficiency improbable, the final production was quite well liked. Much of the movie's success was attributed to expert direction by Henry Hathaway.

Time said: "Far and away the roughest, toughest spy chase yet gleaned from the bulging files of the OSS is Twentieth Century–Fox's *13 Rue Madeleine*. Surpassing its predessessors, *Cloak and Dagger* and *OSS,* the film gets its name from the address of Gestapo headquarters, much of its realistic wallop by paralleling actual OSS training."

With a welcome paycheck in hand, Jimmy returned to Hollywood to begin preproduction work on *The Time of Your Life*. The Saroyan play was a labor of love for Jimmy. His goal was to keep the movie as true to the stage play as was humanly possible. The first step was to sign a theater director, H. C. Potter. Next the Cagneys began rounding up the best possible character actors.

All the action took place on a single set, a San Francisco waterfront bar. A key role was the owner-bartender, Nick, and William Bendix was chosen to play him. Bendix had played the part of the Irish cop in the Broadway production. For the whimsical character of Kit Carson, Jimmy knew exactly the man he wanted, the venerable stage and vaudeville trouper James Barton. Wayne Morris was cast as the slightly retarded Tom, and for the role of the ex-prostitute, Kitty Duvall, Jimmy didn't have to search very far. The role was perfect for his sister, Jeanne. Broderick Crawford played the Irish cop, and the other roles were filled by Ward Bond, Tom Powers, Jimmy Lydon, and the dancer Paul Draper.

Jimmy, as Joe, sits at a table all day drinking champagne and listening to old records. He sends Tom out on a variety of important missions, such as gathering together all the toys he can find; he bets prodigiously on the horses and chews giant wads of gum. Joe is philosophical, intelligent, a ponderous thinker, but always on the up side in his exchanges with others. This was the most sedentary role of Jimmy's career, and perhaps the one most like his real self.

In the Saroyan play, the villain, Blick, is shot at the end, but Jimmy decided to let him live following a bloody beating at the hands of Joe. It was the only time Jimmy moved from his chair for the entire story.

Most of the critics were more than pleased with the carefully produced film, and Saroyan came out of his eccentric funk to shout its praises, but it ended up as the only film in Jimmy's long career to lose money; the sum, he admitted, was half a million dollars. For some inexplicable reason the public wouldn't go near the film.

Jimmy was deeply disappointed, because he felt at the time that this was his most successful attempt at quality movie-making.

The early forties had been all bright lights for Jimmy, culminating in 1942 with the incomparable *Yankee Doodle Dandy,* but from there on the ride was pretty much downhill. It would seem that his timing in embarking on independent production was perfect in every sense. He was riding a crest of popularity, after broadening his image by making a successful musical, but apparently his choice of scripts was too different from the old Cagney image. Moviegoers seemed to want no part of a kind, easygoing Cagney. The fans still loved Jimmy, but they were unwilling to follow him into unknown regions.

Cagney Productions fell upon difficult times, including a lawsuit by Goldwyn over a rental agreement that went awry. The future of the company didn't look good. Jack Warner had always said that Cagney needed Warner Brothers as much as the studio needed him. There was prophecy in his remark: once again Jimmy was listening to Warners' overtures. Their proposition became interesting when they agreed to let Jimmy slip in a pair of Cagney independents that he and the studio would codistribute. This gave Cagney Productions a final breath of life, but Jimmy would return to familiar territory. The territory that Warners had mapped for him couldn't, in fact, have been more familiar. He would be playing a mug to end all mugs in the Warner Brothers picture *White Heat.*

"To let the kids see Cagney as he was in happier days," *Life* said, "Warner Brothers has produced a wild and exciting mixture of mayhem and madness called *White Heat,* in which Cagney plays a bestial killer named Cody Jarrett. Hollywood has, however, grown more sophisticated since the old days, and Cody is presented not merely as a gangster, but, in the studio's words, as a 'homicidal paranoiac with a mother fixation.' Neither the psychiatry nor the plot bothers audiences who have seen the film. They screech with joy when the hero appears pummeling society with both hands and both feet, a tigerish snarl on his lips. The old Jimmy is back again."

The final phrase was the key message. Jimmy had indeed returned to the formula. He had tried more subtle means of entertaining, but this was what the public wanted of him. As far as they were concerned, Jimmy had mysteriously strayed off course, but now he had once again found his bearings.

It was ten years since Raoul Walsh had directed him in *The Roaring Twenties,* and he was called on to capture the same mood in this film. What resulted was one of Jimmy's most memorable hoodlum portrayals, but he held a lower opinion of the film than most of the reviewers, referring to it as "just another cheapjack job." He had tried his best to upgrade the quality of the film, and hoped to land his pal Frank McHugh a role in the film, adding what he considered "much-needed levity." After the Warner brass assured him that they would do as he had asked, they cast a straight actor who did a straight job. Virginia Mayo, as Jimmy's moll, was praised by the critics, as was Edmund O'Brien, as Hank. Margaret Wycherly played Cody's mother to perfection.

The movie was loaded with Cagneyisms. Since Cody was tied emotionally to his mother's apron strings, Jimmy suggested to the director that Cody actually climb onto his mother's lap for solace. "I said, 'Let's see if we can get away with it.' Walsh said we should try it, and it worked. We put it in."

It was Jimmy's idea, in fact, to make Cody a psychotic character. "It was essentially a cheapie one-two-three-four kind of thing, so I suggested we make him nuts. It was agreed, so we put in those fits and headaches."

There are at least two scenes from *White Heat* that remain emblazoned in the minds of movie buffs. One is the scene in which Cody deposits an enemy in a car trunk and later calls to him: "How you doin' in there?" The reply is: "It's stuffy in here. . . . I need some air." "Oh, stuffy, huh," says Cody. "I'll give you some air." He pumps four pistol rounds into the trunk.

The other memorable scene is at the end of the picture, when Cody finds himself atop an oil-refinery storage tank with police in hot pursuit. Just before firing his gun into the tank, to blow himself to powder, Cody cried out triumphantly: "Made it, Ma! Top of the world!"

With the success of *White Heat,* Jimmy said, rather ruefully, to a reporter, "It's what the people want me to do. Some day, though, I'd like to make another movie that kids could go to see." Jimmy must have felt frustrated. The studio brass were assigning the kind of pictures they wanted him to do, and those were invariably the surefire gangster melodramas he deplored. But there was a difference this time: now he was a business partner with the studio.

Jimmy was surprised when his next assignment took him out of the streets and onto flirtation walk. He was given a musical assignment with Doris Day and Gordon MacRae, in a movie called *West Point Story*. Warners may have had fantasies of coming up with another blockbuster Cagney musical like *Yankee Doodle Dandy,* but if so, they missed the mark by a few miles.

The story idea came from a young Hollywood screenwriter named Irving Wallace. Jule Styne and Sammy Kahn were called in to write the songs, and a young dancer named Gene Nelson was hired. Jimmy's present-day assessment of the film: "It was nothing."

This was more or less the consensus of the critics at the time of the movie's release, but it was not a unanimous critical failure. Bosley Crowther of *The New York Times* said: "If everything about *West Point Story* were as good as Jimmy Cagney is in it, this Warner musical show would be the top musical show of the year."

Jimmy played Elwin Bixby, a cocky New York director who comes to West Point to stage the annual show "100th Night." Through a series of circumstances, he masquerades as a plebe, and although he was slightly overweight and fifty years old, Jimmy was believable in the cadet uniform. His energetic dancing helps the illusion. In a number with Virginia Mayo called "Brooklyn," Jimmy did some of the finest dancing of his career. He says that the intricate routine was put together in ten days. Virginia Mayo was at least twenty pounds heavier than most of his previous dance partners, but Jimmy was in good enough condition to contend with it. He says that his old mainstay Johnny Boyle helped him out, and a young disciple of Jack Cole whom Jimmy recalls only as "Godfrey" helped with the choreography. Leroy Prinz was the dance director, but Jimmy and he didn't hit it off very well. "Holy Jesus," he says of Prinz. "He didn't know one foot from the other. He hired guys who could do what he couldn't. He hated me, Jesus, how he hated me. He knew I was on to him."

Jimmy always had high regard for Doris Day, and liked Virginia Mayo very much. Also in the film was Roland Winters; they had worked together in *13 Rue Madeleine* and had become close friends. So the assignment was not an unpleasant one. He was particularly impressed with the dancing ability of Gene Nelson. "Gene

Nelson was one of the best dancers I've ever seen. I watched him go down the aisle in the studio theater, and just lift himself up to the stage without an apparent jump. He sailed upward three or four feet without effort, amazing! I wouldn't know how to do that. He was excellent, beautiful."

Jimmy, in fact, rates Nelson third or fourth among all the male dancers of that time. First place goes to Fred Astaire, which is no surprise, and he gives second place to Gene Kelly. Donald O'Connor would rank high on his list, perhaps on an equal level with Nelson. He singles O'Connor out as a "hoofer—among the best."

West Point Story was released in 1950, and in the same year Cagney Productions made their first joint release with Warners. The property selected was one Warners must have approved ardently. It was formula Cagney all the way, and this time Jimmy could blame no one but himself. In *Kiss Tommorrow Goodbye* Jimmy played Ralph Cotter, a convict who breaks jail and subsequently kills his partner. Then he pummels the partner's sister, played by Barbara Payton, who masochistically falls for him. A pair of crooked cops try to shake him down, but by using a recording device Ralph entraps the cops, who, from then on, are his flunkies.

The reviewers compared the picture with *White Heat,* but it was generally agreed that this one was far less memorable and even more violent. The movie was, in fact, banned in Ohio for its "sordid, sadistic presentation of brutality and an extreme presentation of crime with explicit steps in commission."

The selection of this fare as a Cagney Production was more than likely a simple matter of recouping the financial losses the company had suffered with *The Time of Your life. Kiss Tomorrow Goodbye* did turn out to be successful, and its first half-million in earnings went directly to the bank, to pay off the loss.

The movie was quite well received generally, with praise going to Jimmy, Barbara Payton, and Luther Adler in the role of a shyster lawyer. No mention was made of the actor who played Jimmy's brother: Bill Cagney was cast in the small role. *The New York Times* noted that Jimmy was back in town and back in the same old groove. His new film was like *White Heat, The Times* said, but less entertaining. "As the moll, a superbly curved young lady named Barbara Payton performs as though she is trying to spit a tooth—one of the few Mr. Cagney leaves her.''

Gordon Douglas was the director Jimmy had hired for *Kiss Tomorrow Goodbye.* He was to direct Jimmy's next film too, but this time he would be in Warner Brothers' employ. The film, *Come Fill the Cup,* was based on the life of Jimmy's good friend Jim Richardson, the *Los Angeles Examiner* city editor. The novel from which the script was adapted had been written by another close friend of Jimmy's, Harlan Ware. Nevertheless, this was a Warners, not a Cagney, release. *Come Fill the Cup* is one of the films that Jimmy has positive recollections of. "I liked this one. Gig Young was the drinker in the film—as in real life. He was a funny man, nice to be around. The Massey role had been set for Adolph Menjou, but we couldn't get him for some reason. Their difference was day and night. Menjou, with that flamboyant manner of his, was who the character was. It would have been perfect casting.''

Jimmy played Lew Marsh, a recovering alcoholic who has given up drinking after narrowly escaping death under the wheels of a truck. Charlie Dolan (James Gleason), himself an ex-boozer, lends support to Lew's recovery. Lew regains his job as city editor and is enlisted by the publisher, John Ives (Raymond Massey) to help his nephew, Boyd (Gig Young), who also has a drinking problem. Despite the fact that Boyd is married to the girl Lew loves (Phyllis Thaxter), he accepts the challenge. Boyd, in league with the bad guys, is a difficult subject for reform, and it is his blundering that eventually causes the death of Charlie Dolan. In the climax, the gangster (Sheldon Leonard) who ordered the death of Charlie corners Lew and Boyd. As orchestration for their impending deaths, he orders them to drink the booze he has poured for them. Lew takes the drink but splashes it in the gangster's face. This creates the diversion needed to overpower the thug.

Jimmy's serious preparation for the role resulted in high praise for his performance. Of course, he drew heavily on his experience with his father's alcoholism to develop the characterization, but he also spent many hours studying Jim Richardson, the subject of the story. One of the traits he learned from him was the stiff-legged walk of drunks, who are trying to compensate for rubbery legs.

James Gleason was also highly praised and Gig Young not only received excellent reviews but was nominated for an Academy

Award. He said he would always be grateful to Jimmy for his many kindnesses. "I was called in for a test of the part of Boyd and was expecting one of the Warners stock players to be there to read with me. I couldn't believe it, but Cagney came in to do the test with me. It was unheard of for the star to do that. Jimmy is not only my favorite actor—he's my favorite person."

Jimmy's second film for 1951 was the studio's all-star presentation *Starlift,* in which he did a cameo role. The slapdash story involved stars and military personel at Travis Air Force Base, where Korean War casualties returned home after combat and others were en route. For all the money spent, the production was regarded as a bomb greater in size than any discharged during the war. Jimmy did his moves, spoke his lines, and looked ahead to the next chapters in his life. The film marked the last time he would work under the direction of Roy Del Ruth; their association dated back to *Blonde Crazy* in 1931.

Jimmy made one film in the following year, which was fine with him, but he would have been happier if the single assignment had resulted in something a bit more worthwhile. The studio had led him to believe that the film might be a second *Yankee Doodle Dandy.* The plan was to remake the 1926 silent film *What Price Glory?* as a musical, but John Ford, who had been signed as director, threw out the idea.

"It actually started out as a musical," says Jimmy, "and we had already shot some musical scenes, but Ford didn't like it. The numbers were cut, and the rest of it was done straight." The fact that it was planned as a musical probably accounts for the use of Technicolor (this was only the second color movie of Jimmy's career to date), but color helped little to make the production a success. It turned out to be little more than a Mutt and Jeff act with Dan Dailey, and it did nothing at all to enhance Jimmy's career. It would certainly do nothing to increase his percentages from Warner Brothers, because the movie was a decided flop. Archer Winston of the *New York Post* summed up the critical reaction: "The total result is deplorable, which is shocking when you see the name John Ford as director."

Warner Brothers had spent a fortune on the disastrous *Starlift,* and now they had one more super-disaster that, with all the extras and battle scenes, had cost them even more. Jimmy was not accustomed to working in box-office fizzles, but these were at least the product of somebody else's decisions, not his. No stress—no strain.

Jimmy's extraordinary agility is evident in this still from the 1937 film *Something to Sing About*.

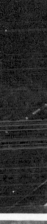

Left and below left: Dance stills from *Something to Sing About*.

Below: Jimmy lays down the law to the Dead End Kids in *Angels with Dirty Faces*.

Jimmy and Frank McHugh pose with each other's wives in this early 1930s photo.

The Cagney home in Beverly Hills, which remains their West Coast residence.

The Cagneys at home in Beverly Hills.

Inside the Cagneys' first home on Hillcrest Avenue in Beverly Hills.

Above: Jimmy and "Bill" at Martha's Vineyard. *Left:* Proving he knows his knots is Jimmy on the dock with his sailboat, *The Martha,* in the background.

The Oklahoma Kid.

Jimmy always loved sailing despite an admitted proclivity to *mal de mer*.

Each Dawn I Die, 1939.

With Pat O'Brien and Anne Sheridan in *Torrid Zone*.

Above: A soundstage chat with Jimmy's good friend and superlative artist, Will Crawford.
Right: Putting away a sparring partner in the 1941 film *City for Conquest.*

Jimmy does a vigorous tap dance routine for a wild-eyed audience
of one—at his Martha's Vineyard stable.

Above: As George M. Cohan in *Yankee Doodle Dandy*—an Academy Award performance. *Right:* From Jimmy's first independent production, *Johnny Come Lately.* In the first row, left to right, are Marjorie Lord, Margaret Hamilton, George Cleveland, and Grace George. *Below:* With Sylvia Sidney in *Blood on the Sun,* 1945.

Somewhere in England on his tour of military units during World War II.

On a USO tour in England during World War II.

Sporting a handlebar
mustache in the 1950s.

The Cagneys in the 1950s.

Jimmy is George M. Cohan once more in the 1955 film *The Seven Little Foys*.

Good pals Pat O'Brien and Jimmy share the company of "Lady" at Jimmy's home in Beverly Hills, 1980.

James Cagney, 1981.

Jimmy and "Bill" receive the key to New York City, 1981.

CHAPTER 23

immy found plenty of time to sit back and evaluate his life during the 1950s. He was perfectly happy to devote himself fully to his Martha's Vineyard farm and the myriad activities that surrounded it. If he had had his way, he would have forgotten about movies entirely, but this was not possible. Under his current contract, he would pick and choose his vehicles at Warner Brothers and could reject any script. But another matter was troubling him: the unresolved state of James Cagney Productions.

In 1953, Jimmy asked his brother Bill to confer with Warners to see what disposition could be made of their remaining properties. A deal was made that gave Warners *Only the Valiant,* a Western that would eventually star Gregory Peck, and *Bugles in the Afternoon,* a Civil War Story that would star Ray Milland. The Cagneys kept the third script; it would be their last independent film. It was the story of a backwoods politican entitled *A Lion Is in the Streets.* Jimmy starred, Bill Cagney was the producer, Jeanne played the strong character role of Jennie Brown, and Ed Cagney was story editor. Since this was the final Cagney production, there was no reason at all that the whole family should not be represented. Raoul Walsh directed the Technicolor film.

Jimmy played Hank Martin, a Huey Long–type demagogue who allows nothing to stand between him and political success, and it turned out to be one of Jimmy's finest portrayals. Inevitably, the film was compared with one on a similar theme, *All the King's Men,* which had won an Academy Award only four years earlier. Jimmy's film was considered the lesser of the two, but it was highly regarded in its own right. Barbara Hale was singled out for her

177

excellent performance as Verity Wade, and Ann Francis was praised as the earthy temptress, Flamingo.

None of Jimmy's movies was released during 1954, so when four of his films splashed across the nation's screens in the following year, it was regarded as a Cagney resurrection. During the flow of publicity, Jimmy assured his fans that he had been around all along. He said, perhaps with a note of irony, that they had simply missed some of his more recent releases.

Jimmy's releases for 1955 were, in proper order, *Run for Cover,* a Paramount picture in the new VistaVision; MGM's *Love Me or Leave Me,* in Eastmancolor and Cinemascope; Warner Brothers' *Mister Roberts,* in Cinemascope and Warnercolor; and Paramount's *The Seven Little Foys,* in Vista-Vision and Technicolor.

Jimmy liked the script of *Run for Cover,* because it seemed to have something that elevated it from the average oater; and he liked his character, Sheriff Matt Dow, because he was essentially a good person; and he liked the directing of Nicholas Ray. But, in the end, he was disappointed. The editors had cut out all of the good stuff, leaving nothing but the clichés, and Jimmy considered the finished film nothing more than one more programmer.

Bosley Crowther of *The New York Times* corroborated Jimmy's assessment and was typical of the reviewers. He suggested that Cagney's sheriff was copied from Gary Cooper's lawman in *High Noon* but said: "There is little to compare with the lean, leathery pictorial poetry and the stunning social comment of *High Noon.* For this William Pine–William Thomas western, directed by Nicholas Ray, is sheer horse opera without freshness or feeling and with practically nothing to say."

This was Jimmy's first association with Paramount. Next, at MGM, he played the challenging role of Gimp Snyder in *Love Me or Leave Me,* based on the life of Ruth Etting. This time he finally hit pay dirt.

By now Jimmy had reached the age of fifty-five. Until quite recently he had been able to retain a youthful enough countenance to compete for typical leading-man roles. But time was beginning to take its toll. The lines in his face were a bit more deeply etched, and there was a suggestion of jowls. The time had arrived for him to expand his scope and work into character roles. There would never be a better such role for Jimmy to experiment with than the portrayal of Martin "The Gimp" Snyder, the crippled Chicago racketeer who strong-armed Ruth Etting into a successful singing career.

Jimmy read the script, by Daniel Fuchs and Isobel Lennart, and could hardly believe his eyes. After twenty-five years of movie-making, this was the first time he had ever read a perfect script. "My God," he says. "We had to go with this one. There was nothing to be added, nothing to be taken away. And all the protagonists were alive."

Jimmy had never met Snyder, but he asked many of his acquaintances to demonstrate the extent of his limp (Snyder had been a polio victim). "What I did was simple," he says. "I slapped the foot down as I walked and turned it out . . . that's all. And I knew that those so afflicted tend to exaggerate the limp when they're tired, so I varied it as I saw fit. That kept it from being monotonous." After seeing the film, Snyder is said to have asked how Cagney learned his limp.

Jimmy had worked with Doris Day in *West Point Story* and they had both been cast in *Starlift*. He had been keenly aware of her talent, but after working with her in *Love Me or Leave Me*, he felt that she was extraordinary. He still speaks of her in superlatives and regrets that she sold out to the *Pillow Talk* kind of movie.

Doris was equally impressed with Jimmy. "He's the most professional actor I have ever known. He was always real. I simply forgot we were acting. His eyes would actually fill up when we were working in a tender scene. You never needed drops to make your eyes shine when Jimmy was on the set."

The critics liked both of their performances as much as they appreciated each other's. The *New York Herald Tribune* said: "It has plenty of songs of the jazz age to gratify the nostalgically-inclined; it has a story to grip those who don't care a Coolidge dollar about the music of yesteryear, and it has a performance by James Cagney that will be remembered for a long time. Cagney has created a fascinating portrait of the Gimp. In every mannerism— heavy limp, coarse speech, taunting sarcasm, flashes of rage—he molds an obnoxious character who tramples over everybody in his lust for power. It's a high tribute to Cagney that he makes this twisted man steadily interesting for two hours."

The film received six Academy Awards, with Jimmy being nominated for Best Actor, his sixth such nomination. Doris Day, unfortunately—and unfairly, many felt—did not receive a nomination.

Jimmy's involvement in his third film of the year began with a call from John Ford early in 1954. He asked Jimmy whether he would like a tropical vacation. What he was leading up to was an offer for Jimmy to play the role of the captain in *Mister Roberts,* which would be filmed partially on location at Midway Island. Jimmy liked the idea that the part would be small, and leisure time in the tropics appealed to him, but what won him over was the information that Spencer Tracy would be playing the part of Doc. As it turned out, the part went to William Powell, whom he ended up liking very much.

When the cast had been chosen, Jimmy met with another surprise. He learned that the young man who would play Ensign Pulver was the same young actor he had mentally "discovered" some months earlier in a television drama. It was on the Kraft Music Hall anthology series that Jimmy had spotted Jack Lemmon, although he didn't know his name until later. He was so impressed with Lemmon's ebullient performance that he wanted his brother Bill to sign him to a contract; he was certain the boy would succeed. When they finally met at the air strip at Midway Island, Lemmon was astonished by Jimmy's remarks.

"The first thing he asked me," Lemmon said, "was whether I was still using my left hand. It had been about a year and a half earlier, when, for my own amusement, I did the lead in that Kraft show as a lefty. Every piece of business was done left-handed, and I told no one—not even my wife, and, as far as I knew, no one ever noticed it . . . except Cagney. His powers of observation must be absolutely incredible, in addition to the fact that he remembered it. I was very flattered."

Four months were spent in Midway, and another several weeks in Hawaii, before the company returned to Hollywood. Jimmy regarded it as a paid vacation. He and William Powell would lounge on the beach between work calls, and there were only a few of those. For the first time in his long career—except for cameo appearances—Jimmy was cast in a subordinate role. He loved it. Only one incident marred an otherwise idyllic assignment.

Jimmy had worked with John Ford five years earlier on *What Price Glory?* As Jimmy remembered it, they had gotten along fairly well, but on greeting him at the airport Ford said a strange thing to Jimmy. He warned that they would more than likely "tangle asses" before the shooting was over. Jimmy was puzzled, but he let it pass. He did not, however, forget it.

Then came a day when Jimmy showed up on the set slightly late. As Jimmy approached, he saw Ford pacing back and forth in what appeared to be seething fury. Jimmy saw that Ford was about to unleash a tirade, but he cut him short. "Now wait a minute," Jimmy recalls saying. "When I started this picture, you said that you and I would tangle asses before this was over. I'm ready now—are you?" Ford took a breath and walked away. "From then on, we got along fine."

Having been forewarned, Jimmy was ready for a Ford offensive; the more he thought about it, the more ready he became. "I would have kicked his brains out," says Jimmy. "He was so goddamned mean to everybody. He was truly a nasty old man." Ford had been at odds with Henry Fonda since the shooting began. Fonda, having played Mr. Roberts on the stage for several years, wanted the movie to be done without Ford's tendency to embellish things. The disagreement erupted into a full battle one night at the naval officers' quarters where they were billeted at Midway. In the middle of the night, Lemmon was awakened by a commotion down the hall. He sneaked down to the open doorway to eavesdrop on Ford and Fonda, who were squared off in their undershorts. Ford, looking up at Fonda, swore and let go with a flurry of flailing fists. Fonda held him at arm's length, trying to appease him. He finally brought the match to a close by gently flinging Ford to the nearby bunk. Lemmon, playing it very much like Ensign Pulver, scurried back to his own room. He could see that eavesdropping at Ford's door was not the way for an aspiring juvenile to make his mark in the movies.

Despite personal differences, the movie turned out to be an enormous success, and despite the bad humor of the director, the cast remembered the experience with joy. Ford, who was actually ill at the time, left after two-thirds of the shooting to have a gall-bladder operation.

One of Jimmy's pastimes on location was drawing caricatures of fellow cast members. After he did Fonda, Lemmon, Broderick Crawford, and Ward Bond, he gave the finished drawings to each of the actors, who more than appreciated his work. He also did one of William Powell but put it aside. "Bill was a caricaturist's delight," says Jimmy. "He had gray hair, and it stuck out over his ears, and he was knock-kneed. I captured him going through a doorway. He was kind of the mother superior of the group, and had a dish in one hand and a towel in the other. I did the drawing of him but thought it was too cruel, so I hid it under some things on the desk. One night he was in there doing some writing after everyone had gone to bed. I heard a silly laugh behind me, and there was Powell. 'Sign it, you son-of-a-bitch,' he said, handing me the drawing. 'Just sign it.'"

Mister Roberts received three Academy Award nominations: Best Picture, Best Supporting Actor (Jack Lemmon), and Best Sound Recording. It was Jack Lemmon who won the Oscar. Jimmy wasn't nominated for his work in *Mister Roberts,* but he was nominated for Best Actor in *Love Me or Leave Me.* The winner was Ernest Borgnine for *Marty.*

CHAPTER 24

If Jimmy Cagney sensed that someone was trying to use him, he could be the coldest fish in an icy pond. Having worked at Warner Brothers for some time, Jack Rose was aware of Jimmy's sensitivities, so he approached Jimmy with trepidation on an occasion in 1955.

"Mel Shavelson and I were trying to do our first job of producing, directing, and writing at Paramount," Rose explains. "We had this idea of doing a feature about the Eddie Foy family, and we wanted Bob Hope to play the lead. This was how it began. The front office wasn't very interested because Hope's last couple of pictures hadn't done too well. We asked them to tell us under what circumstances they *might* be interested. They said, 'First, a tight budget. Secondly, if Hope takes no money, and if you and Mel take no money. We'll give each of you a third of the picture.' So we went to Hope and told him, and he said, 'Fine, let's go ahead.'

"We had bought the story cheaply from Bryan Foy, and there was this tight budget, yet we knew there was a part in the picture that only one man could play. It was the part of George M. Cohan, and our actor was Cagney. When I finally got up the nerve to approach him, I said, 'We don't want to insult you, Jimmy, but we really need you for the part. What we have left in the budget is only about sixty-five thousand dollars.' He said, 'Just forget it,' and our hopes plummeted. But then he said, 'I'll do it for nothing—I don't want any money.'

"He shows up to rehearse a week before the three-day shooting schedule, and when Hope hears about it, he comes in too. So that's why the dance went off so well. After it was all over, I went to Jimmy and said: 'I can't understand this, Jimmy. You don't

183

know Mel and me that well, and you aren't particularly close to Bob. Why did you do the picture?' He says, 'Well, yunkel, when I was in vaudeville Eddie Foy once bought me a cup of coffee.'"

That may have been one reason Jimmy signed on, but he was also very grateful to Bob Hope for having joined him on a Victory Caravan tour without having to be asked twice. And he was indebted to Eddie Foy, Jr., for his cameo appearance in *Yankee Doodle Dandy*. Beyond all these considerations, the role gave him an incentive to shed the extra weight he was then carrying.

However easy the dance number that Jimmy did with Bob Hope looked on the screen, it was anything but that. Jimmy chose to do a step he had been doing for years, but the last time he had tried it was a decade earlier. "It's called the knee-snap. It's a step that gives the knee quite a bit of strain, and during rehearsals my knees were swollen. When it came time to do the number with Bob on the table, I knew it would have to be done in one take. I had to leap up on the table and pull Bob up after me.

"When the cameras started rolling I did the leap all right, but as soon as I landed, pain shot up both legs. I tried not to change expression, and I did the routine with my legs paining almost beyond endurance. After the number, I called Bob into my dressing room and showed him my knees. He couldn't believe it. They were full of fluid, easily twice their normal size. I guess at fifty-six even a longtime song-and-dance man can't expect to bounce around quite the same way he did at, say, fifty."

When Jimmy finished his scene in the picture, Jack Rose and Bob Hope presented him with a silver cup on which was inscribed: "Thanks for the trailer you made for us. We have one for you." They had had a super-deluxe, leather-lined horse trailer custom-made for Jimmy. He considered himself well paid.

After doing three pictures back-to-back, Jimmy was eager to go to Martha's Vineyard for some peace and solitude. For a number of years he had used his forty-five-foot power boat, the *Dahinda*, for his eastern boating. On the West Coast he sailed the *Martha*, which he had bought in 1934 and sold during the war. After that, he used the company-owned two-master, the *Swift*. Although Jimmy was an admitted bad sailor, he could never seem to separate himself from his longing for the sea. Now another vessel came into his life. The *Mary Ann of Chilmark* was a forty-two-foot bug-eye ketch he had had custom-crafted in Nova Scotia. It was a copy of an eighteenth-century oyster boat used by eastern fishermen.

During this visit to Martha's Vineyard he saw a great deal of his good friend Robert Montgomery, who often went sailing with him. To reciprocate, Montgomery invited the Cagneys for a weekend at his farm in Milbrook, New York. It was then that Jimmy came across a farm of 120 acres nestled among the Berkshire foothills in Stanfordville. It was for sale, and Jimmy had to own it. He had paid a paltry $7,500 for his first farm, in Martha's Vineyard, but for the mid-fifties this property was as good a buy at $100,000. Jimmy later bought up adjoining land, until his acreage amounted to 750 acres. He named the property Verney Farms. The first syllable came from his wife's maiden name, Vernon, and the second syllable of his name completed the acronym. The farm included a comfortable white house next to the road, and too many dairy cows. He soon sold them and replaced them with beef cattle. From this point forward, Verney Farms would be the focus of Jimmy's industry and creative planning. The farm in Martha's Vineyard served its purpose well for many years, but what he had now was a farm in its truest sense.

During this period between movies, Jimmy had been honored by Rollins College, in Winter Park, Florida. He was selected to receive a doctorate in humanities, and he surprised the staff at the small college by agreeing to go there to receive it.

"When you get an honorary degree from Rollins," he says, "you are supposed to pick a subject and write a paper on it. So I wrote a paper on soil conservation. I guess this surprised them. They were probably expecting me to show up with Ava Gardner on my arm."

The Cagneys had flown to Florida for the event, and the trip was tranquil. Jimmy had almost decided to like this mode of transportation, but then there was the return trip. The plane ran into extreme turbulence, and just about everyone aboard became airsick. When the plane was safely on the ground at La Guardia Airport, Willie turned to Jimmy and said, "You've got to make me a promise."

"Whatever you want, babe," was his response. "Just name it."

"I want you to promise that you will never take another flight without me."

Jimmy agreed, but didn't know then that she had no intention of ever leaving the ground again. The bumpy trip from Florida was the last either of the Cagneys would make.

Jimmy's next picture would take him to Colorado on location. MGM induced him to play a role that had been planned for Spencer Tracy. It was proposed to Jimmy as though he would be filling in for his friend, who was ill, but that may not have been the whole truth. Tracy and the studio had been feuding around this time, and when *Tribute to a Badman* was offered to Tracy the conflict intensified. He could see no way that the part would enhance his middle-aged career. It did little to enhance Cagney's, but he was praised for his performance. Tracy left the studio, never to return. He had been under contract to MGM for twenty-five years.

MGM liked Jimmy's work well enough to make him another offer. He read the script, whose working title was *Somewhere I'll Find Him,* and liked it. In the film, retitled *These Wilder Years,* he played opposite Barbara Stanwyck for the first time.

Jimmy played a blustery, demanding bachelor who, after many years, sets out to locate his illegitimate son. Stanwyck played the woman in charge of the adoption home that had placed the boy. In his quest, Jimmy comes across a teenage mother (Betty Lou Keim) whose baby was born out of wedlock. The girl reminds him so much of the one he left behind years earlier that he adopts her. When the movie was released, it was dismissed by the critics as a hackneyed, slushy, mawkish, dull soap opera. Jimmy could only shrug.

He did enjoy his time on the set, however, because he and Stanwyck relived their vaudeville years in New York. Stanwyck had even wrapped packages in a Brooklyn store before she got her break. They entertained the crew and cast with their dance improvisations—which, unfortunately for the studio, were not included in the film.

Jimmy did only the two movies in 1956, but he surprised family and friends by agreeing to appear on television twice, though he had always said that TV was of no interest to him whatever. He did a scene from *Mister Roberts* on the "Ed Sullivan Show" and made an appearance on a Bob Hope show. Then, because he had promised Robert Montgomery that he would appear on his series if he ever decided to go on TV, he accepted the lead in a drama called "Soldiers from the War Returning." He played an army sergeant who escorted the body of a pal back home from the Korean

War. This was an important favor to Montgomery, because his network was threatening to drop the series. A strong fall opener was needed to assure high enough ratings to pull the series through; Jimmy's appearance got them.

When asked whether he intended to do television on a regular basis, Jimmy replied: "I do enough work in movies. This is a high-tension business. I have tremendous admiration for the people who go through this sort of thing every week, but it's not for me."

Two of Jimmy's greatest film successes had been in stories about real people, *Yankee Doodle Dandy* and *Love Me or Leave Me.* He wasn't especially seeking biographical parts, but when he was asked to portray the life of Lon Chaney, he accepted. This real-life story would prove successful too.

The reviews of *Man of a Thousand Faces* heaped praise on Jimmy's performance but found the story less than inspiring. *The New York Times:* "Joseph Pevney's direction has a curious affection for clichés, but Mr. Cagney rises above it. He etches a personality."*Life:* "Cagney turns the film into a tender tribute to a fine and troubled man." The *New York Journal-American:* "Cagney submerges his own personality completely into that of the man whom he portrays. The result is a characterization that rates among his best."

Despite the glowing reviews, Jimmy failed to receive an Academy Award nomination. The film made big money for Universal, however, and that satisfied him. Dorothy Malone, as Chaney's first wife, received excellent reviews as did Jane Greer as his second wife. Jeanne Cagney played Chaney's sister, her last film appearance with Jimmy, and Jimmy's own film career was entering its final phase.

CHAPTER 25

here was a second film for Jimmy in 1957, but not as an actor. *Short Cut to Hell* was his debut as a director. It was also his directorial swan song.

For many years, Jimmy had been told by friends in the business that he would make an extraordinary director. After all, he had made his share of contributions to the films he had acted in over the last quarter century. Jimmy didn't doubt that he could do it; the only problem was that he didn't want to. Nothing was less interesting to him.

Then Jimmy's friend A. C. Lyles came to him and asked whether he would consider directing chores in a remake of the Graham Greene novel *This Gun's for Hire*. It would be a low-budget affair, and Lyles, as producer, couldn't offer much money. Jimmy's impulsive answer was yes, but he would assume the task only if there were no money involved at all. He was an actor, not a director, so he would not consider accepting money for talents untested. Jimmy was probably wondering how he would fare. He had never been sufficiently motivated to give it a try, but now he could play director, serve a good friend, and satisfy any curiosity he may have had.

The picture, starring Robert Ivers, Georgeann Johnson, and William Bishop, was released with the title *Short Cut to Hell*. Considering the budget, it turned out all right. The reviews were kind to Jimmy, most of them mentioning the typical Cagney touches in the film. The release gave Lyles a good start as a producer. "We shot it in twenty days, and that was long enough for me. I find directing a bore. I have no interest in telling other people their business."

188

Universal now came to him with another script. They were excited about his acting, after the success of *Man of a Thousand Faces,* and it wasn't difficult for them to remember that Jimmy was also a song-and-dance man. The project was a musical comedy, *Never Steal Anything Small,* based on an unproduced play by Maxwell Anderson and Rouben Mamoulian.

Jimmy put his best foot forward, and so did Universal-International, with their CinemaScope and color, but the production fell far short of expectations. Not even the expensive location scenes filmed in New York City, at a cost of twenty-five thousand dollars a day, could elevate it above mediocrity. The studio was out of its element.

Shirley Jones, Roger Smith, and Cara Williams joined Jimmy in the cast. The script was written in a kind of blank verse, the songs were regarded as highly forgettable, and the movie fans stayed home. Jimmy, now fifty-nine, turned into an ex–song-and-dance man with this movie; it was his fifth and last musical.

Jimmy was next before the cameras a year later, starring in an adaptation of the Reardon Conner novel *Shake Hands with the Devil.* Filmed on location in Ireland, it was produced by Marlon Brando's Pennebaker Productions.

Jimmy played Sean Lenihan, a college professor who is secretly a commandant in the Irish Republican Army. His influence ensnares an American-Irish student, Kerry O'Shea (Don Murray). O'Shea falters, however, because of his growing love for Jennifer Curtis (Dana Wynter), a member of the English royal family. Sean, determined to prevent a treaty he opposes, plans to execute the girl. Although his comrades beg him to reconsider, he turns to shoot her, but Kerry halts him with a fatal bullet.

The film's message, that violence only begets violence, appealed to Jimmy, and his performance was regarded by some as the best of his later work. The international cast included Michael Redgrave, Glynis Johns, and dozens of actors from Dublin's Abbey Theatre. One of the objections by critics was the curious variety of homemade accents intended to sound Irish.

Jimmy had hoped to explore his family tree on this, his second visit to Ireland, but the weather was so miserable that he only captured glimpses of the Irish countryside from behind auto windows, and the rigid shooting schedule left little time for side trips.

A year later Jimmy would be acting in his penultimate film.

He didn't know then that his career was winding down, but he did know that he was tiring of it. On this occasion, however, he was enthusiastic about working with his friend Robert Montgomery. They had planned for years to do something together, as Jimmy had had hopes of working with Spencer Tracy and Fred Astaire. Jimmy would play the lead in a tribute to Admiral William F. "Bull" Halsey, directed by Montgomery.

The story covered five weeks of Halsey's life, during the battle of Guadalcanal in 1942, when the admiral was commander of the Pacific Fleet. The movie, entitled *The Gallant Hours,* concentrated not on the fury of battle but on the admiral, as he suffered his own hell while the battle raged.

There were no big names in the picture except Cagney, but playing Halsey's second-in-command was an actor of television fame, Dennis Weaver, making his screen debut as Lieutenant-Commander Andy Lowe. The movie had a pair of other screen newcomers as well: the sons of Jimmy Cagney and Robert Montgomery played crew members on the command ship.

The picture was a success. Bosley Crowther of *The New York Times* wrote:

> No actual naval battle action is depicted in Robert Montgomery's *The Gallant Hours*. But there is much superb comprehension of the ordeal an admiral goes through when he sends his ships into action, and so much sense of the endless strain of command, that there is a powerful lot more than the mere turmoil of graphic action in this film.
>
> Mr. Montgomery directed with understanding, affection and skill. But it is Mr. Cagney's performance, controlled to the last detail, that gives life and strong, heroic stature to the principal figure in the film. It is one of the quietest, most reflective, subtlest jobs that Mr. Cagney has ever done.
>
> It is, in short, a picture of a man who can say to a boy who shuns the responsibility of leading a squadron of flyers to possible death, "There are no great men, there are only great challenges which ordinary men like you and me are forced by circumstances to meet." It is one of the most affecting pictures of a war hero that we have ever seen.

Jimmy had reached an age at which he could no longer be cast as a young leading man. Even during the prime of his life, his leading-man image was at best offbeat, so character roles came more easily to him than to some other actors. Now the supporting actors provided the love interest. When he made *The West Point Story* he was over fifty but could still play a character who masquerades as a plebe. He admits that he played "kids" much longer than he did other types. In the fifties, he played youthful parts until *A Lion Is in the Streets;* his roles were consistently mature after that.

Most actors are happy to grow gracefully into character roles, and so was he. But the difference between Jimmy and so many others was that he simply didn't care that much about acting. "Just a job," he would say so often; "no stress, no strain." But no matter how often he said it, those around him saw that there was more than a little "stress" and "strain" as the years progressed, and the "job" he was doing was becoming less and less tolerable.

He had announced his retirement so many times that it had become almost an industry joke. Once again he was making noises about retirement, but once again he was offered a role that sounded good, and he found himself accepting it. It would be on location again, this time in Germany. It was the director Billy Wilder who recruited him this time, for the motor-mouthed Pepsi-Cola representative in *One, Two, Three.*

He rather liked seeing Germany, but the part was not the kind he liked best. It was straight comedy, and he had not forgotten the debacle of *Boy Meets Girl* twenty-three years earlier: that was the picture with Ralph Bellamy for which scenes had to be reshot to make it faster and funnier. This role was much the same, with whirlwind pace and back-to-back punchlines from beginning to end. He made it a point to bring all this up with Billy Wilder, explaining that the pace of *Boy Meets Girl* had been so frenetic that the dialogue couldn't be understood. Wilder assured Jimmy that there would be balance, with less emphasis on some lines than others. He had it all figured out, and Jimmy took him at his word.

Jimmy and Willie took a leisurely voyage across the Atlantic and toured France en route to Munich, where most of the film would be made. The vacation was delightful, and Jimmy even had an opportunity to exercise his linguistic talents along the way. He tried to ask road directions in French and wasn't understood at all. He used his expert German on a border-area peasant to ascertain a way across the Rhine, and the peasant laughed loudly: he understood Jimmy well enough but thought that his German, with a strong Yiddish accent, was the funniest thing he had ever heard. They finally found the way to Munich, but Jimmy would find little laughter from that point on.

Jimmy's character in the film was C. P. MacNamara, West German manager of Pepsi-Cola. He is given the unwanted responsibility of babysitting for his boss's daughter, Scarlett (Pamela Tiffin), who is visiting Munich from Atlanta. She falls for Otto (Horst Buchholz), a young Communist from East Berlin. This puts MacNamara on a tightrope: he is trying to sign a deal with the Russians to take on Pepsi-Cola, so dares not offend them, yet he must try to maneuver the boss's daughter away from marrying Otto. She does marry him, however, which gives MacNamara the challenge of changing the lad's image to something more acceptable to the Western corporate brass.

Wilder had promised that the pace would be modulated, but it didn't work out that way, at least not by Jimmy's standards—it was breakneck all the way. For one scene, fifty takes were necessary. This was the scene with Otto and the tailor who was to make him presentable. The miscues were contagious; when one actor blew a line, so would the others. Jimmy became frustrated, Wilder got angry, and that tone continued for the remainder of the shooting.

One, Two, Three became the most unhappy experience of Jimmy's film career. The only highlight was Pamela Tiffin, whom he liked very much. At first she had difficulty working with him, perhaps because of awe. He took her aside and told her what he had learned many years before. "You walk in," Jimmy told her, "plant yourself squarely on both feet, look the other fella in the eye, and then tell the truth." Pamela wrote it all down on a scrap of paper.

He then told her that she was not looking squarely into his eyes when she delivered her line, but flitting from one eye to the other. He suggested that she focus on the downstage eye, the one toward the camera. As the tricks of many years of acting occurred to Jimmy, he passed them on to Pamela, and they rehearsed each scene together. Her improvement was remarkable, and he became convinced that she was an outstanding talent. Today he is mystified that she didn't go further in her career.

Jimmy had made several other predictions of stardom over the years, and his batting average was not the best. Of Pamela Tiffin, Roger Smith, Don Dubbins, Betty Lou Keim, and Jack Lemmon, only Lemmon became a star.

One, Two, Three turned out to be a very successful film. The breakneck speed of it was enjoyed by many of the critics. Some said that the character Jimmy played was abrasive and raucous, and he tended to agree. Actually, Jimmy didn't care one way or the other. He has never seen the film and swears he never will. To see it would bring back the most miserable experience of his later career.

During the making of this film, everything unpleasant seemed to gather in a dark cloud over his head. He had had his fill of temperamental directors who considered their utterances to be missives from heaven, and of actors with inflated self-images. The latter description was reserved for Horst Buchholz, whom Jimmy respected not at all. As he reflected on his career, he realized that he had been fortunate to work with some of the most congenial actors in the business, and some of the most talented. It seemed ironic to Jimmy that such a negative experience with an actor had come only at the end of his career.

"I never had the slightest difficulty with a fellow actor," Jimmy insists. "Not until *One, Two, Three*. In that picture Horst Buchholz tried all sorts of scene-stealing didoes. I came close to knocking him on his ass, which at several times I would have been happy to do."

For the first time in Jimmy's career he threatened to walk out in the middle of a picture, and came very near doing it. He did walk off the soundstage, and when he emerged from the darkness into the clear sunlight he wondered what he was doing in the business. How could he have missed so much sunlight over so many years? He did return to the set, but only his ingrained discipline brought him back.

Jimmy doesn't recall having had all that much difficulty with Billy Wilder on the picture, but Wilder has been quoted as saying that he and Cagney didn't get along. "I never knew what the hell he wanted," said Jimmy. "He was an arrogant guy—a typical Prussian. Billy was more of a dictator than most of the other directors I worked with. He was overly bossy, full of noise—a pain. Still, we did a good picture, as it turned out. I didn't learn until after we were done that he didn't like me."

As a culmination to all his negative feelings about the picture, Jimmy visited nearby Dachau, the Nazi death camp. He was never more glad to return home.

When Jimmy left the Bavarian Studios in Munich he said nothing to anyone, but he knew that he had just completed his film career. This time he meant it—for at least twenty years.

CONCLUSION: IN AND OUT OF RETIREMENT

It was a dripping-hot day in July 1980, as hot and uncomfortable as only New York can be in the summertime. In the Park Slope section of Brooklyn, at Fifteenth Street and Eighth Avenue, masses of humanity had gathered in the street as word spread that scenes from a major movie were being shot that day.

Attention was centered on the balcony of the old armory, where, the prevailing rumor suggested, some actor would soon appear, pretending that he was the pope. This information was brought to the perspiring actor who stood behind the window awaiting his cue. Despite the heat and humidity, he wore a heavy, turn-of-the-century wool suit, mutton-chop sideburns, and a handlebar mustache.

The portly, white-haired actor emerged from inside and took his position on the balcony. In response to the rumor, the actor, with a glint in his eye, blessed the crowd and then made a gesture known well by native New Yorkers: he flicked his right hand backward from beneath his chin with the chin jutting outward. There were resounding cheers and applause. Despite the costume and the facial disguise, and the changes wrought by time, the actor was recognized: James Cagney was back before the cameras after twenty years of self-imposed retirement.

The scene, directed by the Czech-born Milos Forman for the film *Ragtime,* was the beginning of many months of shooting, most of which would be done at Shepperton Studios in London. This scene included the character Rhinelander Waldo, a New York police commissioner of the time, played by Cagney, and another actor, in the street below, playing Harry Houdini. The shooting was completed after eight grueling hours under the sun, but, as it turned out, the entire sequence would be cut from the film. Although this footage would never be seen by the public, it was Jimmy's first appearance before the cameras since the completion of *One, Two, Three* in 1961.

There were twenty years as a private citizen before Jimmy broke his vow to retire permanently, but there was a greater impetus involved than a yen to get back into pictures. Jimmy's physician had ordered him to get back to work. A chance meeting with Milos Forman made Jimmy's return to work easier than might otherwise have been possible. He was having lunch in a restaurant near his home in upstate New York with the young actor Treat Williams. Williams had heard that plans were underway to put together a musical based on Jimmy's life, and he wanted to play the Cagney role. During lunch Jimmy was introduced to Forman, who, almost offhandedly, offered Jimmy a role in his forthcoming film, *Ragtime*. He told Jimmy that he could have any part he wanted, including that of Evelyn Nesbit, if he thought he was right for it. For the first time in at least nineteen years, Jimmy did not say no.

Jimmy had a copy of the E. L. Doctorow novel at home, and that evening he looked through the book to see which parts he could play. There were only two possibilities. "One was the role of an old Jewish man," Jimmy says. "I could have played him perfectly, but he was asleep most of the time." Jimmy settled on the Rhinelander role and let Forman know that he might be interested in playing it. A gentleman's agreement was made over the telephone. Forman gave Jimmy the freedom to back out of the commitment right up to the start of the picture.

These were the mechanics of Jimmy's return to film, but the motivation had been growing since the diagnosis of diabetes some five years earlier and since a slight stroke in 1977. The doctor insisted then that Jimmy get back to work "to recharge my batteries."

Over the years, he had occasionally been tempted to come out of retirement, but Jimmy says that he had only to conjure up a picture of Jack Warner for all temptation to dissolve. The greatest temptation was an invitation to play Doolittle in *My Fair Lady*. After passing up that plum role, it was easier to ignore the others. Jimmy's retirement had been spent in happy obscurity, almost totally isolated, or insulated, from public life. The only publicity splash he received was when he accepted the American Film Institute Life Achievement Award in 1974. Jimmy was the first actor to be so honored. The award had gone to the director John Ford a year earlier.

Jimmy attended the celebration, held March 13, 1974, at the Century Plaza Hotel, along with fifteen hundred of Hollywood's most famous stars and other film-industry luminaries. Frank Sinatra was the master of ceremonies, and the extravaganza, produced by Paul W. Keyes, was shown on television by CBS on March 18.

Charlton Heston, an officer of AFI, opened the program and introduced Sinatra, who carried with him a copy of *Variety*. From it he read a 1921 review of Parker, Rand, and Cagney that described the act as being without laughs and having songs that meant little; however, one of the boys (Cagney) could dance. The actual review was misquoted to say that Jimmy's only chance was "smalltime," instead of that those were the chances of the act. But it served as an appropriate irony on which to launch a stimulating and emotional night of star remembrances, coupled with myriad samples of Jimmy's thirty years of movie acting.

When Frank Sinatra completed his welcome to Jimmy, the first cluster of Cagney film clips came on the screen, from *Strawberry Blonde*, *The Bride Came C.O.D.*, *A Midsummer Night's Dream*, *Picture Snatcher*, *Kiss Tomorrow Goodbye*, *The Roaring Twenties*, *Public Enemy*, *Angels with Dirty Faces*, and *White Heat* (the scene in which Jimmy gave ventilation to his captive by pumping holes in the car trunk with a forty-five). Then John Wayne came on. He said that the latter scene proved how accommodating Jimmy could be, and imaginative. "I'd have probably done something stupid," he said, "like open the trunk."

Next was George C. Scott, in a rare television appearance. He had refused to make an appearance to collect his Academy Award a year earlier, but he was here to honor Jimmy. He introduced another group of movie clips that ended with the historic dance sequence Jimmy and Bob Hope did in *The Seven Little Foys*. Bob Hope then took over and handed out a bouquet of typical Hope quips, among them, "For Cagney, a love scene was when he let the other guy live."

Next Sinatra directed attention to some of Jimmy's friends in the audience: Joan Blondell, Mae Clarke, Allen Jenkins, Frank McHugh, Ralph Bellamy, and California governor Ronald Reagan. He also introduced members of Jimmy's family: Mrs. Cagney, their son and daughter, and Jimmy's sister Jeanne.

Jimmy's former costar Mae Clarke appeared, and she was followed by Shirley MacLaine and Jack Lemmon. Then, the impressionist Frank Gorshin teamed up with Kirk Douglas and George Segal to sing "Give My Regards to Broadway." Doris Day made her contribution following the clip from *Love Me or Leave Me* by singing live the number she sang in the movie, "You Made Me Love You."

At the end of the next group of movie clips was a scene from *Boy Meets Girl* in which Ronald Reagan was cast as a radio announcer. Then Reagan was on hand to say that he made that movie in 1938, and hoped that the Institute would forget his scene when they got around to preserving the film. He said that he had known Jimmy for the better part of his life. "As a matter of fact," he added, "knowing Jimmy Cagney *was* the better part of my life."

Cicely Tyson presented the AFI's three Fellowship Awards in Cagney's name, and Frank Sinatra returned to sing a special version of "My Way," written by Sammy Cahn. In this instance, it was "He Did It His Way," referring to the way Jimmy handled his film career by doing it *his* way, instead of the way Hollywood dictated.

In Jimmy's acceptance speech, he read John Masefield's poem, "Art Is Life Plus." He thanked those responsible for the event and offered salutations to friends of the past or present, and to those absent or deceased. His list included several members of his old Yorkville gang, who had helped mold him into what he had become. During his speech his voice began to break, until he admonished himself, "Hang on, boy."

"About the award," Jimmy said. "I am very grateful for it. But why don't we just say for now that I'm merely a custodian. Holding it for all those wonderful guys and gals who worked over the years to bring about this night for me. So, I really mean this . . . I'm thanking you for them and for me."

As an apparent afterthought, Jimmy issued a correction to Frank Gorshin, who had become a star doing Jimmy Cagney imitations. "Oh, Frankie," he said. "I never said 'MMMMmmm, you dirty rat!' What I actually said was, 'Judy, Judy, Judy.'"

The dinner lasted five hours but was edited down to ninety minutes for television. One columnist suggested that a bomb in the dining room would have brought an end to the movie industry. The assemblage of movie personalities and studio executives was said to be greater than for any event in history. When the show was televised it drew the highest ratings CBS had enjoyed in years, and it was equally successful when it was shown in half a dozen foreign countries. This was a public appearance that Jimmy would never forget.

During the summers, the Cagneys divided their time between Martha's Vineyard and Verney Farms in New York. While at Verney they frequented a nearby restaurant called the Silver Horn. It was a grand old country farmhouse that had been converted into a homey but spacious dining room and bar, decorated with Early American accoutrements. On occasion, the Cagneys would hold parties there attended by their neighbor Robert Montgomery, Jimmy's old pal Frank McHugh, and any other friends that the Cagneys could round up. Some of the parties included fifty or sixty guests, and there was never an attempt to cut corners. For this reason, the Cagneys were regarded by the proprietress of the Silver Horn as good customers, and it was in this category that they remained for at least two years of patronage. Then Marge Zimmermann and Willie Cagney became acquainted.

"She liked the way I decorated my restaurant," Marge said, "and she asked if she could ride along when I went out shopping for things. I explained that I didn't go to antique stores, but to junk shops. She said that was exactly what she had in mind."

That was how they met, and something about Marge's energy and determination seemed to make an impression on Willie. The friendship grew. Marge's husband, Don, a builder and civil engineer, is of German descent; Marge is of Irish and Italian heritage. Don, a quiet man with typical new England aloofness, remained distant from the Cagneys for a considerable time; he wanted no man to accuse him of kowtowing to celebrities. Marge had known Willie at least a year before she became even remotely acquainted with Jimmy. "I first met Jamesy in 1970," she says, "and I used to think he was always depressed. He was, of course, because he was a sick man."

The Cagneys had departed for Los Angeles for the winter, as

was their custom, but during their stay Jimmy placed a call to Marge. He asked if she would keep an eye out for old wood with which to construct an art studio on the farm. Although she told him that she wasn't into that kind of shopping, she promised to ask around. As it turned out, her inquiries resulted in the eventual acquisition by the Cagneys of an old railroad station which was exactly the kind of material Jimmy was seeking. He even acquired the two-seater outhouse that went with it. It was at this point that Jimmy and Don Zimmermann became acquainted, if only in a professional way. Jimmy hired Don to reconstruct the railroad station on a remote and beautiful site within the boundaries of Verney.

Within the next couple of years, Marge was called upon by the Cagneys on numerous occasions for a variety of tasks. On one such occasion Jimmy asked whether Marge could drive him to New York to visit a doctor; he was having severe problems with his eyes. She was too busy with her restaurant at the time, but she was able to convince him that there were competent doctors in the area. He agreed to visit one of them.

"Jimmy had been previously diagnosed as having glaucoma," said Marge, "and was being treated for that with eyedrops. It turned out that his condition was misdiagnosed, that the eyedrops were ruining his eyes. His real problem was diabetes." She says that a glucose tolerance test revealed that the triglycerides in his blood were at an alarming 355, and that if something weren't done about it immediately, he would certainly be susceptible to a massive heart attack.

The Cagneys had always had live-in housekeepers wherever they lived, but after the alarming news from the doctor, Marge was asked to look after Jimmy. She accepted the responsibility, even though operating her restaurant was more than a full-time job. She prepared Jimmy's meals according to a strict diet, and within a few months the trigylcerides, or fat cells, were reduced to 80. The count eventually leveled out at 90 to 100, which was acceptable. All was well, as long as Marge was looking after Jimmy, but without her discipline he tended to cheat. She suspected that he did this consistently during the Cagneys' winter sojourn in Los Angeles.

Jimmy and Willie made trips to the West Coast on two winters while Marge was still tied down to the restaurant operation, and by the time Jimmy was honored by the American Film Institute he was in better shape than he had been in years. Through his diet he had shed some twenty pounds from his overweight frame, and his eyesight had improved measurably with the help of proper treatment and appropriate glasses. When he appeared onstage at the Century Plaza Hotel, he did a brief dance step to illustrate his vitality.

During the Cagneys' winter stay at their Coldwater Canyon home in 1977, Jimmy found himself in serious trouble. He had become lax in his dieting and had skipped his medication on a number of occasions. Whether this was a direct cause is not certain, but one morning in early May, just before their return to New York, Jimmy experienced a loud buzzing in his head, and his legs gave way. He slumped over the kitchen sink, waiting for his strength to return. In a few minutes he felt strong enough to walk out of the kitchen, climb the stairs to his wife's bedroom, and say: "Willie, call a doctor. I've just had a stroke."

At the Good Samaritan Hospital a physician described the attack as transient ischemic anemia, or a minor stroke caused by a spasm of the artery supplying blood to the brain. Jimmy, counting himself lucky, was out of the hospital in two weeks. They returned to New York during the summer, at which time Marge Zimmermann was asked to care for Jimmy on a more-or-less full-time basis. By this time, she had given up the restaurant. She became the constant companion of the Cagneys from that time on: if they went on a trip, Marge went with them; if they were asked to a party, the invitation had to include Marge (she was with them at the twenty-fifth wedding anniversary celebration of Ronald and Nancy Reagan). When the Cagneys made their final visit to Martha's Vineyard as part-time residents, Marge accompanied them.

This was in 1979, and the place was no longer the tranquil refuge of long years past. The changes had been subtle during the thirties and the forties, but later the changes began to accelerate. When Jimmy bought the land, the roads were dust and the countryside was pristine and unblemished by civilization. Now there was an almost carnival atmosphere, with the summer people frenetic in their search for vacation fun. Jimmy would no longer open the door of his house without being accosted by fans or by newspaper and television reporters and crews.

The previous summer Jimmy had felt better about the place. He had spent thirty-five thousand dollars refurbishing his ketch the

Mary Ann. It was refitted with new sails and made sparkling from bow to stern. That was after he took several friends out for a day of sailing, one of his first physical endeavors since his stroke. Marge recalls it well, because she was enlisted to act as a deck hand.

"One day Jimmy told me he was going to take out the boat. I told him I didn't see how he could, because he didn't have a skipper that day. He said he would do it himself. I drove them to the boat, and when we got aboard I was the one elected to get the sails ready. He told all of us what to do, and we went out for several hours of beautiful sailing. From that moment on, he started to get better. He found out he could do things again."

The following year, however, Jimmy made arrangements to give the boat to Columbia University. He gave the Chilmark farm to his son, James junior, and the house at Tashmu was given to his sister, Jeanne. He and Willie moved their furniture to Verney, where they planned to spend their summers exclusively. With this decision made, Jimmy hired Don Zimmermann to scare up more used wood with which to add a new wing to his small hilltop house. Within a year the renovated house had a cozy new living room complete with fieldstone fireplace.

Jimmy's undiagnosed diabetes had changed his physiognomy from that of a very youthful septuagenarian to that of a lagging, depressed old man. Before this unrelenting drain on his system, he had taken pride in his physical condition. He had gained weight but was still able to dance his way back to shape when he wanted to. Once the diabetes took its toll, his energy was sapped and his will to live began to diminish. With the stroke, any hope he might have maintained began to turn to despair. There would be no more dancing, no hiking or horseback riding along his twelve miles of wooded trails. He even lost interest in his favorite of all pastimes, painting. It was when Jimmy's doctor realized his despair that the work-or-else warning was issued. With this warning reiterated daily by Marge and Willie, Jimmy agreed to the offer made by Milos Forman. Although their telephone agreement was tentative, Jimmy knew he would not renege.

The movie location was made more attractive when Pat and Eloise O'Brien were included in the cast. They would share no scenes with Jimmy, but the old team would have plenty of opportunity to share each other's company during the crossing aboard the *Queen Elizabeth II* and throughout the several-week shooting.

If Jimmy entertained any thoughts that he was a has-been, they evaporated when the ship docked at Southhampton: the pier was thronged with hundreds of English movie fans. Cunard Line security officers were swept back by the surging crowds. Cunard officials said that they had never seen anything to compare with it. Over the years many Hollywood stars, including Marlon Brando and Robert Redford, had arrived there, but never had there been such a turnout.

Jimmy and his entourage were booked into the Sheraton Skyliner Hotel in London. The crowds became so insistent that Jimmy often had to be hidden beneath a blanket coming to and from the hotel in a limousine. The fans in the streets held placards: WELCOME TO LONDON; WE LOVE YOU, JIMMY. Marge said that the English fans were the most considerate imaginable, but that the ever-present *paparazzi* could make life miserable. "They were like animals, the way they swarmed over him."

When Jimmy made his first appearance on the set he was greeted by the applause of fellow players and members of the crew. He saluted them, and it was back to work. There were flubs and miscues during the first scenes, but none of the mistakes were Jimmy's. Some of the actors were too much in awe of him to relax sufficiently, or to concentrate. Jimmy's goodwill and easygoing nature soon set them at ease.

Howard Rollins, who played Coalhouse Walker in the picture, said: "I was frightened to meet Mr. Cagney. I asked him how to die in front of the camera. He said, 'Just die!' It worked. Who would know more about dying than him? I'll never forget the other advice he gave me. He said, 'Walk into the room, plant yourself, look the other guy in the face, and tell the truth.'"

There is no mistaking the source of this piece of advice, and it proves that a truth discovered by Cagney is as valid today as it was in the distant past. He gave the same succinct advice to Joan Leslie, Jack Lemmon, Pamela Tiffin, and who knows how many other young actors and actresses. It apparently impressed each one of them in their time.

Before the actual filming began, Marge was beginning to have doubts regarding Jimmy's comeback. She wondered if she had erred in her insistence that he return before the cameras. She had been the person Jimmy had called upon to cue him for his role, and as far as she could see, his readings—mumbled under his breath—were none too good. She had no way of knowing that Jimmy was never one to waste energy before the fact, and she found herself blinking in astonishment when he finally went before the cameras. The old energy, crispness, and electricity were as strong as ever. It was as if he were another person when the cameras were rolling.

"I think he is some kind of genius," said Milos Forman. "His instincts, it's just unbelievable. You don't have to talk to him. I could stay home. One of the qualities of a brilliant actor is that things look better on the screen than on the set. Jimmy has that quality."

Despite painful bouts with sciatica, Jimmy was on the set every day during the nine-week location work. No one outside his intimate group knew that he was ailing. During the stay, Jimmy gave out hundreds of photographs and perhaps thousands of autographs. He posed for pictures with tourists, fans, and dignitaries. He and Pat O'Brien appeared on the Mike Parkinson television show and found the studio smothered with flowers sent by well-wishers. One of Parkinson's questions was whether Jimmy had ever taken acting lessons.

"Never."

"Why not?"

"Why? Why take lessons in perfectly natural things to do? Acting is nothing special. It's a job to do. Do it and sit down, that's all."

At the queen mother's command-performance birthday party at the London Palladium, Jimmy and Pat were backstage with Don Zimmermann while Marge, Willie and Eloise O'Brien watched from out front. Among those scheduled for the performance were Sammy Davis; Danny Kaye; Mary Martin and her son, Larry Hagman; and Peggy Lee. When Jimmy made his unscheduled appearance, the queen mother arose for the first time during the program to applaud. Then, after the show, when she received the performers backstage, she broke protocol to come over to Jimmy. It was a night to remember for everybody involved, but when Jimmy was asked what the queen mother said to him backstage, he answered,

"How the hell do I know?" He had been so nervous that the entire evening played back as a blur.

Over the years of retirement, Jimmy had always received a steady stream of fan letters, perhaps as many as a hundred a week at his various addresses. But after the publicity about *Ragtime,* the pieces of mail increased to the thousands. The Zimmermanns' daughter, Karen, was enlisted to handle it.

Jimmy was never willing to admit that his retirement had become boring, and he has never expressed any particular jubilation over his recent comeback. But those who know him best can judge by certain changes. Previously, he had been steadfast in his refusal to make public appearances. Now, he can be persuaded. There was a time not long ago when he preferred not to hear about work proposals. Today, he listens. He is actively interested in current projects, such as a possible Jimmy Cagney stage musical, and is feeling a renewed enthusiasm for life. He is now willing to look ahead.

After his return from London, Jimmy barely had time to change hats before he was chauffeured to Washington, where he would be one of five recipients of Kennedy Center Honors for "lifetime achievement in the performing arts." He, Leonard Bernstein, Agnes DeMille, Lynn Fontanne, and Leontyne Price were honored in a ceremony at the State Department on December 6, 1980, a White House reception the following afternoon, and a gala that evening at Kennedy Center. The gala was taped for television. President Jimmy Carter said: "James Cagney has touched the heart of America with his roles, ranging all the way from *Public Enemy* to *Yankee Doodle Dandy,* and almost every American has a Jimmy Cagney impersonation."

Several months later, Jimmy appeared at the New York City premiere of *Ragtime,* which led to a series of other public functions. When he was awarded a gold key to the city by Mayor Edward Koch, he responded, "I'm at an age when I cry easily. Thank you very much, sir."

Jimmy threw out the first ball for the second game of the World Series at about the same time. Humiliated by his substandard pitching performance he said, "I aimed the ball here and it came down over there—and me an ex–ball player." The ball plopped lifelessly over the railing but no one knew the pain he was enduring that day from another attack of sciatica.

In 1982 Jimmy was named Man of the Year by Hasty Pudding Theatricals at Harvard, receiving the traditional pudding pot for his "lasting and impressive contribution to the world of entertainment." When the press became overpowering in their need for just one more picture, Marge Zimmermann took charge. She told them to cool down, and wait until after the show, when Jimmy would take care of their needs. They obeyed.

"There wasn't much to it," said Marge. "They had a big poster of Marilyn Monroe with Jimmy's head on it. Jimmy was afraid the kids were disappointed because he didn't do anything, but they loved him. Afterward, I helped arrange it so all of the players in the show could have their pictures taken with Jimmy. His sciatica was bothering him that day too, but you never heard a complaint."

When they attended the Broadway show *42nd Street,* there was supposed to be no fanfare. It was planned that after the performance, the house would be cleared so that Jimmy and his group could exit quietly. As they started to depart, they were surprised to see the curtains open wide. The entire cast was assembled onstage to honor Jimmy with their own applause. Jimmy could not have been more touched, and his tears proved it. "I got up and spoke to them. I don't know what the hell I said. I guess I thanked them for a fine evening."

Jimmy appeared on a number of television talk shows after the release of *Ragtime,* something he had refused to do previously, and he was the recipient of the biggest round of applause in October 1982 when he appeared in a benefit for the Actors' Fund of America at Radio City Music Hall, "Night of a Hundred Stars."

Verney Farms is located on a remote country road near Stanfordville, New York. The nearest city of any size is Poughkeepsie, thirty miles west. To find the place requires intricate directions, but Cagney fans somehow manage to zero in on it with surprising frequency. They aren't fooled by the trim white cottage down the road, where the sign is located. They know that this is the original farmhouse, where the farm manager is housed, and that the Cagney residence is the brown one-story dwelling beyond the willow-draped road that winds up the hill. Marge, ever protective of Jimmy, frequently shoos the intruders away. But if they look all right to her, and if they are genteel and courteous, she may just invite them in for a quick hello.

"The trouble is," says Marge, "that Jimmy will usually say 'Pull up a chair and sit down.' If he had his way, sightseers would be filing in and out all day long." Jimmy recalls an incident that occurred one day when Marge was out of the house. A pair of teenage girls came to the open screen door and peered in at him. "Mr. Cagney?" they asked. Jimmy, not very ambulatory at that time, called out "Willie!" and the girls ran off in fright. "They must have thought I was calling out for help," he said, "but I was just trying to get Willie to answer the door. Poor kids, I felt sorry for them."

Marge takes Jimmy along when she goes on errands in the car or when she goes searching for "junk." The region is dotted with villages just a few miles apart. The optometrist is located in one town, the Chevy dealer in another, and to get the car washed you must drive ten miles in the opposite direction. Marge and Jimmy know the territory, down to the most obscure byways, and the local people know the Cagney station wagon on sight. "Jimmy's always waving to people," says Marge. "He waves to people whether thee him or not—he even waves to the grazing cows."

It is a countryside abounding in working farmers and super-rich celebrities. Meryl Streep has a place not far from Verney; so does Rodney Dangerfield. Milos Forman is only thirty miles away, and George C. Scott is another not-too-distant neighbor. The celebrities are sprinkled among the local folk, and neither group pays too much attention to the other. As with Marge's husband, Don, the local people seldom go out of their way to snuggle up to the famous. If they were bursting at the seams with enthusiasm, they would never let it show. This restraint is what makes Jimmy Cagney feel so comfortable here. He shares the same tendency.

The Cagney home is a simple dwelling of time-weathered wood, and Jimmy surrounds himself with furnishings as time-tempered as the wood used to construct the house. "I don't know why I like antiques," he says. "Must be because they have character, or maybe it's because they're old. Everything here is old—including me."

Including the recent additions constructed by Don Zimmermann, the house consists of seven rooms. The ceilings are low, less than seven feet, the beams are heavy, and the stone fireplace is mammoth. The handsome frosted door separating the downstairs rooms was originally a fixture at Vassar College. The bar is a dry sink, dating from about 1700, that was in the original house at Chilmark. Jimmy removed its zinc liner and had the old wood polished to a sheen. Over the fireplace is an ancient musket of grotesque length. "It's a woman's fowling piece from the seventeenth century," Jimmy explains. "In those days, what the hell, they all did it I suppose—hunt fowl."

There is an exquisite set of antique gold-trimmed glassware from New Zealand and a nineteenth-century maple desk that Jimmy picked up more than forty years ago. Behind Jimmy's easy chair is a magazine receptacle—at least that is its current role in life. When it was crafted in the eighteenth century, it was designed as a baby's crib. In the southwest corner of the room is a huge and ornate grand piano that both Jimmy and Willie play. But anyone could play this piano by merely inserting a music roll: it is a Sohmer player piano of early vintage.

Jimmy doesn't have a magnificent art collection, but his possessions are of high quality. He owns several western sculptures by Charles Russell, "and," he says, "I have some old Bongarth paintings." Sergei Bongrath is the eminent West Coast artist who taught Jimmy to paint in oils. His paintings are said to be worth forty or fifty thousand dollars apiece. As for paintings by James Cagney, Jimmy has exactly two. One of them, in the dining room of his house in Coldwater Canyon, is the impressive oil portrait of an old man. The other, entitled "The Victor," is a remarkable rendition of a battered prizefighter that illustrates perfectly Jimmy's modified views on the boxing profession.

Jimmy rarely signs his paintings, and he accepts no money for his work. He has turned down as much as fifteen thousand dollars for a Cagney original. "How could I face those really good artists who have given their whole lives to it—and still may be having a hard time making a living? I'm just a novice with some name value, and it's not right. No thanks." Jimmy did sell one painting, and it was signed. But that was at an auction for charity. The painting was bought at sixty-five hundred dollars by Johnny Carson.

When asked whether there were any regrets about the way he had lived his life, Jimmy says that there does exist an unfulfilled ambition. "I wanted to be an artist, and now that will never happen. I do these odd jobs now and then—that sometimes turn out all right, but other times, lousy. Art—that's the only thing I started out to do that I didn't finish."

Since Marge Zimmermann came into the lives of the Cagneys her responsibilities have expanded. She now kind of runs things, including the farm. When she assumed its management, only 30 of the 735 acres were under cultivation; now more than half are productive. They raise and sell oats, corn, hay, and straw, and earn enough money to pay for all the employees and the taxes on the property.

There are 125 head of cattle, only a few of which are mixed-bred Scottish Highlanders, once Jimmy's major breed. One of the Highlanders, with its long, reddish hair, has free rein of the acreage and is mistaken for a buffalo when seen from the road. It is so wild that no one has been near it in years.

Nine pure-bred Morgan horses remain. George C. Scott bought two of the original number not long ago and now buys hay from the Cagney farm to feed them. Marge says that six thousand dollars worth of hay was sold last year. Marge insists that she hates farming, but Jimmy, who admires her shrewd management and horse-trading instincts, doesn't believe her. "That isn't true at all," he says. "Actually, I only keep the farm as therapy for her."

It is Marge who acts as an intermediary between Jimmy and the outside world. When requests come in for interviews, television appearances, charity appearances, anything at all—Marge fields them and sorts them out before they reach Jimmy. He trusts her and usually heeds her advice. In Marge, he and Willie have a trusted companion, chief cook and bottle-washer, farmer, business manager, agent, and secretary. It is an arrangement that is perfect as far as the Cagneys are concerned.

At this time there is a project afoot for the filming of Jimmy Cagney's life story; tentative plans are being made for Jimmy to star in a theatrical classic for subscription television; there are parties interested in producing a stage musical based on Jimmy's life; and other proposals drift in with some frequency. "I'll stick it out here," says Jimmy, "and see what happens. If something comes up, fine. If there isn't anything—the hell with it."

When Jimmy is asked whether, during all the years of his career, there were any periods of particular happiness, without hesitation he chooses his early years at Warner Brothers. In particular, during the making of *Public Enemy* he was happy because he had something to work with, and William Wellman was a good director. He says that he had no idea how well he had done after the filming was completed, but the good reviews that came with the picture's release filled him with pride and at least fleeting happiness.

Life seemed good then. He was drawing the astronomical salary of $450 a week, the critics were praising his work, and the future seemed bright. These years between the ages of thirty and forty are remembered as the best, even though life began to get complicated. He did not become happier as his income increased, and his innocence was lost to worries about justice and injustice, about his rights and the treatment he was receiving from Warner Brothers. During those ten years, Jimmy had his most explosive confrontations with the studio heads. Perhaps what he is actually saying is that while those years may not have seemed the best at the time, they should have.

The membership of the Boys' Club has been reduced to three of its original members: Cagney, O'Brien, and Bellamy. The meetings aren't as frequent as they were, but telephone conversations are fairly regular.

Jimmy and Willie celebrated their sixtieth wedding anniversary in September 1982. Together they are living the philosophy of one of Jimmy's earliest poems: "Each man starts with his very first breath/To devise shrewd means for outwitting death."

Asked whether there is any particular way in which he would like to be remembered, Jimmy replied, "No." That is typical Cagney.

FILMOGRAPHY

Sinners' Holiday
Released in 1930
A Warner Brothers and Vitaphone Picture. Directed by John G. Adolfi.
Screenplay by Harvey Thew and George Rosener. Based on the play
Penny Arcade by Marie Baumer.
Cast: Grant Withers, Evalyn Knapp, James Cagney, Joan Blondell, Lucille LaVerne, Noel Madison, Otto Hoffman, Warren Hymer, Purnell B.
Pratt, Ray Gallagher, Hank Mann.

Doorway to Hell
Released in 1930
A Warner Brothers and Vitaphone Picture. Directed by Archie Mayo.
Screenplay by George Rosener. Based on the story "A Handful of
Clouds" by Rowland Brown.
Cast: Lew Ayres, Charles Judels, Dorothy Mathews, Leon Janncy, Robert Elliott, James Cagney, Kenneth Thomson, Jerry Mandy, Noel Madison, Bernard Granville, Fred Argus, Ruth Hall, Dwight Frye, Tom
Wilson, Al Hill.

Other Men's Women
Released in 1931
A Warner Brothers and Vitaphone Picture. Directed by William A. Wellman. Screenplay by William K. Wells. Based on a story by Maude
Fulton.
Cast: Grant Withers, Mary Astor, Regis Toomey, James Cagney, Joan
Blondell, Fred Kohler, J. Farrell MacDonald, Lillian Worth, Walter
Long, Bob Perry, Lee Morgan, Kewpie Morgan, Pat Hartigan.

The Millionaire
Released in 1931

A Warner Brothers and Vitaphone Picture. Directed by John G. Adolfi. Screenplay by Julian Josephson and Maude T. Powell. Based on *Idle Hands* by Earl Derr Biggers.
Cast: George Arliss, Evalyn Knapp, David Manners, James Cagney, Bramwell Fletcher, Florence Arliss, Noah Beery, Ivan Simpson, Sam Hardy, J. Farrell MacDonald, Tully Marshall, J. C. Nugent.

The Public Enemy
Released in 1931
A Warner Brothers and Vitaphone Picture. Directed by William A. Wellman. Screenplay by Kubec Glasmon and John Bright. Based on the novel *Beer and Blood* by John Bright.
Cast: James Cagney, Jean Harlow, Edward Woods, Joan Blondell, Beryl Mercer, Donald Cook, Mae Clarke, Mia Marvin, Leslie Fenton, Robert Emmett O'Connor, Murray Kinnell, Ben Hendricks, Jr., Rita Flynn, Clark Burroughs, Snitz Edwards, Adele Watson, Frank Coghlan, Jr., Frankie Darro, Robert E. Homans, Dorothy Gee, Purnell Pratt, Lee Phelps, Helen Parrish, Dorothy Gray, Nanci Price, Ben Hendricks, III, George Daly, Eddie Kane, Charles Sullivan, Douglas Gerrard, Sam McDaniel, William H. Strauss.

Smart Money
Released in 1931
A Warner Brothers and Vitaphone Picture. Directed by Alfred E. Green. Screenplay by Kubec Glasmon and John Bright. Based on an original story by Lucien Hubbard and Joseph Jackson.
Cast: Edward G. Robinson, Evalyn Knapp, James Cagney, Noel Francis, Morgan Wallace, Paul Porcasi, Maurice Black, Margaret Livingston, Clark Burroughs, Billy House, Edwin Argus, Ralf Harolde, Boris Karloff, Mae Madison, Walter Percival, John Larkin, Polly Walters, Ben Taggart, Gladys Lloyd, Eulalie Jensen, Charles Lane, Edward Hearn, Eddie Kane, Clinton Rosemond, Charles O'Malley, Gus Leonard, Wallace MacDonald, John George, Harry Semels, Charlotte Merriam, Larry McGrath, Spencer Bell, Allan Lane.

Blonde Crazy
Released in 1931
A Warner Brothers and Vitaphone Picture. Directed by Roy Del Ruth. Screenplay by Kubec Glasmon and John Bright.
Cast: James Cagney, Joan Blondell, Louis Calhern, Noel Francis, Guy Kibbee, Raymond Milland, Polly Walters, Charles (Levinson) Lane, William Buress, Peter Erkelenz, Maude Eburne, Walter Percival, Nat Pendleton, Russell Hopton, Dick Cramer, Wade Boteler, Ray Cooke, Edward Morgan, Phil Sleman.

Taxi!
Released in 1932
A Warner Brothers and Vitaphone Picture. Directed by Roy Del Ruth.
Screenplay by Kubec Glasmon and John Bright. Based on the play *The
Blind Spot* by Kenyon Nicholson.
Cast: James Cagney, Loretta Young, George E. Atone, Guy Kibbee,
David Landau, Ray Cooke, Leila Bennett, Dorothy Burgess, Matt
McHugh, George MacFarlane, Polly Walters, Nat Pendleton, Berton
Churchill, George Raft, Hector V. Sarno, Aggie Herring, Lee Phelps,
Harry Tenbrook, Robert Emmett O'Connor, Eddie Featherstone, Russ
Powell, Ben Taggart, the Cotton Club Orchestra.

The Crowd Roars
Released in 1932
A Warner Brothers and Vitaphone Picture. Directed by Howard Hawks.
Screenplay by Kubec Glasmon, John Bright, and Niven Busch. Based on
a story by Howard Hawks and Seton I. Miller.
Cast: James Cagney, Joan Blondell, Ann Dvorak, Eric Linden, Guy Kib-
bee, Frank McHugh, William Arnold, Leo Nomis, Charlotte Merriam,
Regis Toomey, Harry Hartz, Ralph Hepburn, Fred Guisso, Fred Frame,
Phil Pardee, Spider Matlock, Jack Brisko, Lou Schneider, Bryan Sal-
spaugh, Stubby Stubblefield, Shorty Cantlon, Mel Keneally, Wilbur
Shaw, James Burtis, Sam Hayes, Robert McWade, Ralph Dunn, John
Conte, John Harron.

Winner Take All
Released in 1932
A Warner Brothers and Vitaphone Picture. Directed by Roy Del Ruth.
Screenplay by Wilson Mizner and Robert Lord. Based on the magazine
story "133 at 3" by Gerald Beaumont.
Cast: James Cagney, Marian Nixon, Virginia Bruce, Guy Kibbee, Clar-
ence Muse, Dickie Moore, Allan Lane, John Roche, Ralf Harolde, Alan
Mowbray, Clarence Wilson, Charles Coleman, Esther Howard, Renee
Whitney, Harvey Perry, Julian Rivero, Selmer Jackson, Chris Pin Mar-
tin, George Hayes, Bob Perry, Billy West, Phil Tead, Rolfe Sedan, John
Kelly, Lee Phelps, Jay Eaton, Charlotte Merriam.

Hard to Handle
Released in 1933
A Warner Brothers and Vitaphone Picture. Directed by Mervyn LeRoy.
Screenplay by Wilson Mizner and Robert Lord. Based on a story by
Houston Branch.
Cast: James Cagney, Mary Brian, Ruth Donnelly, Allen Jenkins, Claire

Dodd, Gavin Gordon, Emma Dunn, Robert McWade, John Sheehan, Matt McHugh, Louise Mackintosh, William H. Strauss, Bess Flowers, Lew Kelly, Berton Churchill, Harry Holman, Grace Hale, George Pat Collins, Douglas Dumbrille, Sterling Holloway, Charles Wilson, Jack Crawford, Stanley Smith, Walt Walker, Mary Doran.

Picture Snatcher
Released in 1933
A Warner Brothers and Vitaphone Picture. Directed by Lloyd Bacon. Screenplay by Allen Rivkin and P. J. Wolfson. Based on a story by Danny Ahern.
Cast: James Cagney, Ralph Bellamy, Patricia Ellis, Alice White, Ralf Harolde, Robert Emmett O'Connor, Robert Barrat, George Pat Collins, Tom Wilson, Barbara Rogers, Renee Whitney, Alice Jans, Jill Dennett, Billy West, George Daly, Arthur Vinton, Stanley Blystone, Don Brody, George Chandler, Sterling Holloway, Donald Kerr, Hobart Cavanaugh, Phil Tead, Charles King, Milton Kibbee, Dick Elliott, Vaughan Taylor, Bob Perry, Gino Corrado, Maurice Black, Selmer Jackson, Jack Grey, John Ince, Cora Sue Collins.

The Mayor of Hell
Released in 1933
A Warner Brothers and Vitaphone Picture. Directed by Archie Mayo. Screenplay by Edward Chodorov. Based on a story by Islin Auster.
Cast: James Cagney, Madge Evans, Allen Jenkins, Dudley Digges, Frankie Darro, Farina, Dorothy Peterson, John Marston, Charles Wilson, Hobart Cavanaugh, Raymond Borzage, Robert Barrat, George Pat Collins, Mickey Bennett, Arthur Byron, Sheila Terry, Harold Huber, Edwin Maxwell, William V. Mong, Sidney Miller, George Humbert, George Offerman, Jr., Charles Kane, Wallace MacDonald, Adrian Morris, Snowflake, Wilfred Lucas, Bob Perry, Charles Sullivan, Ben Taggart.

Footlight Parade
Released in 1933
A Warner Brothers and Vitaphone Picture. Directed by Lloyd Bacon and Busby Berkeley. Screenplay by Manuel Seff and James Seymour. Songs: "By a Waterfall," "Ah, the Moon Is Here," "Sittin' on a Backyard Fence (by Sammy Fain and Irving Kahal)," "Shanghai Lil," "Honeymoon Hotel" (by Harris Warren and Al Dubin).
Cast: James Cagney, Joan Blondell, Ruby Keeler, Dick Powell, Guy Kibbee, Ruth Donnelly, Claire Dodd, Hugh Herbert, Jimmy McHugh, Arthur Hohl, Herbert Wescott, Renee Whitney, Philip Faversham, Juliet Ware, Herman Bing, Paul Porcasi, William Franger, Charles C. Wilson,

Barbara Rogers, Billy Taft, Marjean Rogers, Pat Wing, Donna Mae
Roberts, Dave O'Brien, George Chandler, Hobart Cavanaugh, William
V. Mong, Lee Moran, Billy Barty, Harry Seymour, Sam McDaniel, Fred
Kelsey, Jimmy Conlin, Roger Gray, John Garfield, Duke York, Harry
Seymour, Donna LaBarr, Marlo Dwyer.

Lady Killer
Released in 1933
A Warner Brothers and Vitaphone Picture. Directed by Roy Del Ruth.
Screenplay by Ben Markson. Based on "The Finger Man" by Rosalind
Keating Shaffer.
Cast: James Cagney, Mae Clarke, Leslie Fenton, Margaret Lindsay,
Henry O'Neill, Willard Robertson, Douglas Cosgrove, Raymond Hatton,
Russell Hopton, William Davidson, Marjorie Gateson, Robert Elliott,
John Marston, Douglass Dumbrille, George Chandler, George Black-
wood, Jack Don Wong, Frank Sheridan, Edwin Maxwell, Phil Tead,
Dewey Robinson, H. C. Bradley, Harry Holman, Harry Beresford, Olaf
Hytten, Harry Strong, Al Hill, Bud Flanagan, James Burke, Robert
Homans, Clarence Wildon, Sam McDaniel, Spencer Charters, Herman
Bing, Harold Waldridge, Luis Alberni, Ray Cooke, Sam Ash.

Jimmy the Gent
Released in 1934
A Warner Brothers and Vitaphone Picture. Directed by Michael Curtiz.
Executive producer, Jack L. Warner. Screenplay by Bertram Milhauser.
Based on an original story by Laird Doyle and Ray Nazarro.
Cast: James Cagney, Bette Davis, Alice White, Allen Jenkins, Arthur
Hohl, Alan Dinehart, Philip Reed, Hobart Cavanaugh, Mayo Methot,
Ralf Harolde, Joe Sawyer, Philip Faversham, Nora Lane, Joseph Crehan,
Robert Warwick, Merna Kennedy, Renee Whitney, Monica Bannister,
Don Douglas, Bud Flanagan, Leonard Mudie, Harry Holman, Camille
Rovelle, Stanley Mack, Tom Costello, Ben Hendricks, Billy West, Eddie
Shubert, Lee Moran, Harry Wallace, Robert Homans, Milton Kibbee,
Howard Hickman, Eula Gay, Juliet Ware, Rickey Newell, Lorena Lay-
son, Dick French, Jay Eaton, Harold Entwhistle, Charles Hickman, Olag
Hytten, Vesey O'Davoren, Lester Dore, Pat Wing.

He Was Her Man
Released in 1934
A Warner Brothers and Vitaphone Picture. Directed by Lloyd Bacon.
Screenplay by Tom Buckingham and Niven Busch. Based on a story by
Robert Lord.
Cast: James Cagney, Joan Blondell, Victor Jory, Frank Craven, Harold

Huber, Russell Hopton, Ralf Harolde, Sarah Padden, J. M. Qualen, Bradley Page, Samuel S. Hinds, George Chandler, James Eagles, Gino Corrado.

Here Comes the Navy
Released in 1934
A Warner Brothers and Vitaphone Picture. Directed by Lloyd Bacon. Screenplay by Ben Markson and Earl Baldwin. Based on a story by Ben Markson.
Cast: James Cagney, Pat O'Brien, Gloria Stuart, Frank McHugh, Dorothy Tree, Robert Barratt, Willard Robertson, Guinn Williams, Maude Eburne, Martha Merrill, Lorena Layson, Ida Darling, Henry Otho, Pauline True, Sam McDaniel, Frank LaRue, Joseph Crehan, James Burtis, Edward Chandler, Leo White, Niles Welch, Fred "Snowflake" Toone, Eddie Shubert, George Irving, Howard Hickman, Edward Earle, Gordon Elliott, Nick Copeland, John Swore, Eddie Acuff, Chuck Hamilton, Eddie Featherstone.

The St. Louis Kid
Released in 1934
A Warner Brothers and Vitaphone Picture. Directed by Ray Enright. Screenplay by Warren Duff and Seton I. Miller. Based on a story by Frederick Hazlitt Brennan.
Cast: James Cagney, Patricia Ellis, Allen Jenkins, Robert Barrat, Hobart Cavanaugh, Spencer Charters, Dorothy Dare, Arthur Aylesworth, Charles Wilson, William Davidson, Harry Woods, Gertrude Short, Eddie Shubert, Russell Hicks, Guy Usher, Cliff Saum, Bruce Mitchell, Wilfred Lucas, Rosalie Roy, Mary Russell, Ben Hendricks, Harry Tyler, Milton Kibbee, Tom Wilson, Alice Marr, Victoria Vinton, Lee Phelps, Louise Seidel, Mary Treen, Nan Grey, Virginia Grey, Martha Merrill, Charles B. Middleton, Douglas Cosgrove, Monte Vandergrift, Jack Cheatham, Stanley Mack, Grover Liggen, Frank Bull, Wade Boteler, Frank Fanning, Gene Strong, Edna Bennett, Clay Clement, James Burtis, Eddie Featherstone, Joan Barclay.

Devil Dogs of the Air
Released in 1935
A Warner Brothers Picture–A Cosmopolitan Production. Directed by Lloyd Bacon. Produced by Lou Edelman. Screenplay by Michael Stuart Boylan and Earl Baldwin. Based on the story "Air Devils" by John Monk Saunders.
Cast: James Cagney, Pat O'Brien, Margaret Lindsay, Frank McHugh, Helen Lowell, John Arledge, Robert Barrat, Russell Hicks, William B.

Davidson, Ward Bond, Samuel S. Hinds, Harry Seymour, Bill Beggs, Bob Spencer, Newton House, Ralph Nye, Selmer Jackson, Bud Flanagan (later Dennis O'Keefe), Bill Elliott, Don Turner.

G-Men
Released in 1935
A Warner Brothers–First National Picture. Directed by William Keighley. Screenplay by Seton I. Miller. Based on "Public Enemy No. 1" by Gregory Rogers.
Cast: James Cagney, Ann Dvorak, Margaret Lindsay, Robert Armstrong, Barton MacLane, Lloyd Nolan, William Harrigan, Edward Pawley, Russell Hopton, Noel Madison, Regis Toomey, Addison Richards, Harold Huber, Raymond Hatton, Monte Blue, Mary Treen, Adrian Morris, Edwin Maxwell, Emmett Vogan, James Flavin, Stanley Blystone, Pat Flaherty, James T. Mack, Jonathan Hale, Ed Keau, Charles Sherlock, Wheeler Oakman, Eddie Dunn, Bill Elliott, Perry Ivins, Frank Marlowe, Gertrude Short, Marie Astaire, Florence Dudley, Frances Morris, Al Hill, Huey White, Glen Cavender, John Impolito, Bruce Mitchell, Monte Vandergrift, Frank Shannon, Frank Bull, Martha Merrill, Gene Morgan, Joseph D. Stefani, George Daly, Ward Bond, Tom Wilson, Henry Hall, Lee Phelps, Marc Lawrence, Brooks Benedict.

The Irish in Us
Released in 1935
A Warner Brothers–First National Picture. Directed by Lloyd Bacon. Screenplay by Earl Baldwin. Based on a story by Frank Orsatti.
Cast: James Cagney, Pat O'Brien, Olivia De Havilland, Frank McHugh, Allen Jenkins, Mary Gordon, J. Farrell MacDonald, Thomas Jackson, Harvey Perry, Bess Flowers, Mabel Colcord, Edward Keane, Herb Haywood, Lucille Collins, Harry Seymour, Sailor Vincent, Mushy Callahan, Jack McHugh, Edward Gargan, Huntley Gordon, Emmett Vogan, Will Stanton.

A Midsummer Night's Dream
Released in 1935
A Warner Brothers Picture. Directed by Max Reinhardt and William Dieterle. Produced by Jack L. Warner. Scenario by Charles Kenyon and Mary McCall, Jr. Based on the play by William Shakespeare.
Cast: James Cagney, Dick Powell, Joe E. Brown, Jean Muir, Hugh Herbert, Ian Hunter, Frank McHugh, Victor Jory, Olivia De Havilland, Grant Mitchell, Nini Theilade, Verree Teasdale, Anita Louise, Mickey Rooney, Dewey Robinson, Hobart Cavanaugh, Otis Harlan, Arthur Treacher, Katherine Frey, Helen Westcott, Fred Sale, Billy Barty.

Frisco Kid
Released in 1935
A Warner Brothers–First National Picture. Directed by Lloyd Bacon. Produced by Samuel Bischoff. Screenplay by Warren Duff and Seton I. Miller. Based on an original story by Warren Duff and Seaton Miller.
Cast: James Cagney, Margaret Lindsay, Ricardo Cortez, Lily Damita, Donald Woods, Barton MacLane, George E. Stone, Addison Richards, Joseph King, Robert McWade, Joseph Crehan, Robert Strange, Joe Sawyer, Fred Kohler, Edward McWade, Claudia Coleman, John Wray, Ivar McFadden, Lee Phelps, William Wagner, Don Barclay, Jack Curtis, Walter Long, James Farley, Milton Kibbee, Harry Seymour, Claire Sinclair, Alan Davis, Carl Hackett, Wilfred Lucas, John T. Dillon, Edward Mortimer, William Holmes, Don Downen, Mrs. Wilfred North, Charles Middleton, Joe Smith Marba, Helen Chadwick, Dick Kerr, Alice Lake, Vera Stedman, Jane Tallent.

Ceiling Zero
Released in 1935
A Warner Brothers–First National Picture. Directed by Howard Hawks. Produced by Harry Joe Brown. Screenplay by Frank Wead. Based on the play *Ceiling Zero* by Frank Wead.
Cast: James Cagney, Pat O'Brien, June Travis, Stuart Erwin, Henry Wadsworth, Isabel Jewell, Barton MacLane, Martha Tibbetts, Joe Allen, Craig Reynolds, James Bush, Robert Light, Addison Richards, Addison Moore, Jr., Richard Purcell, Bill Elliott, Pat West, Ed Gargan, Gary Owen, Mathilde Comont, Carol Hughes, Frank Tomick, Paul Matz, Jimmy Aye, Howard Allen, Mike Lalley, Harold Miller, Jerry Jerome, Helene McAdoo, Gay Sheridan, Dick Cherney, Jayne Manners, Maryon Curtiz, Margaret Perry.

Great Guy
Released in 1936
A Grand National Picture. Directed by John G. Blystone. Produced by Douglas MacLean. Screenplay by Henry McCarthy, Henry Johnson, James Edward Grant, and Harry Ruskin. Based on the Johnny Cave stories by James Edward Grant.
Cast: James Cagney, Mae Clarke, James Burke, Edward Brophy, Henry Kolker, Bernadene Hayes, Edward J. McNamara, Robert Gleckler, Joe Sawyer, Ed Gargan, Matty Fain, Mary Gordon, Wallis Clark, Douglas Wood, Jeffrey Sayre, Eddy Chandler, Henry Roquemore, Murdock MacQuarrie, Kate Price, Frank O'Connor, Arthur Hoyt, Jack Pennick, Lynton Brent, John Dilson, Ben Geary, Dennis O'Keefe, Robert Lowery, Barbie Barber, Gertrude Green, Bruce Mitchell, James Ford, Lester

Door, Harry Tenbrook, Mildred Harris, Bert Kalmar, Jr., Walter D. Clarke, Jr.

Something to Sing About
Released in 1937
A Grand National Picture. Directed by Victor Schertzinger. Produced by Zion Myers. Screenplay by Austin Parker. Songs: "Right or Wrong," "Any Old Love," "Something to Sing About," "Loving You," "Out of the Blue," by Victor Schertzinger.
Cast: James Cagney, Evelyn Daw, William Frawley, Mona Barrie, Gene Lockhart, James Newill, Harry Barris, Candy Candido, Cully Richards, William B. Davidson, Richard Tucker, Marek Windheim, Dwight Frye, John Arthur, Philip Ahn, Kathleen Lockhart, Kenneth Harlan, Herbert Rawlinson, Ernest Wood, Chick Collins, Duke Green, Harlan Dixon, Johnny Boyle, Johnny Miller, Pat Moran, Joe Bennett, Buck Mack, Eddie Allen, Eddie Kane, Edward Hearn, Dottie Messmer, Virginia Lee Irwin, Dollie Waldrof, Robert McKenzie, Alphonse Martel, Bo Peep Karlin, Paul McLarand.

Boy Meets Girl
Released in 1938
A Warner Brothers Picture. Directed by Lloyd Bacon. Produced by Hal Wallis. Screenplay by Bella Spewack and Sam Spewack. Song: "With a Pain in My Heart," by Jack School and M. K. Jerome.
Cast: James Cagney, Pat O'Brien, Marie Wilson, Ralph Bellamy, Frank McHugh, Dick Foran, Bruce Lester, Ronald Reagan, Paul Clark, Penny Singleton, Denny Moore, Harry Seymour, Bert Hanlon, James Stephenson, Pierre Watkin, John Ridgely, George Hickman, Cliff Saum, Carole Landis, Curt Bois, Otto Fries, John Harron, Hal K. Dawson, Dorothy Vaughan, Bert Howard, James Nolan, Bill Teleak, Vera Lewis, Jan Holm, Rosella Towne, Loi Cheaney, Janet Shaw, Nanette LaFayette, Peggy Moran, Eddy Conrad, Sidney Bracy, William Haade, Clem Bevans.

Angels with Dirty Faces
Released in 1938
A Warner Brothers Picture. Directed by Michael Curtiz. Produced by Sam Bischoff. Screenplay by John Wexley and Warren Duff. Based on an original story by Rowland Brown.
Cast: James Cagney, Pat O'Brien, Humphrey Bogart, Ann Sheridan, George Bancroft, Billy Halop, Bobby Jordan, Leo Gorcey, Bernard Punsley, Gabriel Dell, Huntz Hall, Frankie Burke, William Tracy, Marilyn Knowlden, Joe Downing, Adrian Morris, Oscar O'Shea, Edward

Pawley, William Pawley, John Hamilton, Earl Dwire, Jack Perrin, Mary Gordon, Vera Lewis, William Worthington, James Farley, Chuck Stubbs, Eddie Syracuse, Robert Homans, Harris Berger, Harry Hayden, Dick Rich, Steven Darrell, Joe A. Devlon, William Edmunds, Charles Wilson, Frank Coughlin, Jr., David Durand, Bill Cohee, Lavel Lund, Norman Wallace, Gary Carthew, Bibby Mayer, Belle Mitchell, Eddie Bryan, Billy McLain, Wilbur Mack, Poppy Wilde, George Offerman, Jr., Charles Trowbridge, Ralph Sanford, Wilfred Lucas, Lane Chandler, Elliot Sullivan, Lottie Williams, George Mori, Dick Wessell, John Harron, Vince Lombardi, Al Hill, Thomas Jackson, Jeffrey Sayer.

The Oklahoma Kid
Released in 1939
A Warner Brothers–First National Picture. Directed by Lloyd Bacon. Associate producer, Samual Bischoff. Screenplay by Warren Duff, Robert Buckner, and Edward E. Paramore. Based on an original story by Edward E. Paramore and Wally Klein.
Cast: James Cagney, Humphrey Bogart, Rosemary Lane, Donald Crisp, Harvey Stephens, Hugh Sothern, Charles Middleton, Edward Pawley, Ward Bond, Lew Harvey, Trevor Bardette, John Miljan, Arthur Aylesworth, Irving Bacon, Joe Devlin, Wade Boteler, Ray Mayer, Dan Wolheim, Bob Kortman, Tex Cooper, John Harron, Stuart Holmes, Jeffrey Sayre, Frank Mayo, Frank Mower, Al Bridge, Don Barclay, Horace Murphy, Robert Homans, George Lloyd, Rosina Galli, George Regas, Clem Bevans, Soledad Jimenez, Ed Brady, Tom Chatterton, Elliott Sullivan, Joe Kirkson, William Worthington, Spencer Charters.

Each Dawn I Die
Released in 1939
A Warner Brothers–First National Picture. Directed by William Keighley. Associate producer, David Lewis. Screenplay by Norman Reilly Raine, Warren Duff, and Charles Perry. Based on the novel by Jerome Odlum.
Cast: James Cagney, George Raft, Jane Bryan, George Bancroft, Maxie Rosenbloom, Stanley Ridges, Alan Baxter, Victor Jory, John Wray, Edward Pawley, William Robertson, Emma Dunn, Paul Hurst, Louis Jean Heydt, Joe Downing, Thurston Hall, William Davidson, Clay Clement, Charles Trowbridge, Harry Cording, John Harron, John Ridgely, Selmer Jackson, Robert Homans, Abner Biberman, Napoleon Simpson, Stuart Holmes, Maris Wrixon, Arthur Gardner, James Flavin, Walter Miller, Fred Graham, Wilfred Lucas, Vera Lewis, Emmett Vogan, Earl Dwire, Bob Perry, Al Hill, Elliott Sullivan, Chuck Hamilton, Nat Carr, Wedgewood Nowell, Frank Mayo, Dick Rich, Lee Phelps, Jack Wise, Granville Bates.

The Roaring Twenties
Released in 1939
A Warner Brothers–First National Picture. Directed by Raoul Walsh. Produced by Hal B. Wallis. Screenplay by Jerry Wald, Richard Macauley, and Robert Rossen. Based on an original story by Mark Hellinger.
Cast: James Cagney, Priscilla Lane, Humphrey Bogart, Jeffrey Lynn, Gladys George, Frank McHugh, Paul Kelly, Elisabeth Risdon, Ed Keane, Joe Sawyer, Abner Biberman, George Humbert, Clay Clement, Don Thaddeus Kerr, Ray Cooke, Vera Lewis, Murray Alper, Dick Wessel, Joseph Crehan, Norman Willis, Robert Elliott, Eddy Chandler, John Hamilton, Eddie Sullivan, Pat O'Malley, Arthur Loft, Al Hill, Lew Harvey, Joe Devlin, Jeffrey Sayre, George Meeker, Jack Norton, Alan Bridge, Fred Graham, James Blaine, Henry Bradley, Lottie Williams, John Deering, John Harron, Lee Phelps, Nat Carr, Wade Boteler, Creighton Hale, Ann Codee, Eddie Acuff, Milton Kibbee, John Ridgely, James Flavin, Oscar O'Shea, Frank Wilcox, Harry Hollingsworth, Frank Mayo, Emory Parnell, Billy Wayne, Philip Morris, Maurice Costello, John St. Clair.

The Fighting 69th
Released in 1940
A Warner Brothers Picture. Directed by William Keighley. Produced by Jack L. Warner. Executive producer, Hal B. Wallis. Screenplay by Norman Reilly Raine, Fred Niblo, Jr., and Dean Franklin.
Cast: James Cagney, Pat O'Brien, George Brent, Jeffrey Lynn, Alan Hale, Frank McHugh, Dennis Morgan, Dick Foran, William Lundigan, Guinn William, Henry O'Neill, John Litel, Sammy Cohen, Harvey Stephens, DeWolfe Hopper, Tom Dugan, George Reeves, John Ridgely, Charles Trowbridge, Frank Wilcox, Herbert Anderson, J. Anthony Hughes, Frank Mayo, John Harron, George Kilgen, Richard Clayton, Edward Dew, Wilfred Lucas, Emmett Vogan, Frank Sully, James Flavin, George O'Hanlon, George Perrin, Trevor Bardette, John Arledge, Frank Melton, Edward Glover, Frank Faylen, Edgar Edwards, Ralph Dunn, Arno Frey, Roland Varno, Robert Layne Ireland, Elmo Murray, Jacques Lory, Jack Boyle, Jr., Creighton Hale, Benny Rubin, Eddie Acuff, Jack Mower, Nat Carr, Jack Wise.

Torrid Zone
Released in 1940
A Warner Brothers–First National Picture. Directed by William Keighley. Producer, Mark Hellinger. Original screenplay by Richard Macaulay and Jerry Wald.

Cast: James Cagney, Pat O'Brien, Ann Sheridan, Andy Devine, Helen Vinson, Jerome Cowan, George Tobias, George Reeves, Victor Kilion, Frank Puglia, John Ridgley, Grady Sutton, Paul Porcasi, Frank Yaconelli, Dick Boteler, Frank Mayo, Jack Mower, Paul Hurst, George Regas, Elvira Sanchez, George Humbert, Trevor Bardette, Ernesto Piedra, Manuel Lopez, Tony Paton, Max Blum, Betty Sanko, Don Orlando, Victor Sabuni, Paul Renay, Joe Molina.

City for Conquest
Released in 1941
A Warner Brothers–First National Picture. Directed and produced by Anatole Litvak. Associate producer, William Cagney. Screenplay by John Wexley. Based on the novel by Aben Kandel.
Cast: James Cagney, Ann Sheridan, Frank Craven, Donald Crisp, Arthur Kennedy, Frank McHugh, George Tobias, Jerome Cowan, Anthony Quinn, Lee Patrick, Blanche Yurka, George Lloyd, Joyce Compton, Thurston Hall, Ben Welden, John Arledge, Ed Keane, Selmer Jackson, Joseph Crehan, Bob Steele, Billy Wayne, Pat Flaherty, Sidney Miller, Ethelreda Leopold, Lee Phelps, Charles Wilson, Ed Gargan, Howard Hickman, Murray Alper, Dick Wessell, Bernice Pilot, Charles Lane, Dana Dale, Ed Pawley, William Newell, Lucia Carroll.

The Strawberry Blonde
Released in 1941
A Warner Brothers–First National Picture. Directed by Raoul Walsh. Produced by Jack L. Warner and Hal B. Wallis. Associate producer, William Cagney. Screenplay by Julius J. Epstein and Philip G. Epstein. Based on the play *One Sunday Afternoon* by James Hagan.
Cast: James Cagney, Olivia De Havilland, Rita Hayworth, Alan Hale, George Tobias, Jack Carson, Una O'Connor, George Reeves, Lucile Fairbanks, Edward McNamara, Herbert Heywood, Helen Lynd, Roy Gordon, Tim Ryan, Addison Richards, Frank Mayo, Jack Daley, Suzanne Carnahan (later Susan Peters), Herbert Anderson, Frank Orth, James Flavin, George Campeau, Abe Dinovitch, George Humbert, Creighton Hale, Russell Hicks, Wade Boteler, Peter Ashley, Roy Gordon, Max Hoffman, Jr., Pat Flaherty, Peggy Diggins, Bob Perry, Dorothy Gaughan, Richard Clayton, Ann Edmonds, Lucia Carroll, Harrison Green, Eddie Chandler, Carl Harbaugh, Frank Melton, Dick Wessell, Paul Barrett, Nora Gale.

The Bride Came C.O.D.
Released in 1941
A Warner Brothers–First National Picture. Directed by William Keigh-

ley. Executive producer, Hal B. Wallis. Associate producer, William Cagney. Screenplay by Julius J. Epstein and Philip G. Epstein. Based on a story by Kenneth Earl and M. M. Musselman.

Cast: James Cagney, Bette Davis, Stuart Erwin, Jack Carson, George Tobias, Eugene Pallette, Harry Davenport, William Frawley, Edward Brophy, Harry Holman, Chick Chandler, Keith Douglas (later Douglas Kennedy), Herbert Anderson, William Hopper, William Newell, Charles Sullivan, Eddie Chandler, Tony Hughes, Lee Phelps, Jean Ames, Alphonse Martell, Olaf Hytten, James Flavin, Sam Hayes, William Justice, Lester Towne, Richard Clayton, Garland Smith, Claude Wisberg, Lucia Carroll, Peter Ashley, John Ridgley, Saul Gorss, Jack Mower, Creighton Hale, Garrett Craig.

Captain of the Clouds
Released in 1942
A Warner Brothers–First National Picture. Directed by Michael Curtiz. Produced by Hal B. Wallis. Associate producer, William Cagney. Screenplay by Arthur T. Horman, Richard Macaulay, and Norman Reilly Raine. Based on a story by Arthur T. Horman and Roland Gillett.

Cast: James Cagney, Dennis Morgan, Brenda Marshall, Alan Hale, George Tobias, Reginald Gardner, Reginald Denny, Russell Arms, Paul Cananaugh, Clem Bevans, J. M. Kerrigan, J. Farell MacDonald, Patrick O'Moore, Morton Lowry, O. Cathcart-Jones, Frederic Worlock, Roland Drew, Lucien Carroll, George Meeker, Benny Baker, Hardie Albright, Roy Walker, Charles Halton, Louis Jean Heydt, Bryon Barr, Michael Ames, William Fung, Carl Harbord, James Stevens, Bill Wilkerson, Frank Lackteen, Edward McNamara, Charles Smith, Emmett Vogan, Winifred Harris, Miles Mander, Pat Flaherty, Tom Dugan, George Offerman, Jr., Gavin Muir, Larry Williams, John Hartley, John Kellogg, Charles Irwin, Billy Wayne, Rafael Storm, John Gaullaudet, Barry Bernard, George Ovey, Walter Brooks, Ray Montgomery, Herbert Gunn, Donald Dillaway, James Bush.

Yankee Doodle Dandy
Released in 1942
A Warner Brothers–First National Picture. Directed by Michael Curtiz. Producer, Jack L. Warner. Executive producer, Hal B. Wallis. Associate producer, William Cagney. Screenplay by Robert Buckner and Edmund Joseph. Based on an original story by Robert Buckner. Songs: "I Was Born in Virginia," "The Warmest Baby in the Bunch," "Give My Regards to Broadway," "Mary's a Grand Old Name," "So Long Mary," "Yankee Doodle Dandy," "Over There," "Harrigan," "Forty-Five Minutes from Broadway," "You're a Grand Old Flag" (by George M. Cohan); "All Aboard for Old Broadway" by Jack Scholl and M. K. Jerome.

Cast: James Cagney, Joan Leslie, Walter Huston, Richard Whorf, George Tobias, Irene Manning, Rosemary De Camp, Jeanne Cagney, S.C. Sakall, George Barbier, Walter Catlett, Frances Langford, Minor Watson, Eddie Foy, Jr., Chester Clute, Douglas Croft, Patsy Lee Parsons, Captain Jack Young, Audrey Long, Odette Myrtil, Clinton Rosemond, Spencer Charters, Dorothy Kelly, Marijo James, Henry Blair, Jo Ann Marlowe, Thomas Jackson, Phyllis Kennedy, Pat Flaherty, Leon Belasco, Syd Saylor, William B. Davidson, Harry Hayden, Frances Pierlot, Charles Smith, Joyce Reynolds, Dick Chandlee, Joyce Horn, Frank Faylen, Wallis Clark, Georgia Carroll, Joan Winfield, Dick Wessell, James Flaven, Sailor Vincent, George Meeker, Frank Mayo, Tom Dugan, Murray Alper, Garry Owen, Ruth Robinson, Eddie Acuff, Walter Brooke, Bill Edwards, William Hopper, William Forrest, Ed Keane, Dolores Moran, Poppy Wilde, Lorraine Gettman.

Johnny Come Lately
Released in 1943.
A William Cagney Picture. Directed by William K. Howard. Produced by William Cagney. Screenplay by John Van Druten. Based on the novel *McCleod's Folly* by Louis Bromfield.
Cast: James Cagney, Grace George, Marjorie Main, Marjorie Lord, Hattie McDaniel, Edward McNamara, Bill Henry, Robert Barrat, George Cleveland, Margaret Hamilton, Norman Willis, Lucien Littlefield, Edwin Stanley, Irving Bacon, Tom Dugan, Charles Irwin, John Sheehan, Clarence Muse, John Miller, Arthur Hunnicutt, Victor Kilian, Wee Willie Davis, Henry Hall.

Blood on the Sun
Released in 1945
A William Cagney Production. Directed by Frank Lloyd. Produced by William Cagney. Screenplay by Lester Cole. Based on a story by Garrett Fort.
Cast: James Cagney, Sylvia Sidney, Wallace Ford, Rosemary De Camp, Robert Armstrong, John Emory, Leonard Strong, Frank Puglia, Jack Halloran, Hugh Ho, Philip Ahn, Joseph Kim, Marvin Miller, Rhys Williams, Porter Hall, James Bell, Grace Lem, Oy Chan, George Paris, Hugh Beaumont, Gregory Gay, Arthur Loft, Emmett Vogan, Charlie Wayne.

13 Rue Madeleine
Released in 1946
A Twentieth Century–Fox Production. Directed by Henry Hathaway. Produced by Louis De Rochemont. Original screenplay by John Monks, Jr., and Sy Bartlett.

Cast: James Cagney, Annabella, Richard Conte, Frank Latimore, Walter Abel, Melville Cooper, Sam Jaffee, Marcel Rousseau, Richard Gordon, Everett G. Marshall, Blanche Yurka, Peter Von Zerneck, Alfred Linder, Ben Low, James Craven, Roland Belanger, Horace McMahon, Alexander Kirkland, Donald Randolph, Judith Lowry, Red Buttons, Otto Simanek, Walter Greaza, Roland Winters, Harold Young, Sally Mac-Marrow, Coby Neal, Karl Malden, Jean Del Val, Reed Hadley.

The Time of Your Life
Released in 1948
A William Cagney–United Artists Picture. Directed by H. C. Potter. Produced by William Cagney. Screenplay by Nathaniel Curtis. Based on the play by William Saroyan.
Cast: James Cagney, William Bendix, Wayne Morris, Jeanne Cagney, Broderick Crawford, Ward Bond, James Barton, Paul Draper, Gale Page, James Lydon, Richard Erman, Pedro De Cordoba, Reginald Beane, Tom Powers, John Miller, Natalie Schafer, Howard Freeman, Renee Riano, Lanny Rees, Nanette Parks, Grazia Marciso, Claire Carleton, Gladys Blake, Marlene Aames, Moy Ming, Donald Kerr, Ann Cameron, Floyd Walters, Eddie Borden, Rena Case.

White Heat
Released in 1949
A Warner Brothers–First National Picture. Directed by Raoul Walsh. Produced by Louis F. Edelman. Screenplay by Ivan Goff and Ben Roberts. Based on a story by Virginia Kellogg.
Cast: James Cagney, Virginia Mayo, Edmond O'Brien, Margaret Wycherly, Ed Somers, Steve Cochran, John Archer, Wally Cassell, Mickey Knox, Fred Clark, G. Pat Collins, Paul Guilfoyle, Fred Coby, Ford Rainey, Robert Osterloh, Ian MacDonald, Marshall Bradford, Ray Montgomery, George Taylor, Milton Parsons, Claudia Barrett, Buddy Gorman, DeForrest Lawrence, Garrett Craig, George Spaulding, Sherry Hall, Harry Strang, Jack Worth, Sid Melton, Fern Eggen, Eddie Foster, Lee Phelps.

The West Point Story
Released in 1950
A Warner Brothers–First National Picture. Directed by Roy Del Ruth. Produced by Louis F. Edelman. Screenplay by John Monks, Jr., Charles Hoffman, and Irving Wallace. Based on a story by Irving Wallace. Songs: "Still Man" by Mac Julian; "Ten Thousand Sheep," "By the Kissing Rock," "You Love Me," "Military Polka," "Long Before I Knew You," "It Could Only Happen in Brooklyn" by Jules Styne and Sammy Cahn.

Cast: James Cagney, Virgina Mayo, Doris Day, Gordon MacRae, Gene Nelson, Alan Hale, Jr., Roland Winters, Raymond Roe, Wilton Graff, Jerome Cowan, Frank Ferguson, Jack Kelly, Glen Turnbull, Walter Ruick, Lute Crockett, James Dobson, Joel Marston, Bob Hayden, De Wit Bishop.

Kiss Tomorrow Goodbye
Released in 1950
A William Cagney Production. A Warner Brothers–First National Picture. Directed by Gordon Douglas. Produced by William Cagney. Screenplay by Harry Brown. Based on the novel *Kiss Tomorrow Goodbye* by Horace McCoy.
Cast: James Cagney, Barbara Payton, Ward Bond, Luther Adler, Helena Carter, Steve Brody, Rhys Williams, Barton MacLane, Herbert Heyes, Frank Richer, John Litel, Dan Riss, John Halloran, William Frawley, Robert Karnes, Kenneth Tobey, Neville Brand, William Cagney, George Spaulding, Mark Strong, Matt McHugh, Georgia Caine, King Donovan, Frank Wilcox, Gordon Richards.

Come Fill the Cup
Released in 1951
A Warner Brothers–First National Picture. Directed by Gordon Douglas. Produced by Henry Blanke. Screenplay by Ivan Goff and Ben Roberts. Based on the novel by Harlan Ware.
Cast: James Cagney, Phyllis Thaxter, Raymond Massey, James Gleason, Gig Young, Selena Toyle, Larry Keating, Charlita, Sheldon Leonard, Douglas Spencer, John Kellogg, William Bakewell, John Alvin, King Donovan, James Flavin, Torben Meyer, Norma Jean Macias, Elizabeth Flournoy, Henry Blair.

Starlift
Released in 1951
A Warner Brothers Picture. Directed by Roy Del Ruth. Produced by Robert Arthur. Screenplay by John Klorer and Karl Kamb. Based on a story by John Klorer.
Cast: James Cagney, Gary Cooper, Phil Harris, Louella Parsons, Randolph Scott, Jane Wyman, Doris Day, Gordon MacRae, Virginia Mayo, Gene Nelson, Ruth Roman, Patrice Wymore, Janice Rule, Dick Wesson, Ron Hagerthy, Richard Webb, Hayden Rorke, Ann Doran, Tommy Farrell, John Maxwell, Don Beddoe, Mary Adams, Bigelowe Sayre, Eleanor Audley, Pat Henry, Gordon Polk, Ray Montgomery, Bill Neff, Stan Holbrook, Jill Richards, Joe Turkel, Rush Williams, Brian McKay, Jack Larson, Lyle Clark, Dorothy Kennedy, Jean Dean, Dolores Castle, Wil-

liam Hunt, Elizabeth Flournoy, Walter Brennan, Jr., Robert Karnes, John Hedloe, Steve Gregory, Joe Recht, Herb Latimer, Dick Ryan, Bill Hudson, Sarah Spencer, James Brown, Ezelle Poule.

What Price Glory?
Released in 1952
A Twentieth Century–Fox Picture. Directed by John Ford. Produced by Sol C. Siegel. Screenplay by Phoebe Ephron and Henry Ephren. Based on the play by Maxwell Anderson and Laurence Stallings.
Cast: James Cagney, Corinne Calvet, Dan Dailey, William Demarest, Craig Hill, Robert Wagner, Marisa Pavan, Casey Adams, James Gleason, Wally Vernon, Henry Letondal, Fred Libby, Ray Hyke, Paul Fix, James Lilburn, Henry Morgan, Dan Borzage, Bill Henry, Henry "Bomber" Kulkovich, Jack Pennick, Ann Codee, Stanley Johnson, Tom Tyler, Olga Andre, Barry Norton, Luis Alberni, Torben Meyer, Alfred Zeisler, George Bruggeman, Scott Forbes, Sean McClory, Charles Fitzsimmons, Louis Mercier, Mickey Simpson.

A Lion Is in the Streets
Released in 1953
A William Cagney Production. Directed by Raoul Walsh. Produced by William Cagney. Screenplay by Luther Davis. Based on the novel by Adria Locke Langley.
Cast: James Cagney, Barbara Hale, Anne Francis, Warner Anderson, John McIntyre, Jeanne Cagney, Lon Chaney, Jr., Frank McHugh, Larry Keating, Onslow Stevens, James Millican, Mickey Simpson, Sara Haden, Ellen Corby, Roland Winters, Burt Mustin, Irene Tedrow, Sarah Selby.

Run for Cover
Released in 1955
A Paramount Picture. Directed by Nicholas Ray. Produced by William H. Pine. Screenplay by William C. Thomas. Based on a story by Harriet Frank, Jr., and Irving Ravetch.
Cast: James Cagney, Viveca Lindfors, John Derek, Jean Hersholt, Grant Withers, Jack Lambert, Ernest Borgnine, Ray Teal, Irving Bacon, Trevor Bardette, John Mijan, Gus Schilling, Emerson Treacy, Denver Pile, Henry Wills.

Love Me or Leave Me
Released in 1955
A Metro-Goldwyn-Mayer Picture. Directed by Charles Vidor. Produced by Joe Pasternak. Screenplay by Daniel Fuchs and Isobel Lennart. Based on an original story by Daniel Fuchs.

Cast: Doris Day, James Cagney, Cameron Mitchel, Robert Keith, Tom Tully, Harry Bellaver, Richard Gaines, Peter Leeds, Claude Stroud, Audrey Young, John Harding, Dorothy Abbott, Phil Shumacher, Otto Reichow, Henry Kulky, Jay Adler, Mauritz Hugo, Veda Ann Borg, Claire Carleton, Benny Burt, Robert B. Carson, James Drury, Richard Simmons, Michael Kostrick, Roy Engle, John Damler, Genevieve Aumont, Roy Engle, David Van Sickel, Johnny Day, Larri Thomas, Patti Nestor, Winona Smith, Shirley Wilson, Robert Malcolm, Robert Stephenson, Paul McGuire, Barry Regan, Jimmy Cross, Henry Randolph, Chet Brandenberg.

Mister Roberts
Released in 1955
A Warner Brothers Picture–An Orange Production. Directed by John Ford and Mervyn LeRoy. Produced by Leland Hayward. Screenplay by Frank Nugent and Joshua Logan. From the play by Joshua Logan and Thomas Heggen, based on the novel by Thomas Heggen.
Cast: Henry Fonda, James Cagney, Jack Lemmon, William Powell, Ward Bond, Betsy Palmer, Phil Carey, Nick Adams, Harry Carey, Jr., Ken Curtis, Frank Aletter, Fritz Ford, Buck Kartalian, William Henry, William Hudson, Stubby Kruger, Harry Tenbrook, Perry Lopez, Robert Roark, Pat Wayne, Tige Andrews, Jim Moloney, Denny Niles, Francis Conner, Shug Fisher, Danny Borzage, Jim Murphy, Kathleen O'Malley, Maura Murphy, Mimi Doyle, Jeanne Murray-Vanderbilt, Lonny Pierce, Martin Milner, Gregory Walcott, James Flavin, Jack Pennick, Duke Kahanamoko, Carolyn Tong, George Branier, Clarence Frank.

The Seven Little Foys
Released in 1955
A Paramount Picture. Directed by Melville Shavelson. Produced by Jack Rose. Original screenplay by Melville Shavelson and Jack Rose.
Cast: Bob Hope, Milly Vitale, George Tobias, Angele Clarke, Herbert Heyes, Richard Shannon, Billy Gray, Lee Erickson, Paul De Rolf, Lydia Reed, Linda Bennett, Jimmy Baird, James Cagney, Tommy Duran, Lester Matthews, Joe Evans, George Boyce, Oliver Blake, Milton Frome, King Donovan, Jimmy Conlin, Marian Carr, Harry Cheshire, Renata Vanni, Betty Uitti, Noel Drayton, Jack Pepper, Dabbs Greer, Billy Nelson, Joe Flynn, Jerry Mathews, Lewis Martin.

Tribute to a Bad Man
Released in 1956
A Metro-Goldwyn-Mayer Picture. Directed by Robert Wise. Produced by Sam Zimbalist. Screenplay by Michael Blankfort. Based on a short story by Jack Schaefer.

Cast: James Cagney, Don Dubbins, Stephen McNally, Irene Papas, Vic Morrow, James Griffith, Onslow Stevens, James Bell, Jeanette Nolan, Chubby Johnson, Royal Dano, Lee Van Cleef, Peter Ching, James Mc-Callion, Clint Sharp, Carl Pitti, Tony Hughes, Roy Engel, Bud Osborne, John Halloran, Tom London, Dennis Moore, Buddy Roosevelt, Billy Dix.

These Wilder Years
Released in 1956
A Metro-Goldwyn-Mayor Picture. Directed by Roy Rowland. Produced by Jules Schermer. Screenplay by Frank Fenton. Based on a story by Ralph Wheelwright.
Cast: James Cagney, Barbara Stanwyck, Walter Pidgeon, Betty Lou Keim, Don Dubbins, Edward Andrews, Basil Ruysdael, Roy Oliphant, Grandon Rhodes, Will Wright, Lewis Martin, Dorothy Adams, Dean Jones, Herb Vigran, Ruth Lee, Matt Moore, Jack Kenny, Harry Tyler, Luana Lee, William Forest, John Maxwell, Emmett Vogan, Charles Evans, Tom Laughlin, Bob Alden, Michael Landon, Jimmy Ogg, Elizabeth Flournoy, Russell Simpson, Kathleen Mulqueen, Russ Whitney, Lillian Powell.

Man of a Thousand Faces
Released in 1957
A Universal-International Picture. Directed by Joseph Pevney. Produced by Robert Arthur. Screenplay by R. Wright Campbell, Ivan Goff, and Ben Roberts. Based on a story by Ralph Wheelwright.
Cast: James Cagney, Dorothy Malone, Jane Greer, Marjorie Rambeau, Jim Backus, Robert J. Evans, Celia Lovsky, Jeanne Cagney, Jack Albertson, Nolan Leary, Roger Smith, Robert Lyden, Rickie Sorenson, Dennis Rush, Simon Scott, Clarence Kolb, Danny Beck, Phil Van Zandt, Hank Mann, Snub Pollard.

Short Cut to Hell
Released in 1957
A Paramount Picture. Directed by James Cagney. Produced by A. C. Lyles. Based on the novel *This Gun for Hire* by Graham Greene.
Starring Robert Ivers, Georgann Johnson, William Bishop.

Never Steal Anything Small
Released in 1958
A Universal-International Picture. Directed by Charles Lederer. Produced by Aaron Rosenberg. Screenplay by Charles Lederer. Based on the play *Devil's Hornpipe* by Maxwell Anderson and Rouben Mamoulian.

Cast: James Cagney, Shirley Jones, Roger Smith, Cara Williams, Nehemiah Persoff, Royal Dano, Anthony Caruso, Horace MacMahan, Virgina Vincent, Jack Albertson, Robert J. Wilke, Herbie Faye, Billy M. Greene, John Duke, Jack Orrison, Roland Winter, Ongrid Doude, Sanford Seegar, Ed McNally, Greg Barton, Edwin Parker, Jay Jostyn, John Halloran, Harvey Perry, Phyllis Kennedy, Rebecca Sand.

Shake Hands with the Devil
Released in 1959
A Pennebaker Production. Directed by Michael Anderson. Produced by Michael Anderson. Screenplay by Ivan Goff and Ben Roberts. Based on the novel by Reardon Connor.
Cast: James Cagney, Don Murray, Dana Wynter, Glynis Johns, Michael Redgrave, Sybil Thorndike, Cyril Cusak, John Breslin, Harry Brogan, Robert Brown, Marianne Benet, Lewis Carson, John Cairney, Harry Corbett, Eileen Crowe, Alan Cuthbertson, Donal Donnelly, Wilfred Dawning, Eithne Dunne, Paul Farrell, Richard Harris, William Hartnell, John Le Mesurier, Niall MacGinnis, Patrick Mcalinney, Ray McAnally, Clive Morton, Peter Reynolds, Christopher Rhodes, Ronald Walsh, Alan White.

The Gallant Hours
Released in 1960
A Cagney-Montgomery Production. Directed by Robert Montgomery. Produced by Robert Montgomery. Screenplay by Beirne Lay.
Cast: James Cagney, Dennis Weaver, Ward Costello, Richard Jaeckel, Les Tremayne, Robert Burton, Raymond Bailey, Carl Benton Reid, Walter Sande, Karl Swensen, Vaughan Taylor, Harry Landers, Richard Carlyle, Leon Lontoc, James T. Goto, James Yagi, John McKee, John Zaremba, Carleton Young, William Schallert, Nelson Leigh, Sydney Smith, Herbert Lylton, Selmer Jackson, Tyler McVey, Maggie Magennio, James Cagney, Jr., Robert Montgomery, Jr.

One, Two, Three
Released in 1961
A Mirisch Company, Inc., Production in Association with Pyramid Productions, A. G. Directed by Billy Wilder. Produced by I. A. L. Diamond and Doane Harrison. Screenplay by Billy Wilder and I. A. L. Diamond. Based on a one-act play by Ferenc Molnar.
Cast: James Cagney, Horst Buchholz, Pamela Tiffin, Arlene Francis, Lilo Pulver, Howard St. John, Hanns Lothar, Leon Askin, Peter Capell, Ralf Wolter, Karl Lieffen, Henning Schluter, Hubert Von Meyerinck, Lois Bolton, Tile Kiwe, Karl Ludwig Lindt, Red Buttons, John Allen, Chris-

tine Allen, Rose Renee Roth, Ivan Arnold, Helmud Schid, Otto Friebel, Werner Buttler, Klaus Becker, Siegfried Dornbusch, Paul Bos, Max Buschbaum, Jaspar Von Oertzen, Inga De Oro, Jacques Chevalier, Werner Hassenland.

Ragtime
Released in 1981
A Paramount Production. Directed by Milos Forman. From the novel by E. L. Doctorow.
Cast: James Cagney, Mary Steenburgen, James Olson, Elizabeth McGovern, Mandy Patinkin, Howard E. Rollins, Norman Mailer, Pat O'Brien, Eloise O'Brien, Brad Dourif, Debbie Allen, Robert Joy, Donald O'Connor, Kenneth McMillan, Bessie Love.

James Cagney's Short Films

Practice Shots, 1931, with golfer Bobby Jones; *Hollywood on Parade No. 8,* 1933, candid scenes of Cagney, Frankie Darro, and Joe E. Brown; *Screen Snapshots No. 11,* 1934, Cagney, Boris Karloff, Bela Lugosi, Pat O'Brien, Maureen O'Sullivan, Eddie Cantor; *The Hollywood Gad-About,* 1934, Cagney, Gary Cooper, Shirley Temple, Mary Astor, Eddie Cantor, Alice White, Chester Morris, and Walter Winchell; *A Trip Through a Hollywood Studio,* 1935, Cagney, Pat O'Brien, Rudy Vallee, Wini Shaw, Dolores Del Rio, Ann Dvorak, Hugh Herbert, Busby Berkeley; *For Auld Lang Syne,* 1939, tribute to Will Rogers; *Show Business at War,* 1943, Cagney and other stars entertain troops; *You, John Jones,* 1943, Cagney as air-raid warden, with Ann Sothern, Margaret O'Brien; *Battle Stations,* 1944, story about SPARS, with Ginger Rogers.

James Cagney's Radio and Television Appearances

"Lux Radio Theater": "Is Zat So?," 1936; "Ceiling Zero" (with Ralph Bellamy and Stuart Erwin), 1939; "Angels with Dirty Faces" (with Pat O'Brien and Gloria Dixon), 1939. "Revlon Review" (with Gertrude Lawrence), 1940; "Johnny Got His Gun" (1940); "Captain of the Clouds," 1942; "Yankee Doodle Dandy," 1942; "Ed Sullivan Show" (scenes from *Mister Roberts*), 1955; "Robert Montgomery Presents" ("Soldier from a War Returning"), 1956.

James Cagney's Theatrical Appearances

Pitter Patter, Longacre Theatre, September 29, 1920; *Outside Looking In,*

Greenwich Village Playhouse, September 8, 1925 (moved to Thirty-ninth Street Theatre, December 1925); *Broadway,* Broadhurst Theatre, joined cast mid-1927; *Women Go on Forever,* Forrest Theatre, September 7, 1927; *The Grand Street Follies of 1928,* Booth Theatre, May 29, 1929; *The Grand Street Follies of 1929,* Booth Theatre, May 1, 1929; *Maggie the Magnificent,* Cort Theatre, October 21, 1929; *Penny Arcade,* Fulton Theatre, March 11, 1930.

INDEX